Analyze Anything

Also available from Continuum

Analyzing Prose, Richard Lanham

Discourse Analysis: Second Edition, Brian Paltridge

The Nature and Functions of Language, Howard Jackson and Peter Stockwell

The Poetry Toolkit: The Essential Guide to Studying Poetry, Rhian Williams

Analyze Anything

A Guide to Critical Reading and Writing

Gregory Fraser
Chad Davidson

continuum

Continuum International Publishing Group

The Tower Building	80 Maiden Lane
11 York Road	Suite 704
London SE1 7NX	New York NY 10038

www.continuumbooks.com

British Library Cataloguing-in-Publication Data
A catalogue record for this book is available from the British Library.

ISBN: HB: 978-1-4411-5406-4
       PB: 978-1-4411-0730-5

Library of Congress Cataloging-in-Publication Data
Fraser, Gregory.
Analyze anything : a guide to critical reading and writing / Gregory Fraser and Chad Davidson.
    p. cm.
Includes bibliographical references and index.
ISBN 978-1-4411-5406-4 – ISBN 978-1-4411-0730-5 (pbk.) –
ISBN 978-1-4411-5558-0 (ebook (pdf)) – ISBN 978-1-4411-9115-1 (ebook (epub)) 1. English language–Rhetoric. 2. Persuasion (Rhetoric) 3. Critical thinking. 4. Reasoning. I. Davidson, Chad, 1970– II. Title.
PE1431.F73 2011
808'.0427–dc23

                                                                    2011035030

Typeset by Newgen Imaging Systems Pvt Ltd, Chennai, India
Printed and bound in the United States of America

Contents

Acknowledgments

Special thanks to Gurdeep Mattu and the helpful staff at Continuum, who offered valuable criticism and timely advice throughout the writing process. Thanks also to Graeme Harper for his editorial and creative guidance.

Grateful acknowledgment also goes to our colleagues in the Department of English and the First-Year Writing Program at the University of West Georgia, with particular gratitude to Jane and Bob Hill and David Newton for their insights and encouragement. Thanks as well to all of the scholars and friends who contributed exercises to our project, and to our graduate assistants, Randie Mayo and Pam Murphy, for their hard work and many contributions to the text.

Finally, we thank our writing students, who helped refine these ideas, asked pointed questions, and tested out the methods with diligence and enthusiasm. Their importance cannot be overestimated.

Permissions

Dove, Rita. "Adolescence-II." From *The Yellow House on the Corner*. Copyright © 1989 by Rita Dove. Reprinted by permission of the author.

Gildner, Gary. "First Practice." From *Blue Like the Heavens: New and Selected Poems*. Copyright © 1984 by Gary Gildner. Reprinted by permission of the author and University of Pittsburgh Press.

Jones, Stephen Graham. "Discovering America." From *Bleed into Me*. Copyright © 2005 by Stephen Graham Jones. Reprinted by permission of the author.

McGavran, James Holt. "'Insurmountable Barriers to Our Union': Homosocial Male Bonding, Homosexual Panic, and Death on the Ice in *Frankenstein*." Originally appeared in *European Romantic Review*. Copyright © 2000 Routledge. Reprinted by permission of the author and Routledge.

1 Introduction

1. The analytical frame of mind

We are automatically analytical, constantly engaged in acts of reading and interpreting the world around us. We carefully process information and draw conclusions when choosing which car to purchase, which university to attend, or which peers to count as friends. We employ our interpretive skills and reasoning powers to decipher the meanings behind a boss's bad mood, a parent's change of career, a sibling's decision to become vegetarian. Every day—whether consciously or not—we ask "Why?" and work toward plausible responses that allow us to live and flourish under complex, often stressful, conditions. In short, we are forever in an analytical frame of mind.

One of the main purposes of higher education is to help students broaden and deepen the analytical skills they already possess. "An investment in knowledge pays the best interest," wrote Benjamin Franklin, and this kernel of wisdom clearly makes sense to anyone prepared to invest time, money, and energy in pursuit of a university degree.[1] For Franklin, the attainment of knowledge involved copious reading, scientific experimentation, and writing with analytical savvy and wit. In his famous *Autobiography*, he notes that prose writing was "of great use to me in the course of my life, and was a principal means of my advancement."[2]

Like Franklin, we place enormous value on writing as a source of personal and academic growth. We also find that students excel when they learn an effective "method in the arrangement of thoughts," as Franklin put it.[3] In other words, students make the most headway in their coursework and preparations for professional life when they master a reliable method for generating evocative ideas and expressing them in readable prose.

2. The semiotic method

Taught in writing and literature classes for decades, the "semiotic method" (or the "study of signs") has proven especially successful in helping students to build their analytical thinking skills and to strengthen their persuasiveness on the page. One advantage of the approach lies in the fact that "sign study" forms an intricate part of our daily lives—both in and out of school. Signs, indicators, pointers, markers: no matter what name they go by, these phenomena surround us daily, waiting to be decoded. Consider, for example, the act of driving a car. From the network of traffic signals and road signs, we take instructions on when to stop and when to proceed, when to pause for pedestrians, and when to wait for a passing train. The rules of the road constitute a meaning-filled system that manages the flow of traffic and reduces the number of smashups.

The actual traffic signs with their lettering and numbers, however, are not the only elements of the road that send decipherable signals. An eighteen-wheeler slogging up a hill in the slow lane sends a clear message: prepare to pass that behemoth. Meanwhile, the red Corvette whizzing up from behind not only signals other drivers to take increased caution but also carries additional meanings open to interpretation. Does such a sports car represent "quiet reserve" and "economic prudence"? Or does it more convincingly signal "youthful passion," "carefree exuberance," and "risky adventurousness"? Indeed, the red Corvette can mean many different things, to different people, in different contexts. To a police officer, this car might suggest "trouble in the offing." For a man in his forties, the Corvette's potent representation of "sexy flashiness" might suggest a way to overcome a mid-life crisis. For a mechanic, it might embody the epitome of automotive engineering. And for a policeman in his forties who likes to work on cars, it might convey all of these messages at once.

As these examples illustrate, the scope of signs is enormous, and learning to read them well takes practice and commitment. That's because different signs carry varying levels of complexity. In addition, their layers of significance shift and multiply depending on the cultural and historical contexts in which they appear. In fact, whole cultures themselves can be viewed as extraordinarily complicated and ever-shifting systems of signs. Some contemporary theorists go so far as to suggest that, when it comes right down to it, *everything* is a sign, because everything exists within a meaning-making system of some kind. Nothing, in other words, floats free from the realm of signs that lend significance to our social practices and individual lives.

3. Responding to literary signs

Signs surround us all the time, but they are especially conspicuous in advertisements, films, television, and literature. Consider, for example, Lorraine Hansberry's 1959 play *A Raisin in the Sun*. In this drama, a bright, African-American university student named Beneatha—enthralled by progressive ideas and determined to become a physician—does something surprising with her long, straightened hair. She cuts it in a close crop, much to the shock of her family and friends. With a few swift clips, Beneatha "goes natural," returning her hair to what her sister-in-law calls its "nappy" roots.[4] This is a potent statement, or "sign," with which Beneatha simultaneously signals a surging allegiance to her African heritage and a bold defiance of America's dominant white culture in the years following World War II.

A symbol of black pride, Beneatha's "natural" haircut works to criticize white prejudice and power at an especially important site of historical and political contest: the African-American body. A century earlier, many such bodies were literally the possessions of white slave owners. By going "natural," instead of continuing to use tonics and straightening ointments in an effort to mimic the hair of white women, Beneatha strives to obliterate the signs of white culture and to reclaim not only her own body but also the collective corpus of her race. As she herself puts it, "I hate assimilationist Negroes! [They are] willing to give up [their] own culture and submerge [themselves] completely in the dominant, and in this case *oppressive* culture!"[5] Like the hippies a decade later, Beneatha makes a forceful statement with her hair, indicating that she opposes America's "melting pot" mentality.

At this stage, we have begun to analyze a particularly interesting sign in *A Raisin in the Sun*. A thorough interpretation of Beneatha's haircut, however, will need to go deeper. This initial reading is still relatively superficial, because it basically reiterates what the play itself places in the thematic foreground. In other words, Hansberry makes overt—with Beneatha's anti-assimilation-ist speech—one persuasive meaning of the haircut as a sign of resistance to dominant white values and ideals of beauty. If our analysis stopped here, then we would miss the opportunity to explore more complex meanings. Suffice it to say, the playwright has more messages up her sleeve with regard to Beneatha's hair. On one hand, Hansberry signals the rejection of white culture by her young protagonist, but she also stages the *internal* conflicts that faced African-American culture in the post-World War II era. That is, the coiffure additionally becomes a site and sign of contest *within* black com-munities. And with that observation, we start to dive a little deeper.

The movement from *inter-* to *intra*racial conflict comes clearly into view when we examine the responses to Beneatha's action. At the sight of her new haircut, the people around Beneatha immediately question her sanity. Her sister-in-law Ruth asks, "Girl [have] you done lost your natural mind!?"[6] And on the heels of this comment, one of Beneatha's suitors—a rather unlikable fellow named George Murchison—inquires, "What have you done to your head—I mean your hair!"[7] Here, Hansberry has signaled a move from the *external* world (of haircuts and skin tones, for example) to the *internal* realm (of ideas and ideals, prejudices and self-doubts). Now we find ourselves in the midst of a community debate—one that troubled many African-American cultures in the 1950s—and all of a sudden, prompts a series of questions: Is Beneatha crazy to reject America's dominant culture? Is she doing something reckless and potentially dangerous to the future of her race in the United States? Is this a foolish and possibly ruinous signal for her to send? Shouldn't she just be sane and assimilate? Wouldn't it be more reasonable to go along with the crowd and not resurrect the ugly past?

Besides, what is the value of exploring African roots? As George himself tells Beneatha: "Let's face it baby, your heritage is nothing but a bunch of raggedy-assed spirituals and some grass huts!"[8] Couple his comment with another from Walter, Beneatha's older brother, who refers to his own race as the world's "most backward" group of people.[9] Gradually, we come to view Beneatha's haircut not only as a sign of rebellion against white racism but also as a message-bearer that alerts us to doubts and disputes among African-Americans regarding their pasts, their futures, their cultures, and their humanity. Just as Beneatha cuts her hair in an effort to sever her ties with white America and its systems of oppressive signs, George and Walter (in an ironic reversal) strive to cut off their associations with black history. Whose "natural mind," one wonders, has been lost here?

Clearly, new levels of sign complexity emerge as we analyze the meanings behind Beneatha's haircut. Since we have left the simpler semiotic realm of road signs and traffic signals, we can expect to discover many layers of meaning in Hansberry's sign, and we can predict that these significances will be embroidered with subtleties, ambiguities, and potential contradictions. Here is where the analysis of signs becomes a lot more challenging and a lot more fun. In this particular case, we might expand our analysis by considering Beneatha's oppression-defying, heritage-celebrating haircut in the light of other struggles that she faces in the play. In other words, we can situate the haircut alongside some of Beneatha's other noteworthy actions, since all of these signs point to one another and enrich each other's meanings.

As an African-American woman living in a postwar Chicago ghetto, Beneatha finds herself caught in a network of competing sign systems. Everywhere she turns, she is bombarded by conflicting signals that place demands on her as an individual. In addition to receiving constant societal signs of her "natural" racial inferiority, she also absorbs all kinds of messages that prod her to assert her feminine independence, to use her mind to better the world, and to overthrow the restrictive sexism that surrounds her. At one point, Walter barks at his sister: "Who the hell told you you had to be a doctor? If you so crazy 'bout messing 'round with sick people—then go be a nurse like other women—or just get married and be quiet."[10] In many ways, Beneatha's sudden cropping of her hair may be read not only through the lens of race but also from the perspective of gender—as a sign of her female assertiveness in a world still dominated by men. Beneatha, it turns out, intends to live her life "beneath" no one. She aims to pursue a medical profession traditionally occupied by men, and on some psychological level, this may require her to "cut off" her connections to certain images, such as long hair, customarily associated with women. In a reversal of the Samson story in the Old Testament, then, Beneatha's haircut appears to supercharge instead of sap her strength.

4. Responding to cultural signs

As evident from our analysis of Beneatha's hairstyle change, the worlds created in dramas and other literary texts brim with evocative signs vying for attention. But we need not relegate the study of signs to literature. Any university setting—to take the most conspicuous example—displays a dizzying array of meaningful indicators. For instance, consider that young men on campuses all across the United States and elsewhere continue to sport the goatee look—a beard style that includes a moustache and small beard. Though not an especially pervasive sign, it crops up frequently enough to warrant inspection as a fashion phenomenon. Why, we might wonder, would a student choose to wear facial hair only around the mouth and chin? What does this particular style of beard signify in contemporary culture? With theoretical questions such as these, semiotic analysis begins.

The French critical theorist and historian Michel Foucault used the metaphor of an archeological dig to describe the layer-by-layer excavation work of the semiotician. The semiotician's job, then, is to unearth the goatee's various cultural associations and meanings. In present culture, this particular beard appears in many contexts to convey "bad boy" toughness. (Just look at a poster for the 2009 film *The Taking of Pelham 123*, where Denzel Washington and John Travolta both sport gritty goatees.) Check out photos of jazz great Charles Mingus for a sense of the "hip artfulness" embedded in this sign, as well. Furthermore, the beard seems to suggest "rebelliousness," "malicious cunning," "the dark side of reality." (Representations of Satan often feature a goatee.) We might also argue that an "intellectual" element inhabits this sign: a goatee appears to connote "iconoclastic thinking," "taboo concepts." When unpacking this sign in class, students frequently assert that the beard signals a particular kind of anger—a smoldering, interiorized, misanthropic disgust with the world. Such associations become increasingly persuasive if we situate the goatee alongside complementary signs. Imagine a student who, in addition to wearing a goatee, smokes Gauloises cigarettes, reads existential philosophy, and listens to the likes of Mingus, Miles, and Monk—avant-garde heavyweights in the history of jazz.

Then again, a different type of grit and rebelliousness emerges semiotically if the wearer of the goatee drives a pickup truck that sports a gun rack in the rear window and a bumper sticker of the Confederate flag. Similarly, we might find the particular facial-hair style on a protester from the English Defence League—a far-right movement opposed to what it regards as the threatening spread of Muslim extremism in Britain. In these contexts, the goatee belongs to a collection of signs (otherwise known as a "text") that might bespeak a "tough guy" attitude toward left-leaning politics. Suddenly, the same take-no-guff beard signifies a dig-in-the-heels, I'm-no-pushover conservatism. So how can the meanings behind the goatee change so swiftly from context to context, situation to situation?

5. It's all relative

According to semiotics, meanings are not inherent in, or intrinsically connected to, signs themselves. Instead, meanings are relational, situational. What surrounds the sign defines it, and the sign defines what it surrounds. For the semiotician, the links between the goatee and its perceptible messages remain arbitrary, constructed by cultural convention and context. No fixed or final meaning of any sign, in fact, exists. The goatee only signifies "radical," "rough-edged," "hip," "Mephistophelean," and so on because the beard is *relative* to other signs in our culture's current sign system of male facial hair—a network that includes "full beard," "clean shaven face," "moustache only," and more. The goatee's significances, therefore, constitute part of a comparative system, not bonded to the beard itself or to the student who wears it. From a semiotic perspective, no one particular beard can "exist" as a recognizable cultural signal without related signs to lend it meaning and value. In short, the goatee simply cannot "mean" anything without clear similarities to, and differences from, other signs in a perceivable system.

To underscore this vital point, imagine a poster of the cartoon character Lisa Simpson (Bart's sharp-witted sister in the hit animated TV show *The Simpsons*) hanging on one wall of a student's dorm room. Now imagine that two other walls in the room display posters of Charlie "Bird" Parker and John Coltrane. In this relational system, the poster of Lisa might arguably signal the student's love of the jazz saxophone and its famous players. It also suggests a student with a whimsical sense of humor, placing a contemporary cartoon character in relation to icons from the heyday of jazz. But now consider the same Lisa Simpson image flanked by posters of Lucy (from Charles Schultz's *Peanuts* cartoons) and Velma Dinkley (the bespectacled brainiac from the *Scooby-Doo* TV series). Note that the exact same image of Bart's sister suddenly signifies differently, suggesting the student's playful interest in outspoken, intelligent young women in animated programs. Tack up posters for Amnesty International and Oxfam on either side of Lisa, and we might read suggestions of progressive political commitments. The poster of Lisa Simpson does not change in the least, but the neighboring context does, and hence the meanings shift. Semiotics suggests that all meaning emerges in this way—through relationships between signs. By this avenue of thought, meaning is more of a process, an action, a consequence of signs in context.

As an aid to memory, think of this vital semiotic concept as the "Einsteinian Theory of Language and Social Reality," where *everything is relative*. Sign study suggests that nothing possesses meaning on its own: nothing holds pre-existing significance above or beyond the specific sign system—and the particular context, culture, and historical moment—to which it belongs. Thus, our social realities arise from complex webs of endlessly interrelated associations between signs. Nothing inherently "satanic" or "rebellious" exists in the goatee. It only carries these suggestions in conventional comparison to, say, "full beard," which in Western culture tends to signify "respectable," "established," "earnest," "rational," "sober," "wise," "traditional," and "scholarly," among other descriptors.

6. Who's got the power?

In addition, signs never exist apart from intricate interplays of power. (Think back to the earlier analysis of Beneatha's hair crop.) Meaning, in other words, is not only relational in nature but also connected to ideology. Such signs as the goatee are always to some degree "political," where politics is understood to mean not strictly the work performed in legislative bodies such as the US Congress and the British Parliament but the more pervasive clashes—violent, moderate, at times almost imperceptible—that perennially occur between differing ideological positions, value systems, and widely held assumptions or "cultural myths." Who on university campuses typically wears the goatee? Students. And what hidden ideologies does this beard suggest? What cultural assumptions does it seem to embrace or defy? Ultimately, the goatee—like any sign—is a cultural indicator that not only relies on other indicators for identity and meaning, but that also carries ideological baggage. It communicates political, moral, and ethical suggestions (whether the beard-wearer knows it or not).

Consider, though, that some faculty member also wear the goatee: it's not strictly a student phenomenon. This fact begs several additional questions: Which professors? Are they younger? If so, what signals do they send with their beards? Their clothes? What is conveyed ideologically when a professor wears a goatee? Is he suggesting a resistance to traditional approaches to teaching? Is he marking his territory, as it were, and conveying that he is sensitive to student concerns, that he speaks their language, knows their musical tastes, understands them better than the crusty old guard? From a semiotic standpoint, then, all signs reflect subtle power dynamics. Such an awareness can raise the stakes in your written analyses because suddenly you must consider the political dimensions of the signs you intend to investigate. This will move your essays beyond the arena of mere description or personal bias and into the realm of mature, critical thinking, which your professors will demand of you as a serious student and writer.

7. Negative capability

It is additionally important to realize that no guaranteed correlation exists between (a) the messages sent by a sign such as the goatee, and (b) any real-world belief, identity, or intention on the part of the sign's sender. In other words, there is no way ever to know with 100 percent certainty if the student actually endorses the meanings his beard suggests, or if he behaves in accordance with the politics inscribed in the sign. The student may wear a "cutting-edge" beard, and yet hold decidedly retrograde worldviews. No one (not even the student himself, many contemporary thinkers would claim) can *completely* comprehend the relationship between the semiotic signals disseminated and their source in the sender. According to semiotic theory, there can never be any perfect unity or conclusive correspondence between the two. Some gap, some degree of undecidability, always remains. Wearing a goatee doesn't automatically make someone "dark," or "tough," or "cool," even though the beard gives off these vibes.

The same could be said about putting on a smile at a party or family gathering, which does not necessarily imply "happiness." The smiler could easily be pretending, performing, for the sake of appearances. Similarly, the goatee wearer might be "cool," he might not—yet there's no denying that in our present cultural moment, his beard communicates the *message* of coolness. And that, in a nutshell, is what semiotics seeks to study—the various messages sent by specific signs, not so much the ultimate "truth" behind a cultural or literary signal. To determine the student's character and politics—in short, to test the correspondence between the "surface" significations of his beard and his so-called inner identity or self—requires additional signs from him: speech, actions, purchases, work, and so on. A plausible assessment of his "true" identity emerges only through the study of a complex array of signs. Even then, no definitive determination can be made. The union between "surface signal" and "inner truth" will never wholly resolve or fully establish itself, since all signs are overabundant with meanings—intrinsically multiple and incomplete. The answer to "who he is" will always recede, even from him, just as the final meaning of any sign always escapes complete and irrefutable analysis.

To say the least, the implications of semiotic theory can be destabilizing, even frightening, given that they deny the possibility of a "final truth" about any social or literary phenomenon. Yet comfort may come from the realization that, in many ways, these ideas are not necessarily new. Contemporary semiotics sounds cautionary notes about absolute knowledge that date all the way back to the ancients. Didn't Socrates say in the fifth century BC, "I am quite conscious of my ignorance . . . I do not think that I know what I do not know"?[11] What about the Sophists of the same era, who voiced their radical doubts concerning the discovery of final truths? Or consider the Greek philosophers known as the Skeptikoi (their name deriving from the verb *skeptomai*, meaning "to reflect"), who maintained that absolute knowledge is impossible. Thus, semiotics is hardly the first method of thought and analysis to doubt the prospect of authoritative meanings and definitive conclusions. Becoming a seasoned analyst of signs, however, does not necessarily condemn you to pure ignorance in an empty, meaningless world. Quite the opposite, in fact, from our point of view, since semiotics argues for the abundance, rather than the evacuation, of meaning.

Such a pluralist model of thinking, however, also necessitates a level of comfort with multiplicity, ambiguity, paradox, and incomplete comprehension. British Romantic poet John Keats (author of "Ode to a Nightingale" and "Ode on a Grecian Urn," among other canonical works) invented a name for this skeptical mindset: he called it "negative capability." Consider his definition, written in a letter to his brothers George and Tom, dated December 21, 1817—a few years before Keats would die at age 25 from tuberculosis:

> [A]t once it struck me, what quality went to form a Man of Achievement especially in Literature & which Shakespeare posessed so enormously—I mean Negative Capability, that is when man is capable of being in uncertainties, Mysteries, doubts, without any irritable reaching after fact & reason.[12]

Is Keats categorically denouncing "fact and reason"? We don't believe so. After all, like Beneatha in *A Raisin in the Sun*, Keats studied to be a physician and held science (which is based on fact and reason) in great esteem. Instead, the critique seems more pointed at those thinkers and writers who, unlike Shakespeare, force their way to a single, incontrovertible answer—a final, comforting truth. This "irritable reaching" refuses to acknowledge the slipperiness of meaning, to embrace the multiplicity of concepts suggested by any sign.

8. Analyze anything

If this book stopped here—if it only found a place in the limited province of the classroom or even that of university life in general—then it would still hold value. Outside the academic environment, however, the study and interpretation of signs continues, and students will need to take part in this activity no matter what goals they hope to achieve. What is a marketing proposal, for example, if not a close analysis of cultural signs and a set of informed recommendations? What do fashion designers study endlessly if not the ever-changing systems of "hipness" and "style"? Success not only in higher education but also in the world at large requires the close study of signs.

We have titled our book *Analyze Anything* because we firmly believe that all university-ready students can learn to produce effective analyses of any cultural or textual phenomena. We seek to help you organize, develop, and present your analytical findings in crisp prose that will not only impress your peers and professors, but also edify and alter them. Make no mistake: your success in higher education depends on your ability to think innovatively and to write persuasively. Your professors themselves, in fact, are not rarified geniuses but rather practiced interpreters of signs. They have devoted years to reading and writing about the signs that interest them most. They compose formal interpretations (articles, dissertations, books), they attend conferences where they present their analytical findings and arguments, and they come to class prepared to model ways of interpreting the world in its various complexities. As someone now part of the formal academic world, you are invited to learn those same skills in order to write effective essays across a range of courses.

The work you are about to undertake requires no previous training, other than the lifetime of semiotic exposure that you already possess. Energy and enthusiasm, immersion in the study of interesting cultural and textual phenomena, is what we now ask of you. Leave the formal training, the effective "method in the arrangement of thoughts," to us. We have collected the strategies that have worked best for students in our combined 25 years of university teaching. We have also broken down the processes involved in the reading of signs into manageable and discrete units. What's more, we offer a sustainable method that transfers easily into a variety of classes. Your professors may not ask you to write about hair (though it is not out of the realm of possibility), but the tools that you learn in this book apply to the study of any sign—from the scandal created by a polarizing figure such as Lady Gaga to the geopolitical influence of the Obama administration, from a particularly rich pattern in a Toni Morrison or Salman Rushdie novel to an innovative rehabilitation technique for prison inmates. With the tactics introduced in this book, you can analyze anything and, most importantly, you can do so with the level of insight and depth that reveals your full intellectual potential. As a way to suggest the possibilities for aspiring writers, we have included several student essays throughout this textbook. Both of the essays below—by students early in their training—display not only the energy, intelligence, and insight of strong university writing, but also underscore the fact that, with the semiotic method outlined in this book, you too can analyze anything.

9. Student examples

Fashionably Hiding in Foliage

Constance Larrew

During the past decade or so, many young American women have added combat camouflage to their wardrobes. From salacious sequined evening dresses to comfy sweatshirts, battle-ready camo shows up in practically every form of attire—even undergarments. While soldiers must wear these designs for protection during their service, young women make the conscious choice to don fatigue-style patterns, and they often pay a pretty price for their mottled green and brown outfits. But what makes the camouflage pattern that originated in the military a popular motif for young women's clothing? Why are so many fashion bugs hiding nowadays in war-zone foliage?

One explanation may lie with the expression of preparedness for battle. In the United States, as well as other Western nations and those experiencing Western influence, young women seem increasingly inclined to exhibit an image of soldier-like strength and readiness in the face of antagonism. High-school and even university-age girls, often stereotyped as vulnerable and weak, feel a need to signify their refusal to remain docile. Present-day ad campaigns and television shows bombard viewers with alarming statistics regarding the potential victimization of young women, and with this increased concern, many girls take a proactive stand for their dignity and independence. A woman's safety from aggressors is no longer the sole responsibility of her male partner or relatives, so she must rely on her own means of establishing her boundaries and confidence—even to the point of appearing poised for combat. Casual clothes bearing woodland patterns in green and khaki offer a way for young women to signal their ability to defend themselves in dangerous circumstances.

Another reason for the emergence of camouflage as a fashion statement connects to the women's rights movement. The act of dressing in clothes originally designed for men remains a key way for women to test gender boundaries. From coal-mining women in Victorian England to the power suits of female brokers on Wall Street today, women have adopted men's clothing to signify that they, too, possess the skills necessary for the jobs at hand. Men's wardrobes have typically followed designs based on pragmatics. They tend to reinforce particular masculine roles related to labor, whether the tough-clothed trousers worn by miners or the suits and ties in the male-dominated business and political arenas. The construction of men's wear, in other words, is rooted in men's work, whereas women's clothing traditionally and even presently bases itself in aesthetics. Donning the vestments of the "dominant sex" (especially those militarily trained and titled to exercise considerable authority and force) may allow women to assume a more masculine role or at least to situate themselves in that sphere of power. Sporting a pattern linked with the idea of "men doing manly things"—such as grenade-handling and crawling through the mud on a 5-mile obstacle course—carries the implied retort, "If you can do it, so can I." Young women today have grown up in a world where feminist attitudes about gender equality have permeated education, popular media, and family structures, so it would seem natural for them to wear a design that carries ideas of gender modification or transcendence.

Warrior-wear additionally suggests the thrill of action and cunning. Nowadays, a young woman may assert her sexiness and desirability if she effectively suggests her ability to perform difficult feats such as rock climbing or rifle shooting. This idea of allure also borrows heavily from the male repertoire of tools to express virility and suitability as a mate. If one possesses strength and athleticism, whether male or female, the evolutionary model tends to privilege that individual. Indeed, government-sponsored ads for supporting and recruiting into the military reinforce this "fitness" desirability. The singsong encouragement to "Be all that you can be" certainly does not advocate mild motherhood. In this way, "expert marksmanship," "superior climbing skills," and "exceptional cunning" become concepts worthy of striving for, and wearing the uniform (though tailored in decidedly different forms) serves as an invitation to belong among those markers. These tributes to adrenaline-powered activities may translate back into fantasies of sexual prowess, too. The tendency toward assertive or even slightly deviant sexuality also appears to inform the popularity of camouflage clothing for young women, as it satisfies a primal craving to be exceptional in bed.

In a darker vein, a young woman adorned with woodsy battle colors may also inadvertently access the prevalent glorification of violence in contemporary culture. Violent films, television shows, and sports such as boxing all fulfill and perpetuate a longing to take part in rituals of brutality. Numerous theories about the present-day appetite for destruction range from remnants of hunting habits to Freudian "id" drives. Witnessing and especially taking part in violent acts causes increased heart rate and dilated pupils, as well as the release of chemicals affecting consciousness and perception. Violence, in short, provides an addictive rush, and young women who slip into camouflage clothing may experience muted forms of this stimulation. Moreover, sensory deprivation studies have shown strong needs among humans for variation in their environments, so yet another reason for the popularity of camo may involve the desire to break free from the calm monotony of suburban life. Violent imagery may serve, in fact, as a mode of fulfilling a basic need for more and more stimulation. Associating herself with these images, a young woman participates in this realm of action, perhaps communicating that she, too, seeks the sanctioned release of violent energies.

Although adorning herself with a flattering camouflage t-shirt or bodysuit may offer a young woman a stylistic break from traditional feminine expectations and a playful means of crossing the borders of gender and gentility, a troubling irony ultimately remains. For once camouflage becomes a matter of style and fantasy, it starts to disguise the real-world actualities of soldiering and war. Camouflage as a contemporary clothing sign is merely part of a harmless fashion trend, which sanitizes the realities connected to its original purpose. Camo fashion paradoxically calls up images of crafty warfare (the kind that leads to destruction and death) only to clean up these sad and frightening realities by casting them into the safe spaces of shopping malls and bedroom closets. In the end, camo-wear might even threaten to breed complacency toward the lives destroyed by war.

Camouflage remains a style that has outlasted many other recent fashion trends, probably because of its multiple background incentives for wearers. Though most cheerleaders, sorority sisters, and runway models may have inklings of the messages underlying their stylish military garb, various significances likely slip past their notice. Purchasers of camo garments know that the style is still cool, and that is enough for them. The rest, as they say, stays hidden.

Slapping the Fresh Mouth: Dissecting Disciplinein Lorraine Hansberry's *A Raisin in the Sun*

Bryan Murphy

The role of physical discipline as a child-rearing tool in American culture has undergone an ebb and flow of controversy since the days of the schoolhouse hickory switch. In contrast to liberal maxims about child abuse and the effectiveness of the "time-out," prodiscipline elements of our society have adopted "spare the rod and spoil the child" as a tried-and-true mantra. Needless to say, this disciplinary argument nearly always revolves around children and adolescents, since rarely do adults receive corporeal punishment from their parents. In her 1959 play *A Raisin in the Sun*, however, Lorraine Hansberry presents an exception to this general rule when the matriarchal Lena strikes her grown children on two separate occasions, each for a radically different reason. Foremost, Lena slaps her collegiate daughter Beneatha for blasphemy during a heated argument about the existence of God. Lena's second disciplinary measure befalls Walter, her eldest child, who endures repeated blows after he squanders the family fortune on a bad business deal. Both instances occur very near the end of their respective scenes as climactic displays of force, and both call for explanation in a play ultimately devoted to reinforcing the loving bonds—rather than the violent rifts—that characterize the Younger family. Lena's dramatic beatings of her adult children raise important questions not only about physical punishment within the nuclear family, but also about race, violence, and familial structure at the outset of the civil rights movement that would transform American culture during the 1960s.

On the one hand, Lena's forceful discipline of her grown children suggests the frustrating pressures of parenting within a marginalized social group. These burdensome responsibilities, which lead Lena to outbursts of physical violence, seem especially acute given her status as a recent widow. With the death of her husband, Lena stands alone. She remains the sole survivor of a generation that endured incredible hardships under racism—painful adversities second only to the dehumanization of slavery itself. Lena bears the enormous weight of ensuring that her children continue the struggle against racial oppression in Jim Crow America, and this burden may be part of the reason that the play depicts her striking Beneatha and Walter for their philosophical backtalk and botched entrepreneurship. In effect, these scenes show an aging mother desperate to slap sense into, not out of, her grown kids, to alert them forcefully to their heritage within a system of racial violence.

In addition, Lena's display of parental force signals the frantic uneasiness of the sharecropper generation toward the mounting waves of cultural and civil change in the post-World War II era. Beneatha exemplifies this generational strain between herself and her mother in her constant call for critical reasoning. For a young, empowered thinker like Beneatha, intelligence remains the chief virtue, replacing old notions of piety and righteousness. "It's all a matter of ideas," declares Beneatha, "and God is just one idea I don't accept" (51). From a position of social bondage—one to which Lena and others like her have grown accustomed—the notion that "ideas" can trump traditional "absolutes" such as the presence of God simply does not register. Indeed, after striking Beneatha, Lena says of her children:

There's something come down between me and them that don't let us understand each other and I don't know what it is. One done almost lost his mind thinking 'bout money all the time and the other done commence to talk about things I can't seem to understand in no form or fashion. (52)

Through her generational lens, Lena cannot fathom the changes that inform her children's lives and decisions, and these shifts trouble Lena to the point of aggression. In her time, God proved an immovable source of stability in the lives of oppressed African-Americans. In addition, Lena's era offered little financial mobility. For this reason, the very prospect of Walter's business proposal seems alien to Lena, and the generational lack of understanding fuels her torrent of slaps.

Despite the difficulties of commanding the house alone and comprehending the social changes unfolding around her, Lena nonetheless places herself as head of this family. Thus when she strikes Beneatha, her strength and resilience become amplified, not only by the slap itself but also by her stern repetition, "In my mother's house there is still God" (51). While the relevance and centrality of religion in people's lives fluctuates throughout history, Lena's stressing of God's existence through violence and verbal repetition helps to cement the foundation of the family through its essential religious bond. Such latent significances find resonance, too, in the way in which Hansberry herself promoted strong familial ties rooted, it seems, in stern mothering. In a radio interview, Hansberry affirmed the importance of familial structure: "we might well long for the day when knowledge of the debt all society owes to organized womanhood in bringing the human race closer together, not pushing it farther apart, will still laughter in the throat of the uninformed" (qtd. in Carter 160). When situated alongside these comments, Lena appears to embody Hansberry's "organized womanhood." Her repeated smacking of Walter further solidifies the place of the powerful matriarch, since shortly thereafter Lena's son experiences a coming of age against the shady Lindner character. When Walter tells Lindner of their proud and hard-working legacy, the stage directions imply a deep satisfaction in Lena: "Mama has her eyes closed and is rocking back and forth as though she were in church, nodding the Amen yes" (148). In this moment, the text reinforces the notion that Lena's discipline has paid off. Indeed, Lena yields her aggressive stance only when Walter undergoes his ascension to family head. In response to Lindner's plea to curb her son's obstinacy, for example, Lena retorts, "I am afraid you don't understand. My son says we was going to move and there ain't nothing left for me to say" (148–9). With Walter's finally assuming the position of father figure, Lena has brought the family together with her "organized womanhood" and may now rest.

Lena's violent behavior against her adult children may also function as a metaphor for the frustrated energy of African-American women in their struggle for civil equality. In the same interview cited above, Hansberry notes, "obviously the most oppressed group of any oppressed group will be its women, and when they are twice oppressed often they will become twice militant." The use of the word "militant" carries revolutionary overtones and signals a call to arms for the cause of civil liberty. Through her display of maternal discipline, Lena becomes both the embodiment of Hansberry's call to action and the representative of a "twice oppressed," "twice militant" woman. The play uses Lena's open palm, in other words, to cast the African-American woman as a formidable force, demanding long overdue respect and unconditional equality. Lena's outbursts, then, behave as a microcosm of a larger social context traditionally relegating black women to silent resignation in their marginal status. Through Lena the powerful mother, Hansberry dramatizes the hope that African-American women might emerge from the margins, with "militant" energies if necessary, to direct those of the younger generations in need of guidance.

In the figure of Lena, who lashes out momentarily with acts of parental policing, the play additionally raises complex questions about free will and its containment. If Hansberry's drama explores themes of freedom from oppression and violence, then why does it show Lena aggressively monitoring the free choices of her intellectual daughter and her entrepreneurial son? Beneatha's view of reality involves the fluidity of individual ideas, and yet Lena quashes her in this regard, asserting, "There are some ideas we ain't going to have in this house" (51). Lena's opinion of Beneatha's plans to become a doctor also conveys an aura of condescension and oppressive doubt. When Beneatha first discusses her choice of profession, Lena retorts, "Course you going to be a doctor, honey, God willing" (50). This condescending tone implies a paradoxical tendency in Lena to restrict freedom and contain choice. Similarly, Lena judges her son Walter by contrasting him with big Walter—a rather problematic idea of the perfect man. On several occasions, she criticizes her son by shorting him in comparison to his father, as when she declares, "I'm waiting to hear how you be your father's son. Be the man he was" (75). By judging Walter and suggesting his inability to make informed choices about his own future, Lena seems to repeat the restrictive actions that have historically characterized white relations with African-Americans. Cleverly, Hansberry appears to stage Lena's aggressive acts of containment in order to pose the question: How can the African-American community attain civil justice if they do not reject the trends of their oppressors?

Despite such complex themes of power and punishment, choice and containment, Lena's beatings also point toward a plainly painful cause: futility. The play carefully sidesteps, for example, the notion that the physical reprimand of Beneatha in any way changes her mind or, even less likely, reaffirms the existence of God in her. The punishment—and indeed embarrassment—of Lena's daughter, in fact, might merely reinforce her sense of the oppressive nature of religion, and thus push Beneatha further away. And while Walter appears to mature following his mother's discipline, he nonetheless squanders the family fortune. The prospect of a new home may seem like a felicitous resolution to the Youngers' problems, but Walter's blunder ensures that the dream of a comfortable life promised by the life-insurance money will not materialize any time soon. Moreover, Walter's decision to inform Lindner of the family's desire to move does not seem wholly motivated by his mother's reprimand. Since the text showcases a rather impetuous streak in Walter throughout, this ultimate decision to stand firm in the face of Lindner's veiled threats and racist rhetoric might represent nothing more than Walter's continued spontaneity. Arguably, in fact, Walter may not have changed at all. He may have simply opted to perform maturity for his mother and, hence, soften her disdain for his wrongdoings. With this possibility in mind, the violent actions of Lena become fruitless, failing to elicit their desired effects. If such a critique of violence inhabits Hansberry's play, then the drama fits perfectly into the canon of nonviolent civil rights rhetoric, which suggests that cultural progress may only occur through diplomacy, understanding, and peaceful demonstration.

Lena's choice to discipline her grown children speaks to the difficult challenges surrounding African-American culture as it vied for a renewed position and an important voice within post-World War II society. Thus, the powerful, climactic acts of familial violence in the play gesture not simply at maternal anxieties and generational strife among the Younger family itself, but also toward larger issues of racial solidarity under enduring oppression, and toward the promise of a nonviolent civil rights movement. Most importantly, however, the sheer complexity and multiplicity of meaning within these two disciplinary instances serve to explode any racist assumptions regarding a "primitive" African-American culture. For Hansberry, it seems, such issues of culture and literary achievement are not just black and white.

Works Cited

Carter, Steven R. "Images of Men in Lorraine Hansberry's Writing." *Black American Literature Forum* 19 (1985): 160–2.

Hansberry, Lorraine. *A Raisin in the Sun*. New York: Vintage, 1959.

2
Choosing a Sign to Analyze

1. What should I write about?

Have you ever struggled to choose a topic (or "sign") for a writing assignment? Have you faced indecision or even apathy when trying to select a focus for an essay? If so, then you are not alone. Writing at the university level can improve your critical thinking skills and your ability to argue persuasively. It can also, however, cause anxiety. Often, roadblocks in sign selection arise from the desire to impress others. Naturally, it seems, we all want to land on a phenomenon that will dazzle our readers and show us to be intelligent observers of the world. We seek the "perfect find" that will lead us to fresh ideas and meaningful conclusions. And we hope to locate an angle whose interest and uniqueness will render the writing process effortless, if not finally enjoyable. Such miraculous discoveries, however, rarely come about. Instead, successful sign selection requires experimentation, patience, and hard work. Finding the "right" sign to analyze, in other words, begins with a commitment to explore an eclectic range of prospects.

Signs surround us all the time, springing from televisions and computers and radios, permeating books and films. They crop up in the places we inhabit and visit every day: our homes, shopping malls, workplaces, restaurants—the list goes on and on. In fact, part of what makes sign choice potentially intimidating lies in the sheer amount of material available for inspection. Ultimately, the hand-wringing that often accompanies sign selection appears to stem from radical freedom, the liberty to choose from an endless font of possibilities. The dizzying array of signs to investigate, however, does not necessarily have to cause unease—especially when you possess reliable methods for narrowing the semiotic field and settling on a phenomenon that will pass muster in a university setting.

Below, we have compiled a series of tools for isolating interesting signs in literature and wider culture. By no means exhaustive, these tools for approaching literary and cultural material typically lead to greater dexterity and precision in sign selection, and they often help alleviate the worries that many students experience at the outset of the writing process.

2. Specificity

If you take just one piece of advice from this textbook, let it be this: aim for as much specificity as possible in all facets of your thinking and writing. In selecting signs to examine, you will avoid major pitfalls by demanding particularity and uniqueness. Think of this specifying action as climbing a ladder, each rung of which represents a more incisive articulation of the sign under analysis. Suppose, for example, that you are interested in "representations of race on television"—a provocative arena for interpretation, to be sure. For a typical assignment of five to seven pages, however, this sign would prove difficult to manage. The examination of such an all-encompassing semiotic area could easily lead to sweeping generalizations that lack precision. To narrow the focus so that it better fits the parameters of a brief assignment, simply "climb the ladder of specificity." Here's how:

- We start on the bottom rung with "Representations of Race on TV." A sign at this level of abstraction and breadth could steer a scholar's entire career, yielding several books. In all likelihood, it will problematically lead to generalized commentary in a relatively short paper.
- We ascend to the next rung with "Representations of Black Characters on TV." This would be a wonderful sign for analysis . . . for a book-length study. Several volumes, in fact, have already been published, including *The Black Image in the White Mind: Media and Race in America* by Robert M. Entman and Andrew Rojecki; *Representing Black Britain: Black and Asian Images on Television* by Sarita Malik; *Revolution Televised: Prime Time and the Struggle for Black Power* by Christine Acham; *Primetime Blues: African-Americans on Network Television* by Donald Bogle; and *Tuning Out Blackness: Race and Nation in the History of Puerto Rican Television* by Yeidy Rivero. Once again, we need to climb.
- We take another step up the ladder to "Representations of Black Women on TV." We're getting closer. This sign selection would work nicely for a master's thesis or doctoral dissertation (typically ranging from 50 to 300 pages). The individual instances of this sign—the number, in other words of black female characters on TV—are too numerous to cover adequately in a short paper. We would never have room for in-depth analysis, since we would spend most of our time inventorying the appearances of black women on TV.
- Next rung: "Representations of Black Women on TV Detective Shows." We're closer now. This semiotic focus probably lends itself best to an academic article or upper-division student paper of at least 15 pages in length.
- Let's climb one more rung: "Representations of Black Women in Positions of Power on TV Detective Shows." At this point, we have ascended to a level of specificity that will work for a study of about five pages. The paper could analyze, for example, the presentation of characters such as Lieutenant Anita Van Buren on NBC's long-running *Law & Order*, Captain Kate Perry in the TNT series *Saving Grace*, and crack sleuth Precious Ramotswe, the heroine of HBO's *The No. 1 Ladies' Detective Agency*. Wouldn't that make for an interesting and highly focused project? Compare its precise semiotic parameters to the impossibly rangy "Representations of Race on TV" located at the bottom of the ladder.

For practice, let's try a second example:

Ladder Position	Sign for Analysis	Action to Take
Rung 1	Disaster films (like *Titanic*, *The Perfect Storm*, *Airport*, etc.)	Climb . . .
Rung 2	End-of-the world films (such as *War of the Worlds*, *Children of Men*, *Mad Max*, etc.)	Climb . . .
Rung 3	Global environmental catastrophe films (such as *Deep Impact*, *Armageddon*, *Meteor*, etc.)	Better, but climb . . .
Rung 4	Films about human-generated eco-apocalypse (like *The Day After Tomorrow*, *Wall-E*, *Waterworld*, etc.)	Better still, but climb . . .
Rung 5	The dearth of films in which human ingenuity triumphantly saves a planet threatened by environmental recklessness (such as *The Core*)	This focus will work well for a five- to seven-page study. The sign is especially interesting, since the big-budget film industry centered in Hollywood typically capitalizes on "the happy ending."

One more example for good measure:

Ladder Position	Sign for Analysis	Action to Take
Rung 1	Sports	Way too general. Climb . . .
Rung 2	Olympic sports	Too low. Climb . . .
Rung 3	Newly inducted Olympic sports (ice dancing, team figure skating, golf, etc.)	Good, but keep climbing . . .
Rung 4	Youth-culture sports new to the Olympics (snowboarding, BMX cycling, freestyle skiing, etc.)	Better, but try one more rung . . .
Rung 5	Fierce opposition to youth-sport inclusions in the Olympics (editorials, for example, that suggest a contamination of the Olympic image by these nontraditional events)	This focus would easily fuel an analysis of five to seven pages.

Identifying signs that drive you to explore their multiple meanings, that invite strong interpretation, and that pique the interest of your readers calls for patience and practice. Try generating long lists of potentially interesting phenomena as you study your cultural surroundings, watch films and TV programs, and read texts for class—and do so actively, climbing the ladder of specificity as you work to identify individual signs. With time, you will develop in the art of sign specification, just as repeated effort will improve your ability to play the guitar, build muscle tone and lose weight, tackle complex math problems, and so forth.

3. Scrutiny

Along with specificity in sign selection, strong writers also apply scrutiny. As one way to hone your investigational skills, start to examine the world of advertising, which provides ample opportunities to test out this helpful tool. All ads convey deep-seated social values and hidden assumptions. They carry invisible ideological messages and unspoken worldviews. And all of them overflow with analyzable signs waiting for your closest attention. In the words of social critic Alvin Toffler, author of the best-selling 1970 book *Future Shock*, advertisers set out to meet "the consumer's subtle, varied and quite personal needs for beauty, prestige, individuation, and sensory delight."[1] With that in mind, study the clever slogans, the eye-catching imagery and ear-grabbing sounds, and the ingenious mechanisms for both producing and promising to fulfill a broad spectrum of consumer desires.

Take, for instance, these semiotic candidates visible to a scrupulous eye:

- American-made products with fictitious, foreign-sounding names such as Häagen-Dazs ice cream (made in New Jersey), TRESemmé hair-care products (a Missouri-based company), and Starbucks "frappuccino" (invented in Seattle)
- the trend in corporate logo design toward sleek, lowercase letters ("iPod," "illy" espresso, "bing," and "swatch," among others)
- the number of ads that deliberately cross genres to resemble film trailers, music videos, video games, and so forth
- Hollywood megastars who tend to avoid appearances in American advertisements but willfully take part in foreign commercials (George Clooney for Swiss-based coffee manufacturer Nespresso, Kevin Costner for Valle Verde shoes, John Travolta for Telecom Italia, etc.)
- Michelin tire ads that feature cute, smiling babies, while subtly leading viewers to imagine small children being hurt in accidents caused by inferior tires

Playing the semiotic scrutinizer yields results, too, in the realms of media and popular entertainment:

- the increase in cartoons for adult viewers, and the fact that many of these animated shows include numbskulled father characters (*The Simpsons*, *Family Guy*, *King of the Hill*, among others)

- the longstanding popularity of "retro" TV series such as *Happy Days* (broadcast from 1974 to 1984 but set 20 years earlier), *Mad Men* (which premiered in 2007 but depicts the advertising industry in the early 1960s), and *That '70s Show* (which ran from 1998 to 2006)
- films and television programs that cast the traditionally adult vampire into youth-culture contexts (the *Twilight* series, the Swedish film *Let the Right One In*, *Buffy the Vampire Slayer*, *True Blood*, etc.)
- fantasy films and their literary precursors that establish an equation between an uncorrupted natural world and the moral superiority of its inhabitants (*Lord of the Rings*, *Avatar*, *The Chronicles of Narnia*, etc.)
- the lasting appeal of TV shows with disabled heroes such as Adrian Monk, the ace detective with obsessive-compulsive disorder, and Dr. Gregory House, the genius physician with a damaged leg and a Vicodin addiction

You can also scrutinize the products of mass consumption for peculiarities of analytical interest:

- pretorn jeans that cost the same as (if not more than) perfectly undamaged ones
- vintage powdered soap and hand towels in restaurants such as Ted's Montana Grill
- herbalized" shampoos (including Suave "with 100% natural rosemary and mint")
- absurdly overstuffed fast-food items, despite persistent warnings about the dangers of overeating and the unhealthiness of fatty foods
- Ben & Jerry's ice cream flavors that promote progressive politics ("Imagine Whirled Peace," "Mission to Marzipan," and the studiously ironic "Fossil Fuel")

Scrutiny frequently pays dividends in the identification of signs from popular and consumer culture, but it may be most useful in the analysis of literature. Often, students organize their essays around broad themes and all-too-obvious elements in plays, stories, and poems. To fight this tendency, we encourage students to read their assigned texts with scrutiny, and then create inventories of unique and provocative details. Such small semiotic particulars can frequently form the basis of an innovative essay, leading to unanticipated interpretations that exhibit distinctiveness and flair.

For practice, let's apply the scrutiny tool to a well-known (and often mis-read) poem by four-time Pulitzer Prize-winner Robert Frost:

The Road Not Taken

Two roads diverged in a yellow wood,
And sorry I could not travel both
And be one traveler, long I stood

And looked down one as far as I could
To where it bent in the undergrowth;

Then took the other, as just as fair,
And having perhaps the better claim,
Because it was grassy and wanted wear;
Though as for that, the passing there
Had worn them really about the same,

And both that morning equally lay
In leaves no step had trodden black.
Oh, I kept the first for another day!
Yet knowing how way leads on to way,
I doubted if I should ever come back.

I shall be telling this with a sigh
Somewhere ages and ages hence:
Two roads diverged in a wood, and I—
I took the one less traveled by,
And that has made all the difference.[2]

You have likely read this poem before, or at least encountered the phrase "the road not taken" or "the road less traveled by." The poem's enduring popularity bespeaks its role in defining a particular American identity that involves rugged individualism and the rejection of herd mentalities. Without much trouble, we can support these notions with various textual citations. The speaker begins at a crossroads in a "yellow wood," and immediately we understand the time of year to be autumn. Winter looms, which lends a degree of finality to the decision at hand. What's more, the narrator acknowledges—with the phrase "how way leads on to way"—that subsequent responsibilities and opportunities in his life will likely distract him from returning to test out the alternative path. Suitably, the speaker feels "sorry" and yearns briefly to have it both ways—to travel both roads as "one traveler." From these details, we surmise that the decision requires deep consideration, necessitating a "long" pause for assessment.

Once the speaker decides, however, his actions are swift. He takes the "other" road, which appears to him as "grassy" and needing the "wear" that his footsteps will provide. The promise of striking out and forging a path for others to follow seems at play here. Why choose the beaten track, the poem appears to imply, when you can blaze your own? This brand of intrepidness and self-confidence reinforces powerful definitions of "Americanness" expressed by writers and philosophers such as Henry David Thoreau and Ralph Waldo

Emerson. In his 1841 essay "Self-Reliance," for example, Emerson declares, "Whoso would be a man must be a nonconformist"[3] and "A foolish consistency is the hobgoblin of little minds."[4]

In keeping with this ideal of steadfast autonomy and strong personal conviction, Frost's speaker seems rightfully self-satisfied as the poem unfolds. He mocks the rejected road—the one that others would follow—suggesting that he will keep it "for another day!" the exclamation point after his commentary perhaps a sign of the ridiculousness of ever desiring to reverse his decision. (This is, after all, a person of action, an Emersonian "nonconformist," a true American.) Then, a smug note enters the text, as the speaker imagines "with a sigh" some future moment at which he will look back to the crossroads in the secluded forest. At this point, the poem appears to celebrate the resilience and fortitude of its speaker, as he triumphantly repeats the opening: "Two roads diverged in a wood, and I— / I took the one less traveled by." By pausing on that repetitive "I"—separating the personal pronouns with a dash and line break—the speaker emphasizes his heroic place at the center of this narrative of decisiveness. He has made the difficult choice, and he is proud of having done so. As he declares in the poem's final line, his savvy selection "has made all the difference." His life has been transformed, it would seem, by this one pivotal decision.

Perhaps this reading of Frost's "The Road Not Taken" as a tale of self-reliance and an anthem to American individualism sounds familiar to you. Certainly, the excerpts that we quoted support an interpretation of the poem as a quintessential American parable. Yet maybe at this stage, calling upon your powers of scrutiny, you have started to think, "Wait a minute. In order to read the poem from that perspective, you had to skip over other important parts of the text." The nineteenth-century German philosopher Friedrich Nietzsche insisted on the slow reading of philosophical treatises. The same applies when approaching literary works, so the caution to "Wait a minute" makes good sense in this case. The merits of slowing down and reading attentively only become stronger when we realize that Frost himself considered "The Road Not Taken" a "very tricky" poem—one that requires the skills of a dedicated semiotic sleuth. In fact, Frost once noted to his friend and fellow poet Louis Untermeyer, "I'll bet not half a dozen people can tell you who was hit and where he was hit by my Road Not Taken."[5] This statement suggests that there is more to the poem than first meets the eye.

Still, how do we approach the processes of slow reading and semiotic scrutiny, especially with literary works that "hit" us in often imperceptible ways?

How, in other words, can the scrutiny tool help us tackle "tricky" texts and isolate interesting signs for analysis? Our experiences have shown that students excel in literary sign identification when they create careful inventories of textual elements that arouse curiosity and give the reader pause. Such a catalog of semiotic markers invariably leads to deeper understandings of the texts under examination, and also sets the stage for effective sign selection. A collection of ten up-close phenomena in Frost's "The Road Not Taken," for example, might include the following pointers to meaning:

1. The first stanza repeats "And" as the first word of lines 2 through 4: the poem curiously stacks this conjunction.
2. Line 13 contains a somewhat unexpected exclamation point, and thus a sudden shift in tone.
3. The poem includes several conditional and qualifying words such as "could," "perhaps," "Though," "really," "Yet," "doubted if," and "Somewhere."
4. The first-person speaker, the "I" of the poem, vanishes from lines 5 to 12 and "divides" between lines 18 and 19.
5. The text tends to repeat the same word in a short span: "way leads on to way" and "ages and ages hence" are the most apparent examples, but "one" appears in lines 3 and 4, and it crops up again in line 19. The text also repeats the same word or phrase over larger stretches, as with "took," "both," "travel," and "Two roads diverged in." The poem seems obsessed with recycling language.
6. We half expect "yellow" to precede "wood" in line 18, but it never appears (although its linguistic ghost, or trace, seems to hover in that line).
7. The poem oddly equates the two paths (they are "really about the same" and they "equally lay in leaves" that have not been trampled) even while it emphasizes their "difference."
8. All description of the wood stops at line 12, about halfway through the poem.
9. The poem highlights verbs of possession such as "kept" and "took."
10. The text begins with an act of private observation during a past experience in a specific place; it ends, however, with an act of public declaration in an imagined future and an unspecified locale.

This list of detailed phenomena is hardly exhaustive. A scrupulous reader could identify many more indicators of meaning in the text. Notice, though, that we have avoided signs such as "the color yellow" and "the season of autumn," since these could be found in any number of texts and, thus, do not seem especially tied to Frost's poem in particular. We have also set aside "abstract" signs including "doubt," "choice," "nature," "the terror of decisions," and "existential angst." Instead, we have maintained a high degree of scrutiny in our list. We do not yet know the possible meanings behind these signs, but that should not trouble us at this early stage of the analytical process. First, we want to devote time and effort to hunting for complex, interesting, and highly focused phenomena. Such precision and scrutiny in sign identification typically paves the way for essays that distinguish themselves as fresh rather than stale, sharply focused rather than featureless and general.

Having created an inventory, we can now concentrate on a particular item or cluster of items. Out of this list of ten signs, for example, the seventh identification seems especially revealing with regard to the celebratory reading of the poem that we offered above. We noted that the speaker takes the "other" road, the one that was "grassy" and in need of "wear," yet we had to steer around the fact that the traffic on the two paths appears "really about the same," and that both roads "equally lay / in leaves no step had trodden black." Frost's narrator, in other words, may state that he took "the road less traveled by," but his language—on close scrutiny—suggests parity between the paths. Suddenly, we sense a curious discrepancy between what the speaker first claims and what the signs in the poem actually present. Consequently, the brazen self-satisfaction that we noted at the end of the poem starts to sound more equivocal and ambiguous. Is the "difference" necessarily triumphant? Couldn't the speaker's final decision have led him down the wrong path to ruin? That would make "all the difference" too, wouldn't it? Both interpretive roads "equally lay" before us.

Close scrutiny would suggest that the poem ultimately takes *neither* position (exultant or evacuating, delighted or despairing) but instead calls attention to how the speaker mythologizes his choice after the fact. Contrary to popular belief, Frost's "tricky" text seems less about making choices than about the desire to appear as though a definitive decision has been made. Ultimately, we cannot know whether the poem intends to convey a triumphant or a despairing "difference," whether the narrator's choice of roads brought about success or destruction. The poem refuses to let us decide definitively either way, because the ambiguity in the word "difference" ensures (very cleverly) that the opposite reading always shadows whichever interpretive path we take. (The same might be said of the word "sigh.")

By slowing down, trusting our powers of scrutiny, and building a strong semiotic inventory, we discover just how problematic it becomes to read "The Road Not Taken" strictly as a tribute to American individualism and bold decision-making. We start to grasp the poem's complexities, in fact, in the manner of professional scholar Frank Lentricchia, who has referred to Frost's text as "the best example in all of American poetry of a wolf in sheep's clothing."[6]

4. Chronology

Focusing on the chronology of a particular phenomenon—plotting its evolution, its alterations over time—can also lead to strong sign selection. Take, for instance, the cinematic representations of that icon of British spy thrillers, Agent 007. Based on Ian Fleming's book series launched in the 1950s, the James Bond film franchise is one of the most successful in history, having spawned twenty-two motion pictures in all, with the last five alone grossing more than two billion dollars. Given numbers of this magnitude, we might assume that one key to the Bond sensation lies with the protagonist's time-lessness—his uncanny ability to remain popular after half a century on the silver screen. No matter how dangerous or difficult the assignment, Bond still brings his enemies to justice, still drives the gadget-filled cars, still woos the female leads. And yet, we know that Bond is not identical in every film. Representations of the hero have transformed over time. Sean Connery led the way through six of the first seven films, from 1962 to 1971. He passed the reins to Roger Moore, who starred in the blockbuster series for the next seven films, ending his tenure in 1985. Since then, the moviemakers seem to have foundered a bit in locating the perfect Bond, with duties shared by Timothy Dalton (two films), Pierce Brosnan (four), and the present torchbearer Daniel Craig (two and counting).

Needless to say, it is not simply the change in actors that modifies the films. Rather, Bond's character—his portrayal as the international secret agent *par excellence*—has shifted with the years. Just examining the two major players alongside the current tough guy, we can begin to notice this metamorphosis. Sean Connery represented the rugged Scotsman—unpolished and gritty, often condescending to women, and not above baring his knuckles for a backroom brawl. Moore, on the other hand, wears the sheen of the upper class. He seems aristocratic, debonair. The Moore Bond would sooner sip cocktails and chat an evening away than engage in fisticuffs. In addition, he seems vulnerable to the advances of enticing women, something to which the Connery Bond appears less susceptible.

With Daniel Craig, the franchise reintroduces a rough-and-tumble version of the hero, even intensifying this facet of his character. Craig's 007 seems remorseless in his violent reprisals, and he is stoical and deceptive with women. If a romantic fling must ensue, then its treatment by both actor and director appears perfunctory, merely a nod to convention. Today's Bond, the newer films imply, cannot waste time at parties or distract himself with trysts.

What's more, the justice to which the new Bond has sworn his allegiance, as well as the methods by which he enforces his service, appear every bit as dubious as the motives of his villainous foes. He operates on the margins of legality, and he often utilizes questionable tactics in his quest to rid the free world of its latest menace. Why is it, we might ask, that this contemporary Bond possesses a strangely compromised morality? Why is our favorite British spy now keen to engage in vindictive violence? Why does he never fully trust the agency under which he works? Such a portrayal differs markedly from the salt-of-the-earth Connery or the bon vivant Moore, and this peculiar shift in the portrait of Agent 007 over time seems ripe for a semiotic analysis rooted in chronology.

For a second example—one also rooted in depictions of gender—consider "The Girl" in the well-known advertisements for St. Pauli Girl beer. Aimed at a certain male demographic, she is alluring but also wholesome, unattainable yet not forbidding, and she seems to reside—unattached, no doubt—in some quaint Bavarian hamlet unmarked by specific name or time. Unmistakably accommodating (she is, after all, a beaming barmaid doling out beer), she is buxom, kind, and—it's impossible to miss—iconically blonde. Her hair color, a potential sign for analysis, might prompt us to ask what significances underlie the ubiquitous blondeness of the models who appear in ads for this pricey German import. But while this focus could certainly drive a successful analytical study, we might produce more interest (and avoid the obvious) by exploring the chronology behind the advertisements. In this case, our tool would help us clear away the more recent history of St. Pauli Girl ads to reveal the interesting fact that, since 1977, all of the models have been blonde except during 1989 and 1990, when her image suddenly went brunette. That brief shift away from blondeness is also a sign—one that fuels a different sort of investigation based from the start in a particular historical moment. Why, we might wonder, would the corporation approve such a noticeable change in its advertising campaign? Why depart from the well-established blonde norm? And why was the departure so short-lived (the models have been fiercely blonde ever since)? Such questions derive primarily from a chronological consciousness that steers away from the unignorable sign of blondeness to a less detectible phenomenon, setting the stage for an essay that tackles the St. Pauli Girl mystique from a fresher angle.

The word "chronology" combines the Greek "chronos" (meaning "time") and "logos" (meaning "word," "speech," "logic," or "reason"). Thus, when you study a sign's chronology, you can think in terms of its "time logic." What, you might inquire, is the particular logic behind a sign's changes over time? What reasons underlie the sign's recognizable shifts? What do alterations in the sign suggest about the culture or text in which it resides? In fact, we can search for several types of chronological patterns, identifying how specific signs:

- perform subtle cycles and repetitions
- make abrupt shifts and deviations
- exhibit meaningful vacillations
- engage in significant evolutions and devolutions
- show gradual emergences or disappearances.

As a way of illustrating some of these more specific ways to chart a sign's chronology, let's consider the short story below, written by Blackfeet Native American author Stephen Graham Jones:

Discovering America

Because I'm Indian in Tallahassee Florida the girl behind the counter feels compelled to pull the leather strap ($1.19 per foot) around her neck, show me her medicine pouch, how authentic it is. "Yeah," I say, "hmm," and don't tell her about the one-act play I'm writing, about this Indian in the gift shop at the bottom of Carlsbad Caverns. His name isn't Curio but that's what the lady calls him when she sighs into line with her Germanic accent and her Karl May childhood. "You should do a rain dance or something," she tells him, she's never seen heat like this, like New Mexico. In the play she's sweating, he's sweating, and there's uncounted tons of rock above them, all this pressure.

In Tallahassee it rained all the time.

I stayed there for eleven months, nineteen days, and six hours.

Because I'm Indian at a party in Little Rock Arkansas, a group of students approaches me out of a back room of the house, ceremony still thick on their breath. In a shy voice their leader asks me what kind of animal my spirit helper is, and when I can't quite get enough tact into my mouth to answer, they make a show of respect, say they understand if I can't tell them, really. They tell me theirs, though: a grasshopper, a dragonfly, three wolves, and somewhere in there I become that tall, silent Indian in Thomas Pynchon's "Mortality and Mercy in Vienna," right before he goes cannibalistic in the middle of an otherwise happening party. The working title of the play I'm still writing is *The Time That Indian Started Killing Everybody*, and standing there with my beer I don't revise it.

In Little Rock there were all kinds of bugs I hadn't seen before.

I stayed there for five months, four days, and twenty-two hours.

Because I'm Indian in Odessa Texas the guy who picks me up off the side of the road asks me what kind. He's an oilfield worker. His dashboard is black with it. When I say *Blackfeet* he finishes for me with *Montana*, says yeah, he drilled up there for a while. Cold as hell. "Yeah," I say, thinking this is going to be an all right ride. He drives and tells me how when he was up there he used to ride a helicopter to the rig every morning, it was *that* cold. In trade I tell him how the National Guard had to airlift hay and supplies a couple of winters back. He nods as if this is all coming back to him, and then, with both arms draped over the wheel real casual, asks me if they still run over Indians up there? I turn to him and he explains the sport, even hangs a tire into the ditch to show me how it's done.

In Odessa the butane pumps go all night, and it's hard to sleep.

I stayed there for three months, fourteen days, and fourteen hours.

Because I'm Indian the guys at the warehouse in Clovis New Mexico add a single feather to the happy face that's been carved into the back of my locker ever since I got there. It's not like looking in a mirror. Every time it's not like looking in a mirror. My second week there we're sweeping rat droppings into huge piles, and when I lean over one to see what Butch is pointing at he slams his broom down, drives it all into my face. That weekend I start coughing it all up, become sure it's the hantavirus that's been killing Indians all over. My whole check goes into the pay phone, calling everyone, talking to them one last time, reading them my play, the part where Curio kills one of the gift-shop people the old way, which means he hits him across the face with a log of Copenhagen, then follows him down to finish it, out of mercy.

In Clovis they don't turn their trucks off so you can talk on the phone, so you have to scream.

I stayed there for four weeks, one day, and two and a half hours.

Because I'm Indian in Carlsbad New Mexico the crew I'm working with calls me Chief, motions me over every time there's another animal track in the dirt. "I don't know," I tell them about the tracks, even though I do, and for a couple of hours we work in silence, up one row, down another. Once I find strange and cartoonish tracks in my row—traced with the sharp corner of a hoe—but I pretend to miss them, pretend no one's watching me miss them. All this pretending. Towards the end of the day I pass one of the crew and, without looking up, he asks if I've scalped anybody today, Chief? I unplant a weed from his row, look up for the briefest moment, long enough to say it: "Nobody you know." He doesn't laugh, and neither do I, and then later that night in a gas station I finish the play I started writing in Florida. It starts when the clerk wipes the sweat from his forehead, says how damn hot it is. And dry. I neither nod nor don't nod, just wait for him to say it.

In Carlsbad New Mexico the law is sluggish, slow to respond.

I stay there for sixteen hours, nine minutes, and fifty-two seconds, and when
the rain comes it's not because I danced it up, but because I brought it with me.[7]

Jones's story seems particularly well-suited to a study of semiotic chronology,
since the narrative format is explicitly repetitive and serialized. Each of the
five "mini-stories" begins with the phrase "Because I'm Indian"; each takes
place in a specific place in the United States and offers a single-sentence sum-
mary of the locale (e.g., "In Odessa the butane pumps go all night, and it's
hard to sleep"); and each concludes with the exact amount of time that the
narrator spends in various cities and towns. These recurrent signs, however,
are unmistakably visible: Jones deliberately situates all of them in the narrative foreground. In order to find a suitable focus for an interpretive essay, we
need to push past the obvious by looking at subtler ways in which signs function chronologically throughout the text.

Notice, for instance, the manner in which the story begins and ends
with references to a rain dance. With close attention to detail, we realize
that the opening mention of the dance serves a clear dramatic function
within the narrator's developing stage play: its reference builds interpersonal pressure between the misnamed protagonist, "Curio," and the
woman "with her Germanic accent and her Karl May childhood." (May,
a German writer who lived from 1842–1912, published several novels set
in the American West, four of which centered on a fictional Apache chief
named Winnetou.) In short, Jones's initial reference to rain dancing works
to underscore cross-cultural tensions and to evoke stereotypical notions
about Native Americans.

Yet a meaningful shift occurs at the conclusion of the tale with regard to the
rain dance. At this late juncture, the narrator identifies the rain dance only to
reject its validity and import, stating, "when the rain comes it's not because I
danced it up, but because I brought it with me." The latter passage minimizes
the significance of the rain dance in order to conjure a godlike power within
the narrator to possess and carry storms wherever he travels. This suggestion
of the narrator's superhuman power blatantly surpasses a force historically
linked to Native Americans, whose ritual ceremonies could reputedly cause
changes in the weather. The traditional rain dance seems almost quaint in
comparison to the narrator's far greater sway—his self-professed ability to
hold onto and dispense rainstorms at will. Consequently, the narrative purpose of the rain dance transforms over time, and such an alteration represents
an interesting sign that warrants inspection. With regard to sign selection, the

key factor here is the specific *change in narrative function* of the rain dance, not simply the "rain dance" as a freestanding image.

As another example, consider the trend in Jones's story to spotlight the act of murder. We initially notice this phenomenon in the second episode, when the narrator imagines himself as "that tall, silent Indian in Thomas Pynchon's 'Mortality and Mercy in Vienna,' right before he goes cannibalistic." Directly after that reference, the narrator discloses the name of his new one-act play: *The Time That Indian Started Killing Everybody.* The oilfield worker speaks of running down Indians for sport in the subsequent frame; the next segment finds Curio killing someone "the old way" (i.e., clubbing the person to death); and the final section hints at the lethal prospect of scalping. Note that the murders—in all of these examples—belong to the mental realms of memory and imagination. Not one of them, in other words, actually takes place in the real time of "Discovering America," as told by Jones's narrator. These murders are part of the past or future, of recollection or speculation, fantasy or fiction.

Then, however, we arrive at the final movement of the tale, where an interesting shift takes place in Jones's narrative treatment of murder:

> [L]ater that night in a gas station I finish the play I started writing in Florida. It starts when the clerk wipes the sweat from his forehead, says how damn hot it is. And dry. I neither nod nor don't nod, just wait for him to say it.

What exactly happens here as the story draws to a close? To what, precisely, does the "It" refer in the sentence beginning "It starts when the clerk wipes the sweat from his forehead"? Does "It" refer to the one-act play, or does something else begin at this moment? This odd use of the pronoun "It" seems provocative, since the narrative style of "Discovering America" is not especially interested in tricks and strange sentence structures—of the kind that we might encounter in more obviously experimental writers such as Virginia Woolf, William Faulkner, and Thomas Pynchon, whom Jones actually mentions in the story. We will need to comprehend this moment—this apparent rift in logic in a text that is otherwise perfectly logical—as we progress with our sign identification.

At first glance, we might naturally assume that the "It" refers back to the "play," given the pronoun's placement directly following the narrator's declaration of having finished his one-act drama. It initially seems, in other words, that the narrator is talking about the start of his play. This reading does not work, however, because we are now in the gas station with the narrator (and not with Curio in the gift shop) when "It starts." Such a shift in settings—from a gift shop to a gas station—is impossible in a one-act play, which by convention contains only a single setting, one and only one locale. The "It," then, must refer to something else. If so, then what starts immediately after the narrator completes the script of *The Time That Indian Started Killing Everybody*?

To answer that question, we need to examine the story as a whole, specifically the way in which Jones begins and ends his tale. When we look back to the start of "Discovering America," and compare it to the ending, we find a set of revealing parallels:

- In the first paragraph of the story, the narrator mentions that his one-act play is set in a gift shop at Carlsbad Caverns. At the end of the story, Jones's narrator has made his way to Carlsbad, New Mexico.
- The one-act drama unfolds in the retail environment of a gift shop, with Curio and the white woman waiting to purchase novelties in paragraph one. At the end, the story's narrator stands in line to pay for his gasoline.
- In the play, the weather is extremely hot and bothersome: the white woman has "never seen heat like this" and she is "sweating." The same insufferable heat pervades the end of the story, where "the clerk wipes the sweat from his forehead, says how damn hot it is. And dry."
- Because of the arid heat, the white woman in the play tells Curio, "You should do a rain dance or something." The same prejudicial statement is apparently what Jones's narrator expects the gas-station clerk to utter at the end of the story. All he has to do is "wait for him to say it."

But how might this inventory of parallels help us decode the ambiguous "It" that "starts" as the story comes to a close? For one thing, they call attention to an especially important similarity in the text—that between the narrator and the protagonist of his play. Indeed, it becomes impossible, once we have parallelism in mind, to overlook the fact that the two figures relentlessly converge. If the two men are so similar, if they overlap so unmistakably, then we can only assume that the story's narrator is equally homicidal. We know from the title of the narrator's play that his protagonist eventually embarks on a murderous rampage. We can, therefore, surmise that the "It" at the story's close is a bloody onslaught performed by the narrator. The gas-station clerk, in other words, is a goner.

All this leads us back to our sign identification. Prior to the final scene, all mentions of murder remain squarely in the province of the imagination—they are relegated to the past or offered as speculation. This last murder, however, takes place in the real time of the story's narration. (We almost see the homicide occur.) What's more, reading the final violent act as performed by the narrator sheds light on the concluding lines of the text:

> In Carlsbad New Mexico the law is sluggish, slow to respond.
>
> I stay there for sixteen hours, nine minutes, and fifty-two seconds, and when the rain comes it's not because I danced it up, but because I brought it with me.

Our narrator is quiet and composed, even in the moments before and directly after his assault on the clerk, for he knows that "the law is sluggish and slow to respond." No one will catch him, since he won't be around long enough for the police to pick up his trail. And by tracking the amount of time Jones's narrator spends in each location—durations that become progressively briefer—we realize that the actual murder of the store clerk has driven him onward. This Indian, the story makes clear, is still out there.

Plotting the references to murder in "Discovering America" provides a unique focus for analysis rooted in chronology, and we might phrase that focus, or sign, in a variety of ways that underscore its "time logic":

- the shift from murder in the remembered past to homicide performed in the narrative present
- the movement from killing that is only speculated upon or acted out in a dramatic script to slaughter actually performed in the protagonist's real life
- the switch from strictly imagined to actual murder at the close of the story
- the change from murder talked about to murder enacted
- and so on

By charting the references to homicide in Jones's story, we come to understand the text's puzzling closure and render it more coherent. We also set the stage for an interesting semiotic study because we clearly identify a curious chronological phenomenon that will no doubt lead to provocative interpretations. And though tracking the murders in Jones's story might appear on the surface more difficult than, say, the St. Pauli Girl or James Bond signs with which we opened our discussion of chronology, all three interrogate the same types of "time logic." They each identify, in other words, a meaningful semiotic shift over time: the demeanor of a beloved spy, the hair color of a marketing icon, and the references to murder in a contemporary short story.

5. Juxtaposition

Another key way to locate analyzable phenomena in both literature and culture involves teasing out particular—ideally, peculiar—relationships between signs. Many times, semiotic juxtapositions of this sort produce irony, which typically leads to interesting essay topics. Irony takes many shapes, all of which share an impulse to reverse, to flip the tables on expectation, to run against the grain and emit oppositional energy. The most basic form is "verbal irony," where a speaker deliberately means the opposite of what he or she literally expresses. (If storm clouds pour down rain, and your best friend looks out the window and says, "Gorgeous weather, huh?" then she has offered up a piece of verbal irony. Your friend obviously means "lousy weather," but she expects you to grasp the irony, to hear the literal language in an "upside down" fashion and pick up on the inverse suggestion.) When we seek juxtaposition in identifying phenomena to analyze, we effectively "double up" with signs, setting one against the other, making them converse and interact in dynamic ways. By setting two or more signs in relation to one another—while also identifying some ironic, paradoxical, or unlikely element about that relationship—we lay the groundwork for complex investigations of significance. We also tend to capture the interest of discerning readers and spark our own critical imaginations.

As an example, take the rather recent phenomenon of the luxury box at many professional sports arenas. Can we think of a particular relationship or juxtaposition that renders the sign less obvious, more paradoxical or ironic? By lending scrutiny to our sign and cataloging its particular characteristics, we might note that the professional sporting arena seems, at least on the surface, devoted to the spectacle of the human body in competitive play. Indeed, the priciest seats in these forums have traditionally been those closest to the action. At the field level, we feel the bone-jarring hits, hear the crack of the bat, the swoosh of the ball; we might even catch a bead of sweat from a star ·player. The signifier of privilege, of "luxury," in other words, has historically involved *proximity* to the players. Sitting close to the field, we feel inside the game; we almost become a member of the team. In fact, some might argue that famed New York Knicks fan Spike Lee—with his courtside seats and high media profile—becomes a kind of "sixth player," badgering the officials after a bad call, hectoring the opposition, passionately encouraging his beloved squad.

The rise of the luxury box, however, appears to reverse this relationship. Now, proximity is overthrown by distance, competitive air by air-conditioning, the grunts and dust of the game traded for the in-suite bar and catered food. In fact, these luxury boxes often come equipped with multiple flat-screen televisions, so that attendees can enjoy the game without the annoying real-world interruptions of . . . the game. Granted, these high-priced private viewing areas serve many motives. The corporations that possess the means to rent them, for example, utilize the extravagant space to impress prospective clients, seal business deals, and reward their own personnel. To wealthy companies, in other words, these exclusive seating options resemble conference rooms more than bleachers. Still, this trend in sports culture—one that prompts owners to demolish and rebuild otherwise structurally sound stadiums in order to cash in on the fad—changes the way we perceive professional athletics. "Take me out to the ball game," with the luxury box in mind, assumes entirely different meanings.

The juxtapositional strategy above locates a paradox: one can go to the game without, in effect, going to the game. Still other juxtapositions and relationships exist throughout our social worlds: provocative symmetries and parallels, knotty tensions, interesting enigmas, curious dichotomies. And the same goes for literary signs. Below are some juxtapositional relationships—you might even think of them as "formulae"—to help you hone your sign-selection skills in the literary arena:

1. Stranger in Town
   Formula: In a text devoted to X, why do we find Y?
   Example: While Marianne Moore's often anthologized poem "The Fish" deals mainly with images of aquatic life and marine surroundings, it also curiously employs metaphors from the domestic sphere: hand-held fans, spun glass ornaments, decorative cornices, and so on. Why?

2. Ghost in the Machine
   Formula: In a text devoted to X, why *don't* we find Y, especially when we think we should?
   Example: Joseph Conrad's *The Heart of Darkness* never mentions the slaughter of elephants in the Congo, even though the entire novel serves as a critique of the ivory industry established by Belgian colonial powers. Why this strange absence?

3. Little Sibling
   Formula: Considering a text that foregrounds X, why do we find Y, a related but less noticeable form of the dominant focus?

Example: While *The Great Gatsby* highlights homicidal violence in Jazz Age New York, it simultaneously underplays instances of suicide. To what ends?

4. War of the Worlds

Formula: Why does the text appear to pit two opposing yet related sign systems (X and Y) against one another?

Example: Homer's *Odyssey* celebrates bardic tales of men singing to men but represents the Sirens' song—*women* singing to men—as destructive and evil. How come?

5. The Big Flip

Formula: In a text grounded in X, what accounts for the paradoxical presence of Y?

Example: Franz Kafka's *The Metamorphosis* positions Gregor as the victim of an oppressive manager, an ungrateful family, and a diabolical transformation. But he, too, displays signs of tyranny and oppression over others. What's that all about?

Looking closely at these formulae, you might notice how each of them calls attention to a particular form of paradox. They all highlight some specific irony embedded in the juxtaposition, underscoring a peculiar reversal of expectation or common consensus.

6. Fusion

In his canonical "Lines Composed a Few Miles Above Tintern Abbey, On Revisiting the Banks of the Wye during a Tour, July 13, 1798," British Romantic poet William Wordsworth writes of being

> A lover of the meadows and the woods,
> And mountains; and of all that we behold
> From this green earth; of all the mighty world
> Of eye, and ear,—both what they half create,
> And what perceive[8]

In this celebration of the creative imagination—a power as varied, sublime, and "mighty" as the forces of the natural world—Wordsworth implies a hybrid sense of perception. In his thinking, we "half create" what we "behold," an idea that especially resonates with the act (indeed, the art) of fusion in sign selection. Deploying this tool, the semiotician cleverly unites several observable phenomena, making them adhere in such a way that a new, more multifaceted sign emerges. With fusion, you become half perceiver, half creator—identifying disparate signs of interest and then constructing an appropriate term that unifies the elements in some creative fashion. The endeavor is, we might say, *poetic*, since it requires both inspection and invention, reason and imagination.

To clarify this last and most complex of our five tools, let's look at the phenomenon of reality TV shows. Since "reality shows" is far too broad to qualify as a strong choice, we need to climb the ladder of specificity if we hope to locate a sign suitable for university-level analysis. With that in mind, we might consider the more specific phenomenon of "reality shows that feature celebrities." Taking a further step might reveal a juxtapositional irony inherent in celebrity reality shows. Think about it: don't reality programs traditionally feature everyday folks? Why, in a genre of television programming usually devoted to "real" and average people, do we find entertainment stars, who strike us as anything but commonplace? Forerunners to reality programming, such as *COPS* (in which the camera crew follows police officers on unscripted calls), focus on "ordinary people." In addition, reality shows as we currently understand them—globally syndicated series such as *Big Brother*, *Survivor*, and the various *Pop Idol* competitions—reinforce the idea that the viewing public desires, in some sense, to view people like themselves. So why do some reality shows focus on figures at whom the spotlight has been pointed all along?

This is a fruitful area, to be sure, for semiotic investigation. Yet we might seek out an even sharper angle. Proceeding up the ladder of specificity leads to a particular subset of "reality shows that feature celebrities"—namely, programs where rock stars receive the coverage. Series such as *The Osbournes* (chronicling the domestic life of infamous Black Sabbath front man Ozzy and his family) and *Gene Simmons Family Jewels* (the wry A&E series following the exploits of the former Kiss bass player and vocalist) fit the category, as does *Bret Michaels: Life As I Know It* (centered on the lead vocalist for the 1980s-rock outfit Poison). What's more, our powers of scrutiny suggest that these figures are not just *any* rock stars; more precisely, they are all rather washed-up hard rockers. We have now entered some pretty provocative terrain, since our focus contains not only specificity and scrutiny but also a fusion of reality shows grouped under the concept of "Heavy Metal Has-Beens."

Still, we could take this sign selection one step further, given the similarity of the three shows cited above. The degree of difference between the items united by our cohesive concept, in other words, is rather slight. This is not to say that the sign selection isn't strong. It is. But it could actually gain power by establishing greater tension between the elements subject to fusion. In short, a more challenging deployment of this tool might call for increased divergence between the catalogued phenomena. Starting with these three rock-star-centered TV shows, we could look outside the genre of reality programs for more semiotic material to import into our "half-created" category. We might recall, for instance, the smash mockumentary *This is Spinal Tap* (1984), Rob Reiner's satire of the pretensions and outlandish lifestyles enjoyed by famous rock stars. We could also call upon musical acts—such as Weezer and Pavement, maybe even Kid Rock—whose identities rely on an ironic relationship to the established aura of rock stardom.

Diverging even further, we could place Rock Star energy drinks under our new and expanded collection of signs. If you are not familiar with the product, it resembles Red Bull and many other supercaffeinated beverages, and bills itself as "the world's most powerful energy drink." With its ostentatious logo (a giant star with two capital Rs back to back) and slogan ("Party like a rock star"), the product seems to cash in on a particular brand of parody. For though we might easily understand how energy drink names such as Hype, Energy, and Red Bull connote their desired effect—the shot of caffeine, the boost, the pick-me-up—Rock Star doesn't offer that clear connection. In fact, the notion that a drink has been engineered for the life of a rock star seems mocking. Far from aligning itself with ideas of nourishing the ideal physique or maximizing the body's potential for endurance and training, Rock Star appears more interested in a theatrical performance. It promises (and also parodies) the idea that we may inhabit the flamboyant identity (and not the body) of a rock star.

Taken as a group, these fused signs carry a good deal of satire. Though all appear to play on the common wish for stardom—for legendary rock-and-roll status—they simultaneously parody that longing, making it comically explicit. The "stardom" sold to us in these specific forms seems campy and kitschy, complete with built-in irony and a preformed tongue-in-cheek quality. Savvy marketers and writers understand the appeal of irony and satire, parody and performance, and how such wittiness plays to our intelligence. In this "rock satire" example, then, the elements grouped under the umbrella sign seem more disparate. We include television programs, a film, a few music groups, and even an energy drink. The mark of the analyst who fuses several different items under one unifying term is quite apparent, since we "half-created" the sign from a divergent set of phenomena. These types of fusions—unlikely combinations, hybrid groupings—test our abilities as sign engineers, asking us to look for curious convergences, stray associations, subtle bonds.

For an example of fusion from the literary realm, we might turn to a classic novel such as F. Scott Fitzgerald's *The Great Gatsby*. In studying and searching for meaningful signs in this 1925 work, we might initially be drawn to images that Fitzgerald clearly spotlights—the green light at the end of Daisy Buchanan's dock, the giant eyes of Dr. T. J. Eckleberg, the Valley of Ashes, the cars, parties, mansions, and so on. Yet all of these signs seem too obvious and overt, which means that they have already been discussed and analyzed at great length. Often enough, however, we can deploy our semiotic tools to lend nuance and uniqueness to signs that might have lost their luster through overexamination. Consider, in this regard, Gatsby's mansion. While the protagonist's lavish home would fall flat as a sign in its own right (it remains a highly foregrounded object that, by itself, does not capture any relational complexity), we might test out fusion possibilities and situate Gatsby's mansion among a complex grouping of related signs in the text. To begin, we need to apply scrutiny to the novel and inventory its particular descriptions of the Gatsby estate. We know, for example, that the house is a replica of a European aristocratic dwelling, since Nick Carraway, the book's narrator, supplies this background:

> There was nothing to look at from under the tree except Gatsby's enormous house, so I stared at it, like Kant at his church steeple, for half an hour. A brewer had built it early in the "period" craze, a decade before, and there was a story that he'd agreed to pay five years' taxes on all the neighboring cottages if the owners would have their roofs thatched with straw.[9]

The "'period' craze" mentioned in this passage refers to a fad among wealthy Americans to construct extravagant homes modeled on the manorial estates of past European aristocrats. The rich American brewer, in this instance, has chosen an architectural design from the feudal period in European history—a time prior to the rise of a middle class, when moneyed lords wielded power over an oppressed peasantry. The brewer who had the mansion built, and later sold it to Gatsby, clearly wished to recreate that centuries-old social order, as indicated by his desire to have the roofs of neighboring cottages "thatched with straw." His approving nod to a previous social arrangement, one in which the aristocracy faced few populist threats to its privilege, represents an interesting textual phenomenon in

Fitzgerald's book (which is deeply interested in class structures and their consequences). By taking cues from continental architecture, by bowing to the Old World's alleged cultural supremacy, the brewer and his imitative mansion set up Europe as a mark of excellence, signifying power and prestige better than anything American-made.

Such an observation could provide a unique fusion opportunity. We need only to locate other signs that celebrate Europe and presume its elite status. These might include, for example:

- Gatsby's shirts, which are tailored and shipped to him by his "man in England"[10]
- the "Adam study" attached to Gatsby's bedroom suite; the name refers to Robert Adam, an eighteenth-century Scottish architect and interior designer[11]
- the decor in Myrtle Wilson's apartment, which is "crowded to the doors with a set of tapestried furniture entirely too large for it, so that to move about was to stumble continually over scenes of ladies swinging in the gardens of Versailles."[12] One of the largest palaces in the world, and the royal château of French monarch Louis XIV (1638–1715), Versailles is renowned for its expansive gardens
- the rumor that Gatsby is "an Oxford man"[13]—that is, that he attended Britain's oldest surviving university (it was founded in the twelfth century) and arguably the most distinguished institution of higher learning in the English-speaking world
- the home of Tom and Daisy Buchanan, "a cheerful red-and-white Georgian Colonial mansion, overlooking the bay";[14] the architecture refers to designs that emerged in Britain roughly between 1720 and 1830, during the successive reigns of George I to George IV

We could place this series of interrelated signs under a "fusion" term such as "Glorifying Europe in *The Great Gatsby*" or "Old World Tributes in *The Great Gatsby*." What's more, by situating this fusion within its uniquely American context—Fitzgerald's novel is often considered one of the masterpieces of *American* literature—the sign bristles with interest. What are these celebrations of Europe doing in such a quintessential American text? At this point, we do not know why the novel reveals such an interest in European fashions and trends, and we need not worry about issues of interpretation yet. For now, we want to focus on finding—and indeed "engineering"—a sign with a high degree of interest and complexity.

Climbing toward greater specificity, lending intense scrutiny, plotting evocative chronologies, discovering curious juxtapositions, and performing difficult forms of fusion: all of these acts will help you arrive at compelling phenomena that generate lively and insightful interpretations.

Familiarizing yourself with each of these five tools, gaining competency with all of them, ensures that your essays begin with clearly demarcated parameters that will capture your readers, stimulate your critical imagination, and guide your speculations about meaning. The tools discussed above have aided countless students in their quests to become savvy analysts and persuasive writers, and we are confident that they will help you, as well. On that positive note, let's now look at a method for testing the strength and workability of your sign selection. It, too, has proven beneficial to numerous students determined to excel in the art of analysis.

7. The VOICE test

We have explored several strategies for locating a specific sign to analyze in an essay. Now comes the time to test the effectiveness of our selection. How do we know if the sign we have isolated will truly meet the grade? How can we proceed with confidence in our choice? In answering these vital questions, we advise students to put their prospective signs through a series of tests. The "VOICE" method discussed below offers five reliable appraisals of a sign's viability and interest. The individual letters of the word stand for:

- Visibility (Can you observe and describe the sign in concrete detail?)
- Originality (Has the sign been explored too often in the past or does it seem fresh?)
- Import (Is the sign worthy of analysis? Does it seem important enough to merit in-depth inspection?)
- Complexity (Is the sign sufficiently complex and multifaceted?)
- Energy (Does the sign carry some energy-producing tension or "charge"? Is it dynamic, ironic, or paradoxical in some way?)

Visibility

First, your sign must be "above the waterline"—like the tip of an iceberg, clearly visible to anyone on board a passing ship. Relying too heavily on abstract concepts in sign identification ("Women's Issues" or "Social Class Conflict" or "Sexuality") typically leads to generalized interpretation. The visibility test keeps you from dipping too far into invisible ideas in your sign selection. "Hope" or "the American dream" or "conspicuous consumption" in *The Great Gatsby* fail to provide enough visibility. They seem, to use the iceberg analogy, "below the waterline." They do not literally "appear" in the novel as much as remain underlying "themes" or "ideas" with which the novel wrestles. They are latent rather than manifest, conceptual rather than perceptible.

Consider, for instance, the following moment in Fitzgerald's text, where the narrator speaks with a rather shady underworld character named Meyer Wolfsheim:

> "I see you're looking at my cuff buttons." I hadn't been looking at them, but I did now. They were composed of oddly familiar pieces of ivory.
>
> "Finest specimens of human molars," he informed me.
>
> "Well!" I inspected them. "That's a very interesting idea."
>
> "Yeah." He flipped his sleeves up under his coat.[15]

In this small excerpt, the text calls attention to a grisly piece of jewelry worn by Wolfsheim. Any reader can see that his bizarre cufflinks appear in the text, so as a sign, they pass the visibility test. In fact, these strange accoutrements achieve high marks in terms of visibility because they are neither too abstract (and hence invisible) nor too conspicuous (and thus overly spotlighted and even cliché).

Originality

We might also argue that the focus on Wolfsheim's cufflinks passes the originality test. If we asked a hundred readers to find interesting textual phenomena—or signs—in *The Great Gatsby*, how many would return with this strange piece of jewelry? Not many. Instead, a high percentage would more than likely focus on the infamous "Valley of Ashes," the ostentatious clothes and automobiles, the green light on the Buchanans' dock. The novel, in fact, calls special attention to these signs, offering them on a silver platter. On the other hand, Wolfsheim's human-molar cufflinks seem less available on first, second, or even third readings. Consequently, this sign passes the originality test. (For a look at a complete essay devoted to this very phenomenon, see student Kellen Ward's "*The Great Gatsby* and the Meaning of . . . Molars?" which we reprint at the end of this chapter.)

Import

The test of import asks questions such as the following: "Does the sign seem relevant to the text or culture in which it is situated?" "Is it too extraneous or trivial?" "Is it important to an understanding of the text or culture as a whole?" "How significant is the sign in terms of its relation to the wider culture and time period in which it appears?"

As an example, take the curious fact that the monster in Mary Shelley's *Frankenstein* never receives a proper name. Throughout the narrative, Victor strictly refers to his creation in patently dehumanizing terms such as "the creature,"[16] "the miserable monster whom I had created"[17] and even just "it." With respect to import, we might argue that the book seems deeply concerned with issues of paternity and lineage, which lends significance to the monster's namelessness. In addition, the title of the novel itself speaks to the importance of naming. Our sign, then, would pass the test of import in relation to the text at large, to Shelley's writing and thinking, and to British Romantic literature more generally.

Or consider again the sign of Meyer Wolfsheim's human-molar cufflinks. Aside from a high degree of visibility and originality, the sign also holds import, since it connects well to the novel's immediate historical context. Fitzgerald's depiction of Wolfsheim as a kind of half-savage immigrant (whose human-molar cufflinks suggest a cannibalistic bent) carries disturbing importance in terms of class- and race-based distinctions and anxieties in Jazz Age New York. By learning more about those cufflinks, in other words, we gain a deeper awareness of the difficult ethnic, racial, and class-based tensions present in America in the 1920s.

Complexity

In testing a sign's relative complexity, we can draw an analogy to Olympic diving. That is, if your sign were a dive, then what would be its "degree of difficulty"? What "rating" would the judges ascribe to it? How involved, in other words, is your sign? Think back to the phenomenon of "black women in positions of power on TV detective shows," which we developed earlier using the specificity tool. Look at its component parts and actions. In order to zero in on the sign, we had to overlay instances of race (black), gender (women), occupation (positions of power), media (television), and genre (detective shows). In diving terms, this sign involves several "spins and turns" and "choreographed muscle movements." It is nothing like the old "cannonball" that many of us practiced as kids. A cannonball demands very little from its practitioners, whereas the dives performed in Olympic competitions possess high degrees of complexity and several dynamic moves.

When striving for complexity in your sign selection, however, you also want to balance the "degree of difficulty" with the need for clarity and precision. Remember that you ideally want to hit the dive cleanly, without making an unsightly splash—otherwise, the score from the judges will drop dramatically. Just as a cannonball would prove laughable in any serious diving competition, so too would a fantastically complex dive, one so convoluted that the athlete fails to pull it off. Note, for example, the almost absurd complexity of the following semiotic focus: "black women police lieutenants over forty years old on network TV detective shows broadcast from 8:00–9:00 p.m. on Wednesdays." Complexity for complexity's sake, in other words, can often lead to obscurity, confusion, and frustration. We invite you, instead, to think of complexity—and indeed all of the elements of the VOICE test—as a sliding scale, one that you can manipulate up (toward greater intricateness) or down (toward clearer contours and definition). The point is to find a proper balance. It is possible to be too simplistic, but it is also possible to overengineer a sign. This test encourages you to gauge your sign's complexity relative to the need for clarity and precision in its identification.

Energy

If your sign has successfully passed the tests above—if it is visible but not obvious; if it is original but carries import to the text and its wider cultural and historical contexts; if it is many-contoured and multifaceted—then it probably generates a good deal of energy, as well. By "energy," we mean a kind of "charge" embedded in the sign, a dynamic and stimulating quality that propels your critical imagination. Celebrated British Romantic poet, artist, and printer William Blake argued that "Opposition is true Friendship," and this adage makes good sense for the selection of signs.[18] That is, you may think of signs as oppositional forces, pushing and pulling at their texts and contexts, creating energy out of that opposition. In this way, a sign's potential energy may stem from how much it resists its surroundings or creates contradiction, paradox, or irony.

As an example, let's return to a sign from the world of women's fashion. At the end of our introductory chapter, we include an essay by student Constance Larrew, who writes on the trend among young women to wear fashionable clothing that incorporates military camouflage patterns. Since her chosen phenomenon involves the opposing systems of fashion signs and military signs, it harbors its own internal energy or oppositional force. It seems, in other words, "ironic" that military gear—highly pragmatic and uniform—could become a fashion statement for women. But what if we desire even more energy? In that case, we might look at the related trend of *pink* camouflage apparel. You may have seen this fashion phenomenon or can at least imagine it. This additional specification seems to carry greater energy, because we customarily associate camouflage with violence, stealth, hardness, animal aggression, and so on—all traits traditionally linked with masculinity. When we think of pink, we likely return with the complete reversal of those associations: femininity, softness, beauty, innocence, and so forth. The sign "pink camouflage," in other words, seems especially energized, in that it yokes starkly opposing sign systems, fuses competing associations, marries unlikely significations.

As you can see, the VOICE test offers a rigorous series of hurdles that your sign must overcome in order to pass muster. Over the years, our students have found it incredibly helpful. Try not to worry about interpreting or finding supportive research for your analysis at this stage. For now, simply set your mind to locating and engineering signs that you find provocative and, perhaps more importantly, that will fascinate your readership. Ask yourself: "Does this sign stimulate me to interpret its multiple meanings?" The VOICE test can help you reach an answer.

8. Student example

Gatsby and the Meaning of . . . Molars?

Kellen Ward

F. Scott Fitzgerald's *The Great Gatsby* typically conjures images of extravagant parties, luxurious homes, lavish cars, and the reckless excesses of socialites during the Jazz Age of the 1920s. It is safe to assume, then, that most readers do not remember any special mention of human teeth in the novel. Nonetheless, a curious reference to molars occurs during a luncheon where the narrator Nick Carraway meets up with Meyer Wolfsheim and Jay Gatsby. As the three men sit at the table conversing, Nick takes note of Mr. Wolfsheim's cuff links. Aware of Nick's stare, Wolfsheim replies, "I see you're looking at my cuff buttons.

[. . .] Finest specimens of human molars," to which Nick responds, "That's a very interesting idea" (81). Without further commentary on this bizarre clothing accessory, the luncheon proceeds as if nothing unusual has transpired. Yet the passing mention of Wolfsheim's uncommon cufflinks—meaningless as the remark may seem at first—actually calls greater attention to their presence, and immediately begs the question as to why the novel features this strange fashion item. What underlies the text's depiction of Meyer Wolfsheim—a Jew, an underworld power broker, and "the man who fixed the World's Series back in 1919" (78)—as someone proud to wear cuff buttons made out of "the finest specimens" of human teeth? What thematic significances can be assigned to this odd piece of jewelry?

It would initially seem that, through the strange cufflinks on Wolfsheim's shirt, the text offers a critique of the excessive displays of material wealth in American culture during the Roaring Twenties. Most of the characters in the novel, including Daisy and Tom Buchanan, believe that a person's value as an individual directly aligns with the accumulation of luxuries. The characters tend to base their friendships and associations on people with the flashiest possessions and the most money. Through the enormous houses, fancy parties, and expensive clothes, the characters seem to display their wealth in outlandish ways in order to signal their cultural superiority. On the way to lunch, for example, Nick and Gatsby see a group of young black men headed to a funeral. While passing by, Nick thinks to himself, "I was glad that the sight of Gatsby's splendid car was included in their somber holiday" (111). Such a scene demonstrates the cultural need to showcase material opulence, even during times of tragedy and misfortune. Along with driving pricey cars, many of the characters dress themselves in diamonds and other precious stones as a means to highlight their social status. Similarly, Daisy fawns over Gatsby's wardrobe of hand-tailored imported shirts. Fitzgerald, however, dresses Wolfsheim with the most "spectacular" fashion statement of all. Since the idea of wearing real human teeth is peculiar and eccentric, the novel draws attention to the molars in order to criticize the rampant materialism of postwar American culture. Driven by the idea of amassing material possessions, and coupled with the desire to be considered part of the elite, some people, the text illustrates, even wear human molars. The novel highlights this odd clothing item, then, to elucidate the obsessive longing for all things eye-catching and hard to obtain.

The drive for luxurious lifestyles and fancy materials flourished after World War I—a time when cultural celebration reached a zenith. Also during this time, however, many people faced the deaths of loved ones from the war overseas, and many fell into party-hard lifestyles as an escape mechanism. Fitzgerald realized the overwhelming sense of death in the country and incorporated this into his work. Thus, the human molars also suggest the undeniable presence of death and decay in the novel and, indeed, in the nation after the war. Fitzgerald provides many images of death in *The Great Gatsby*: the running over of Myrtle by Daisy, the shooting of Gatsby by Wilson, Wilson's suicide, and more. Though Fitzgerald includes Wolfsheim's horrifying molar cufflinks, he does not offer any speculation as to where the teeth came from. Given that Wolfsheim is involved in organized crime, one might logically infer that the teeth were extracted from the mouth of a business partner or customer who failed to deliver on a promise and found himself in fatal trouble. Such a suggestion underscores the rampant but less conspicuous violence taking place in American culture at the time. With this in mind, the representations of death have moved from the battlefields of Europe to the social spheres of the postwar homefront. By highlighting this class conflict, Fitzgerald suggests that, even though America emerged on the victorious side of "The War to End All Wars," the desire to overcome and overtake simply made its way back to American soil. The novel carefully uses the molars, then, to highlight Wolfsheim's success in the postwar class struggle, and to reveal the violent extent to which some may go to attain social prowess.

The overt display of cultural power dates back to the earliest civilizations. In many Native American and African tribes, the wisest and most successful men adorned themselves with human and animal bones. By dressing these cultural elites in bones, the tribes displayed them as higher in status. The fascination of Western culture with "primitive" societies reached new heights during the Modernist era. During this time, European and American societies became intrigued by the practices and rituals of native civilizations, and reflections of this interest appeared in the arts. One thinks, for example, of the painting by Picasso titled *Les Demoiselles d'Avignon* (in which the women's faces resemble African masks). By placing human molars on the cuffs of Meyer Wolfsheim's shirt, Fitzgerald reflects upon this societal infatuation with "primitive" tribal practices. The human molars act as a badge for Mr. Wolfsheim to illustrate his supremacy and prestige as a potential chief and wise man in the new society. Gatsby believes Wolfsheim to be very knowledgeable in the world of organized crime, gambling, and bootlegging, and he places his mentor on a pedestal. He is so admiring of Wolfsheim, in fact, that he invites Nick to meet the older man. The human molars signal to Nick that Mr. Wolfsheim must be of another status altogether. Fitzgerald adorns Wolfsheim in human bones to demonstrate his wisdom and importance to figures like Gatsby—vulnerable in youth, and later corrupted—and to raise the troubling question of which "wise" men the postwar nation will turn to for direction. Needless to say, the novel worries about making into social leaders the criminal and murderous Wolfsheims of the world.

As modern Westerners dwelled on the primitive practices of native tribes, they also grew captivated by an idea known as "social Darwinism." A widespread misconception based on poor understandings of the biological studies of Charles Darwin, social Darwinism found its way into mainstream America as a means for upper-class citizens to express and justify their superiority over other social classes. The teeth on Wolfsheim's shirt, then, recall this particular form of brutality and barbarity in American culture. Since Wolfsheim is considered an elite within the "new money" class, Fitzgerald provides him with human teeth to display his victory over others. In so doing, the author questions the "cannibalism" among the characters by suggesting that their drive for social domination could eventually escalate into the consumption of one another and the wearing of each other's bones as trophies.

The idea of social Darwinism, and the relentless striving for social supremacy, however, not only applies not only to the upper, middle, and lower classes. It plays out, as well, with respect to the struggles between ethnicities and races. The novel additionally mentions the human molars as a means of highlighting the anti-Semitism of American society in the first quarter of the twentieth century—especially toward Jews in powerful, wealthy positions. The text's emphasis on Wolfsheim's molar cufflinks demonstrates his powerful status—which would have been increasingly worrisome to the empowered WASPs steering the nation. During and directly before the 1920s, many Jews began emigrating from Europe in order to start a new life and fulfill their own American Dream. These immigrants, however, were often met with hostility and hatred. Early in the novel, Tom Buchanan expresses his distaste for other social groups by stating, "It's up to us, who are the dominant race, to watch out or these other races will have control of things," meaning that if the traditionally dominant WASPs are not careful, they will be overrun by other ethnic groups. This was the attitude of many people in the early years of the century, and with the publication of books such as *The International Jew*, a four-volume anti-Semitic work, Jews felt the danger of raising their heads in public and being blamed for the problems in America. By placing a Jewish man in a powerful position in the world of organized crime, and adorning him with human-molar jewelry, perhaps Fitzgerald attempts to paint a picture for his readers of the stereotypical image of the Jews in the 1920s. Fitzgerald carefully situates Wolfsheim in the world of crime, since people like Tom believe that Jews and nonwhite minorities are responsible for everything wrong with the nation. Fitzgerald adds teeth to Wolfsheim's suit because some individuals in early twentieth-century America believed Jews to be lacking in moral integrity and essentially subhuman. By conjuring this terrifying image of one of the only Jews in the novel, Fitzgerald attempts to show his society the outlandishness of their prejudice.

While complex images and subtle themes pervade *The Great Gatsby*, it is interesting that Fitzgerald inserts such a strange pair of cufflinks. In the final analysis, it would seem that the text uses this passing reference to warn American culture about the overindulgence of material possessions; the barbaric, warlike push for social supremacy; and the overwhelming sense of racism in the culture. Could it be, the novels seems to ask, that the loss of American cultural unity after World War I might occur as quickly and easily as losing a tooth?

Work Cited

Fitzgerald, F. Scott. *The Great Gatsby*. New York: Scribner, 1925.

3

Questioning and Staging the Sign

1. Creating questions to fuel your analytical quest

Once you have selected a sign to analyze and ensured that it passes the VOICE test, you will then want to lay a plan for interpretation. This crucial process begins by establishing a field of inquiry or set of related theoretical questions. These linked queries will fuel your critical imagination to travel—or quest—into reasoned argumentation about the meanings and motivators behind your chosen sign. Interestingly, the words "question" and "quest" both trace their roots to the Latin "quaerere," which means "to ask" and "to seek." Strong semiotic analysis almost invariably begins with well-formulated questions that lead the writer on a meaning-seeking expedition, a voyage toward persuasive responses about significance.

Thinkers of all kinds have long valued the place of questioning in the processes of intellectual journey and discovery. "He that questioneth much," claimed sixteenth-century British philosopher Francis Bacon, "shall learn much."[1] More recently, Nobel laureate Albert Einstein declared that "the important thing is not to stop questioning," not to lose "a holy curiosity."[2] As these observations suggest, the generation of provocative questions can promote critical inquiry and set the stage for edifying investigations. Yet what constitutes a "theoretical question," let alone a "holy" one? And what counts as a well-formed "field of inquiry"? For starters, consider a few analytical queries raised by reporters for the *New York Times*:

> From a study of why many contemporary American women wear blatantly sexy Halloween costumes:
>
> "Why have so many girls grown up to trade in Wonder Woman costumes for little more than Wonderbras?"[3]
>
> From an essay that investigates the photographic image of Marxist revolutionary Che Guevara on products such as key chains and bikinis (the article was published on the fortieth anniversary of the Argentinean activist's death):
>
> "What exactly does the sheer proliferation of [Guevara's image] mean in a decidedly capitalist world?"[4]
>
> From an article on the ways that psychotherapists decorate their offices, and the effects of those choices on the mental health of patients:
>
> "So what do therapists think about when they decorate an office?"[5]

In each of these examples, the writer shines the spotlight on a specific and interesting phenomenon—the rise of risqué Halloween costumes for women, the rash of Che Guevara images reproduced on consumer goods, the décor choices of practicing therapists—and inquires about its meanings in contemporary culture. While the three examples treat vastly different signs, each poses a core inquiry about significance, a driving theoretical question that provides a navigational guide for the writer's interpretive quest. Seasoned analytical writers, however, rarely stop with a single phrasing of their primary question. Instead, they generate a "field of inquiry," a unified collection of related queries that builds curiosity about the sign, revs up the interpretive mind, and solidifies the focus of the analysis.

2. Building a field of inquiry

By creating a "block" of questions devoted to the chosen sign, writers lay the foundation for their analyses. Below are some supplemental rephrasings of the questions that we culled from the *Times*. By adding two interrogations of our own in this exercise, we establish a field of inquiry that effectively spurs interpretation:

> Example 1
> "Why have so many girls grown up to trade in Wonder Woman costumes for little more than Wonderbras?" How are we to understand this curious fashion statement made each year by many women? What meanings and motivators lie behind the choice by contemporary women to don risqué outfits on Halloween—a holiday typically associated with kids, candy, and innocent dress-up?

> Example 2
> "What exactly does the sheer proliferation of [Guevara's image] mean in a decidedly capitalist world?" What varied significances might the face of Che Guevara carry when emblazoned on consumer goods? Why does the portrait of a Marxist radical continue to appear with such frequency, particularly in countries that still consider "Communism" a dirty word?

> Example 3
> "So what do therapists think about when they decorate an office?" In what specific ways does a therapist's choice of office décor signify? Why does the outward appearance of an office matter in a profession devoted to the inner life?

Notice, first, that each additional question focuses on the same phenomenon. Sustaining the spotlight on one sign—making it the star or protagonist of analysis—will keep the study from veering in unrelated directions during the interpretation process. In this way, the field of inquiry keeps essays coherent and probing (delving more and more deeply into one specific sign), rather than unorganized and meandering (wandering out to extraneous phenomena and steering off course).

Observe, too, how our supplementary questions prompt analytical responses that will be plural rather than singular, heterogeneous rather than homogenous. The pluralizing terms "meanings and motivators," "varied significances," and "specific ways" all underscore diversity and multiplicity. But we need to remember that multiplicity lies in the meanings of the sign, not in multiple signs. An effective group of theoretical questions focuses on *one* unique phenomenon and helps the analyst approach it from a *variety* of interpretive angles.

Finally, viable fields of inquiry almost always include at least one question driven by the word "why." Interpretive writing for university classes—especially, perhaps, English courses—positions "why" as the crucial question of analysis. In a British literature class, for example, a student might generate a field of inquiry such as the following: "Why does Samuel Beckett's 1958 play *Endgame* contain so much repetitive language, where characters ask and answer the same questions, in the same ways, throughout the one-act drama? Why does Beckett place such emphasis on redundant forms of inquiry and response? Why, in short, does the play highlight cyclical modes of communication?" Such a collection of highly related "why" questions sets the stage for reasonable speculations about meaning, and ushers the writer and readership into the all-important realm of theory.

The call for "why," however, does not prohibit the use of other question words. As in the *New York Times* examples above, we can construct inquiries where alternative prompts function as synonyms for "why." The questions below, for instance, serve as "why" substitutes that successfully trigger interpretation:

> What does this phenomenon mean?
> What are the multiple significances of this sign in this specific place and time?
> What lies behind this fascinating phenomenon?
> What is this textual curiosity all about?
> When did this sign originate, and what accounts for its persistence?
> How can we make sense of this phenomenon?
> How can this sign be read and understood?
> Where does this sign lead us intellectually and emotionally?
> To where do the roots and tendrils of this phenomenon reach, and how might this coverage be significant?

The point is this: you can never go wrong if you "supply the why" in the field of inquiry, but also remember that other question words possess value for the critical writer, particularly when adjusted toward theoretical aims. If your questions remain focused on one sign, gesture toward plural significances, and successfully supply the why, then chances are your field of inquiry will promote deep thinking and help in your intellectual quest for meanings.

Our discussion, however, need not conclude with these three distinguishing features of strong analytical inquiries. The art of questioning involves myriad subtleties and challenges, and becoming adept at raising the kinds of queries that will energize both you and your readers takes time and practice. With that in mind, we include below a set of discussions designed to strengthen your sense of question-raising as part of analytical writing in higher education.

3. Hints for developing a strong field of inquiry

Privilege the theoretical over the practical in your questions

As you generate a field of inquiry to help probe the meanings of your sign, be sure to differentiate between practical and theoretical questions. Practical questions—though important to your understanding of how the chosen sign operates—are different from theoretical ones. Use the former to pin down the specifics of your sign within the text or cultural setting. Deploy the latter—the theoretical questions—to help search for answers to the sign's meanings and importance.

If your study involves a literary sign, for example, practical questions might include:

> Who (or which character) in the literary work is associated with this sign?
> Where is the sign located in this text?
> When do I encounter related signs?
> How many instances of the sign exist within the chosen work?

The formulation of practical questions is especially constructive in the reading and prewriting phases of sign analysis. If you actively engage the phenomenon under inspection, and take copious notes about its specific characteristics, then you will prepare yourself to develop more insightful and persuasive theories about significance.

As a clarifying example, consider another sign from F. Scott Fitzgerald's *The Great Gatsby*—namely, the unlikely pastoral metaphors often ascribed to urban environments in the book. By "pastoral," we mean the literary convention of idealizing rural life. (The term derives from the Latin *pastor*, which means "shepherd.") Recalling our discussions of sign selection, you might note that this identification involves some oddity or strangeness: the sign seems interesting and worthy of inspection because the novel applies these pastoral metaphors to cityscapes, as opposed to the more expected farms and pastureland. Narrator Nick Carraway, for example, refers to a drive around Manhattan as "so warm and soft, almost pastoral, on the summer Sunday afternoon that I wouldn't have been surprised to see a great flock of white sheep turn the corner."[6] To help with the logistics of the sign, we might ask the following practical questions:

> Where do these pastoral metaphors appear in the novel?
>
> Who is responsible for uttering them?
>
> What are the particular circumstances surrounding the appearance of these pastoral turns of phrase? (Are they uttered only at large festive gatherings, or when a specific character is alone, or during a particularly intimate moment between two characters?)
>
> When, in relation to other events in the novel, do these rural idealizations occur? (After a particularly traumatic or pleasant episode, or in the buildup toward a lavish party or secret meeting?)
>
> How much attention does the novel pay to rural metaphors of the city?

These are wonderful ways to explore the fundamental facts about the chosen phenomenon. As questions, however, they are not theoretical because they do not promote interpretation in an open-ended fashion. Rather, they are practical and can be answered inarguably. Look at each question again and ask yourself if you could answer it with irrefutable data. If you answered yes, then you are in the practical realm.

A collection of theoretical questions, on the other hand, might include the following inquires, all of which lead into the realm of interpretation, where our responses are matters of persuasion rather than simple, verifiable fact:

> What multiple significances underlie the pastoral metaphors of the city in *The Great Gatsby*?
>
> Why do these curious placements of the rural within the metropolis appear in a Modernist novel?
>
> Why in describing the city do we find Fitzgerald's characters utilizing figures of speech that recall idyllic country existence?
>
> What underlying motivators explain the odd way in which the novel applies rural similes to urban locales?

How might Fitzgerald's deployment of pastoral metaphors in describing metropoli-
tan settings speak to larger thematic concerns of the text?

Understanding the distinction between, and different uses of, practical and
theoretical questions ensures that your analytical studies achieve their ultimate goals, and that you reach your full potential as a semiotic interpreter.

Offer stylistic diversity in your questions

A lively field of inquiry also avoids redundancy and maintains reader interest
by presenting a variety of phrasings for the sign and a range of interrogation
strategies. Look, for instance, at the following list of questions focused on the
rather recent popularity of stadium-style churches in the American South:

What are the multiple significances of the megachurch phenomenon in the American
South?
Why the proliferation of stadium-sized churches in the Southern states?
What meanings lie behind the continued success of such massive places of worship
for American Southerners?
Why are megachurches currently thriving in states such as Georgia, Mississippi, and
Louisiana?
How might we account for the particular popularity of these colossal houses of rev-
erence in the Southern United States?

This list of questions avoids needless repetition by rearticulating the sign in
various forms. Crafting multiple reiterations of the same fundamental question establishes a unified field of inquiry while capturing the reader's attention through stylistic variation.

Be careful, though, not to let changes in language and attention to style
steer you away from your specific sign. Each question, though phrased differently, still needs to spotlight the same phenomenon—otherwise, your study
might lose direction. Note that the following questions invite this danger:

Why is church attendance so much higher in the American South?
Why are the majority of megachurches Evangelical?

Though still theoretical and interested in religion, the Southern United States,
and the popularity of church-going in this region, these inquiries move off the
original focus and promote an incoherent investigation. We might imagine

different studies that deal with higher church attendance in the South or the tendency of megachurches to arise within a particular Christian denomination. Both are fascinating and worthy signs for analysis. They are, however, different from the original identification: the popularity of megachurches in the American South. As such, these divergent questions might obscure the focus and court disorganization.

For practice, consider the following list of stylistically diverse analytical questions, and try to identify those inquiries that stay on track, and those that stray, from the following sign: "the mainstream popularity of tattoos in contemporary culture."

Why have tattoos suddenly become part of mainstream culture?

Why have tattoos "come out," achieving widespread public approval in recent years?

Why do young men "get inked" more frequently than young women?

What accounts for the sudden shift of tattoos from a marginal to mainstream status in contemporary culture?

What forces underlie the choice by many young women to get flowery tattoos?

Why are lower back and solar plexus tattoos more popular with women, while arm and neck tattoos remained favored by men?

Why have tattoos entered into vogue—increasingly functioning as fashion statements?

How can we understand the current popularity of tattoos in contemporary culture?

What hidden motivators, if any, are associated with the relatively recent spread of tattoos?

Most of the inquiries above concentrate on the mainstreaming of tattoos in contemporary culture, but others diverge into different (if still interesting) semiotic terrains. While the location of tattoos on men's and women's bodies, for example, carries its own interest, that focus problematically veers from the original sign. In building a field of inquiry, then, be sure to address all of your related questions to one—and only one—specific phenomenon.

Stay objective and scientific in your questions

As an analyst of signs in both literary and cultural spheres, you will also want to remain as objective and scientific as possible. This means that your questions should appear rational and level-headed. Imagine a biologist, poised to begin an investigation dealing with rats, asking, "Why do we care anyway, since these vermin are disgusting?" Rather, the biologist, as an impartial observer, might inquire, "What accounts for the rat's curious ability to digest *x*?" or "Why has a large portion of the rat population in a particular city suddenly died off?" These are unbiased investigatory prompts that avoid individual emotion and subjective outlooks.

Or consider again the sign of megachurches in the American South. Just as a rat-loathing biologist seems implausible, so too does a social scientist or historian who asks, "Why do people go to these silly warehouse churches, when organized religion is obviously a sham?" The opposite could scarcely work either: "Why don't more people attend these fabulous communal spaces, since they offer true spiritual enlightenment and promote salvation?" In both instances, the questions invite subjectivity, court personal opinion, and highlight bias. By avoiding value judgments and opinion, your questions will help to legitimize your arguments while simultaneously ushering you into rational studies of ideology, cultural beliefs, dominant assumptions, history, and so on.

We sympathize, however, with students who feel compelled to include implicit statements of value or morality in their questions. In fact, the editorial pages of our newspapers, the politically slanted radio and talk shows, the blogosphere and internet news sites all tend to promote hard-and-fast positions rooted in perceived wrongs and rights. Uninformed consumers of this information often consider it factual and beyond reproach. Being a mature thinker and writer, however, means exploring and questioning the received opinions that permeate our lives. When we delve into the belief systems and values, the underlying "psychologies" of culture, we often find that complex issues defy easy understandings and neat divisions into two opposing camps. Nonetheless, this common "either-or" mentality seems ubiquitous, especially with respect to issues that specific cultures regard as "touchy." Consider the following examples:

> Hip-Hop is either a revolutionary political and artistic means of "keeping it real" or the morally depraved noise of thugs.
> Nose and lip piercings are either disgusting self-mutilations or beautiful expressions of personal freedom.
> Conservative politicians are either evil fear-mongers or the saviors of traditional ideals.
> Facebook and Twitter are either hip, innovative ways of interacting with the world or the death of face-to-face social engagement.

"Either-or," "good-bad," "right-wrong," "moral-immoral," "evil-benevolent," "stupid-smart," "negative-positive": these binary constructions reduce and simplify incredibly complicated signifiers of meaning; they render the world in stark polarities, operate on the extremes, and offer black-and-white outlooks shorn of subtlety and complexity. In your analyses, you will want to avoid the types of questions that force you down one of two preformed paths. Instead, work toward fields of inquiry that remain unbiased and objective. This will help you think more like a scientist about your chosen signs and their meanings.

Promote multiple answers in your questions

You also want to keep your questions open-ended and not "front-loaded" with answers. In other words, try to avoid early interpretations of your sign during the question-generating stage. Consider, for example, this problematic inquiry regarding megachurches:

> Why have many megachurches modeled themselves on stadiums in order to appeal to men between the ages of 20 and 45?

The claim that megachurches have become popular because they appeal to what we might call "an underrepresented demographic" of church-goers—namely, males aged 20 to 45—marks the beginnings of an intriguing interpretation. It offers a plausible reason as to why these coliseum-like religious venues have gathered momentum in the late twentieth and early twenty-first centuries. (For, the reasoning might run, by approximating a rock concert at an arena—complete with massive video display, live band, and thousands of people ecstatically singing and swaying to the music—the megachurch attracts the kind of men who enjoy grand spectacle.) Still, that claim represents just one possible avenue of investigation and restricts the possibility of other viable interpretations. Problematically, this question comes with a "conclusion in hand," an interpretation embedded in the inquiry, and as a result, it forces a single way of thinking about the sign. No doubt, this is a valuable idea. In the question-generating phase, however, you ideally want to privilege inquiries that invite multiple claims about the sign's meanings.

Now consider a more open-ended version of the question regarding the recent appeal of the megachurch:

> To whom in specific do these enormous Southern churches appeal, and how might that attraction be significant?

In this case, the question remains open-ended. While you might investigate how such churches draw men between 20 and 45 by approximating a sporting event or concert, you might also want to discuss how they appeal to those habituated to large warehouse-shopping and mall culture. In this second way of reading the sign, then, you would focus less on the particular sex and age of the church-goers and more on their predilections in terms of consumption. And what about the attraction of these massive temples for those increasingly isolated by the suburbs and the internet? In this third analytical approach, you could concentrate not on sex and age, or on patterns of consumption, but on a broad-reaching cultural isolationism. Stadium-like churches, it would seem, promise their congregations near anonymity. Believers may come to worship, the megachurch appears to say, without being singled out or put on the spot. Such a large structure bears little resemblance to a quaint parish chapel, where everyone knows (and keeps tabs on) everyone else. The megachurch offers a vast sea of people, in other words, in an anonymous rush of religious praise.

Because it is open-ended, the question above spurs even further analysis. For instance, these massive churches might also tap into a prevalent "bigger is better" mentality, suggesting that the more extravagant the church, the more prosperous and enviable those who attend it. This additional reading seems particularly interesting, given that many of the largest, most lavish churches in the country have historically been located in the North. New York City alone boasts the largest Catholic cathedral in the United States (St. Patrick's) and by some measures the largest cathedral in the world (the Cathedral of St. John the Divine, which belongs to the Episcopal Diocese of New York). These churches are, aside from houses of worship, enormous symbols of wealth and prosperity. With the rise of economic powers such as Dallas, Houston, and Atlanta in the latter half of the twentieth century, the megachurch phenomenon appears additionally to reflect increased flows of capital in the Southern US states. At the same time, however, at least one fundamental difference remains between the Northern and Southern versions. Whereas historians would situate the grand cathedrals of the North in the "high-church" tradition (associated with the prescribed rituals, clerical organization, and architectural grandeur of Catholicism and, to a degree, Episcopalianism), those of the South typically fall under the "low-church" heading—which downplays those very tendencies and leans toward the Evangelical. (Note that the terms "high" and "low"—while they appear to promote moral judgments—refer in this case to specific and objective spiritual practices.) And since the low-church tradition has historically sought to define itself against the perceived excesses of its Catholic counterparts, the fact that many Southern churches have opted to "go grand" presents an interesting paradox.

As you can see, rearticulating your questions in an open-ended fashion helps to generate multiple responses to any sign. Such interpretive rangi-ness—with all of its exploratory energy—typically sets the stage for stronger, more revelatory analytical essays.

Sidestep a "character focus" in your questions

While it is quite tempting to think of literary characters as living, breathing human beings, your theoretical questions need to assume that the figures inhabiting novels, plays, and poems remain literary constructs that authors fashion and manipulate. The degree to which the author and his or her char-acters seem to merge—especially in the case of, say, *The Autobiography of Benjamin Franklin*, Ralph Ellison's *Invisible Man*, or the poetry of Sylvia Plath—will always be of great interest. Still, authors and the characters in their literary productions are never irrefutably the same. Furthermore, we cannot suppose that these characters are sentient—making choices and pos-sessing feelings. Rather, the author imbues them with particular features, cre-ating the linguistic illusion of people who live, breathe, and feel.

All this seems commonsensical enough, but consider how easy it is to slip into the trap of thinking about characters as actual people with conscious-ness and free will. Below is a list of questions dealing with Daisy's decision to choose Tom over Gatsby at the end of *The Great Gatsby*. See if you can discern their character-based focus:

> What is Daisy feeling when she chooses to stay with Tom?
> What are Daisy's expectations of Tom when she selects him over Gatsby?
> What underlying motivators drive Daisy's decision?
> What role does public opinion have in helping Daisy decide which man to choose?
> What unspoken tensions make Daisy pick Tom?

All of the questions above treat Daisy as if she were a real person with feelings and expectations. She has the power to make decisions, she may experience tension, she can be swayed by public opinion. In pursuing these questions, you may end up with a psychological profile of Daisy instead of a probing analysis of Fitzgerald's strategic representations of Daisy in the novel. In cre-ating your field of inquiry, then, try to think less "characterologically" than "textually." That is, focus less on *Daisy*'s choice of Tom over Gatsby and more on the way *the novel* presents Daisy's selection. In other words, strive to frame your questions not around Daisy's choice and its meaning for her and her life, but around the semiotic function of her choice in Fitzgerald's literary project. What, in short, does her decision mean with respect to the larger thematic concerns of this novel, written by this author, in this specific cultural and historical context?

Though the avoidance of "character-based" questioning is particularly important in establishing a field of inquiry for literary texts, it also makes sense when applied to cultural signs. For example, consider the following question:

> Why does my brother wear an expensive North Face jacket, since he's not a climber or even much of an outdoorsman?

Here, the question unnecessarily limits the focus to one specific individual. Such a question could easily breed personalized interpretations rooted in subjectivity:

- because Uncle George gave it to him, and he admires George
- because he has no money and a friend offered it to him
- because our last name is North
- because his favorite actor wore a similar jacket in a recent film
- because his girlfriend thinks he looks good in it

Consider, however, these rephrasings of the question, which expand the scope of the sign and read it as a broader cultural phenomenon:

> What are the multiple significances of extreme mountaineering equipment when worn casually by young people?
>
> Why this particular mode of dress by this particular demographic at this specific place and time?
>
> Why have brands such as the North Face and Patagonia (traditionally worn by climbers and explorers) become a clothing trend for teens?
>
> Why have young men and women turned to pricey outdoor wear as a fashion statement?
>
> What accounts for the popularity of expensive, rugged apparel among those who do not engage in demanding wilderness activities?

These revisions successfully navigate around the character-based logic of the original question starring "my brother." They are no longer concerned with why that one particular person might choose to wear a North Face jacket but have shifted instead to focus on a clothing choice by an entire demographic. The questions, in other words, are more interested in scientific (and hence objective) answers as to why many young people don high-priced mountaineering gear, precisely when these teenagers are not themselves explorers or climbers.

Now that you have studied the makings of strong analytical queries and learned how to establish a viable field of inquiry, you are ready to think about staging signs. Up to this point, you have read about discrete tasks within the analytical process: isolating specific signs and posing questions that will trigger interpretation. In the next step of the process, you will work on generating prose that captures the intricacies of the chosen sign and invites readers to follow your reasoned speculations about meaning.

4. Staging your sign

How much interest would the film *Philadelphia* hold if the lawyer played by Denzel Washington possessed no preconceived notions about homosexuality, no prejudices? What engaging tensions would we find in *The Sound of Music* without the backdrop of Nazi totalitarianism? Just as in screenplays and dramatic scripts, your critical studies also require "staging," so as to generate audience interest—to hook your readers (as well as yourself, as chief interpretive writer). In order to do so, you will need to consider the three key parts of almost all successful dramas: a "star" or protagonist; a "situation" or cultural and historical setting; and a "problem" or conflict to address and potentially resolve. In films and stage plays, these narrative features make us wonder, "What will happen to the hero given the present situation? How will he or she get out of this bind?" In a similar way, you can spotlight your sign like the star of a drama, situate it within a specific place and time, and pose a curious interpretive problem or puzzle associated with the phenomenon.

Few students ever receive instruction along these lines, however, largely because thinking of critical analysis as a kind of "creative drama" seems counterintuitive, perhaps even misguided. For decades, creative and critical writing have largely been considered mutually exclusive domains. On closer inspection, however, it becomes clear that the finest creative writers—novelists and dramatists, poets and screenwriters, song writers and comedians—devote a great deal of time to thinking critically about how signs function in culture. Likewise, the best critical writers strive for new and creative avenues of exploration into their chosen fields. In short, creative writers take their task of critical inquiry seriously, while critical analysts seek out creativity throughout their methods of investigation. This cross-fertilization—this willingness to blur the boundaries between the critical and creative arenas—promises great dividends as you work to stage your sign and bring your study to life. Ensuring that your staging focuses on a specific sign or "star"; that it locates the sign in a particular cultural and historical context or "situation"; and that it highlights a specific interpretive predicament or "problem" will help to dramatize your analysis, animating it for you and your readership. With that in mind, we turn to specific discussions of these three crucial facets of the staging process.

Making the sign the star

If you have taken pains to select a highly evocative sign that passes the VOICE test, then you should already possess an able protagonist. Your sign, in others words, has excelled in a series of auditions and established itself as the top choice—the star with a lead role in your investigation. In the initial phase of staging, then, you want to shine the spotlight on your chosen hero. Take, for example, the phenomenon of "sexy schoolgirls" in Spike Lee's film *25th Hour*, and observe how student Lauren Bullington establishes her sign's presence as the star:

> In his 2003 film *25th Hour*, Spike Lee repeatedly focuses on images of sexualized schoolgirls. Mary, for example, struts around in her skin-tight clothes and barely-there miniskirt, while Naturelle coyly drags from her cigarette as she sits on a playground tire swing. A group of girls in plaid shower Monty's dog with affection in one of the film's early scenes, and later, Lee presents two young students outside the Coventry Preparatory School, their short skirts highlighted by the camera angle, their cigarettes curling smoke. In addition to their frequent appearance, the schoolgirls in *25th Hour* exhibit risky behavior and exude sexual energy. Mary attends class with a belly tattoo that is impossible to ignore, and after seductively reciting poetry in class, she flirts with her teacher in the faculty lounge—a place with a "no student" policy. Similarly, Naturelle turns her simple snack of honey on a spoon into a tantalizing game, inviting Monty to join her in the bathtub.

In this initial phase of the staging process, Lauren effectively highlights her sign. There is no doubt whatsoever about her analytical focus—she clearly reveals the "star" of her study. Rather than generalize, she offers concrete examples and clear-cut evidence of its presence in the film. Consequently, she puts her chosen sign on stage for readers to view, showing its specific characteristics and contours.

No fewer than seven precise illustrations of Lauren's sign appear in the writing above. By the end of her first paragraph, the presence of "sexed-up schoolgirls" in Lee's film is inarguable. Notice, too, how Lauren deploys a high percentage of strong, active verbs—"struts," "drags," "showers," "flirts," and so on—a clear indicator of a student who takes seriously the work of creating interest in her study by making her sign move, act, and react. As a result, Lauren succeeds in making her sign the hero of her study, illustrating where it occurs in the text, establishing its presence from many angles, and proving that it constitutes an important part of the movie.

Situating the sign

Making the sign the star is fundamentally an objective act. Lauren's paragraph rests on facts, since no one can argue that the sign of "sexy schoolgirls" does not exist in *25th Hour*. In moving to the second part of staging—the situation or context—Lauren widens the spotlight to show more of the stage. No longer does she consider the sign in isolation but now views it as an interactive element within a larger drama. Take a look at how Lauren now situates her sign, revealing the broader backdrop of the film and locating Lee's sexed-up schoolgirls in their precise semiotic surroundings:

> These schoolgirls, however, do not appear in a teen romantic comedy or kooky frat flick—movies known for innocent sexual discovery and carefree fun. Lee's *25th Hour* deals instead with serious issues related to crime and punishment, social justice and the assignment of blame. Monty, a convicted drug dealer, attempts to wrap up loose ends before his incarceration. His close friend Frank embodies the stereotypically amoral stock broker out to profit at any cost, while his other chum Jake comes across as a schoolteacher with questionable ethics. If that were not enough, Lee sets his film in the aftermath of 9/11, the tragic day when New York City was attacked by militants who regarded the United States as an unjust world power.

All of a sudden, Lauren's sign bristles with import and piques curiosity. Sexy schoolgirls might not seem strange in many other movies or texts, but here—in this particular film, by this particular filmmaker, in this specific historical context—the sign does not appear easily decodable. The situation provides contrast, contradiction, and, as a result, interest.

Notice, however, that Lauren remains noninterpretive, simply presenting factual observations. All that has changed is the coverage of her spotlight. Whereas in the first section—making the sign the star—she trained her lens on her sign in isolation, she now widens the scope to show the sign in its surroundings. The situation provides engaging contrast, renders the sign strange and even slightly out of place in three important ways. First, she offers a genre context. That is, her sign seems odd given the weight of the genre—a serious dramatic film as opposed to a romantic comedy or slapstick romp. This is not a carefree summer film for teenagers but a thought-provoking look at criminality and its allure. Lauren then illustrates how the sexed-up schoolgirls contrast with other characters in the film. The youthful charm and charisma of the girls seem alien to the troubles of Lee's adult male protagonist and his morally dubious friends. Finally, Lauren exposes the cultural and historical situation of post-9/11 New York. Again, the analogy to a stage set is apt: the stage lights slowly reveal more detail and situational specificity, which lend genuine interest to her sign.

Posing the problem

The final act of staging involves "posing the problem" that will drive interpretation. Often enough, the so-called problem of a critical essay entails a peculiar or tense relationship between the chosen phenomenon and its setting, between star and situation, sign and context. Think back to the *New York Times* questions, which we cited early in this chapter. One example focused on the popularity of consumer items—such as t-shirts and key chains—featuring the image of Marxist revolutionary Che Guevara. "Why," we wondered along with the *Times* reporter, "does Che Guevara's face show up on a range of capitalist goods in a decidedly anti-communist country?" The "problem," "tension," or "conflict" seems obvious enough in this case: it has to do with the incongruous relationship between sign and context. For Marxists mourning Guevara's death in 1967, wearing a t-shirt emblazoned with Che's face would hardly seem strange or ideologically inconsistent. We expect followers to display images of their fallen hero. When a range of products bearing Che's image, however, appear nearly half a century later—in a country whose politics often run aggressively counter to Guevara's socialist vision—we suddenly have an interesting "problem." The "tension" or "conflict," in other words, emerges when we find his image on consumer goods in a stridently capitalist and anti-communist setting.

Establishing a semiotic problem sharpens the edge of a study. The sign's complexity is highlighted in relation to its contexts. And after the hard work of choosing a viable sign and situating it against an evocative backdrop, posing the critical problem often means simply restating the driving theoretical questions. This is the strategy that Lauren deploys when posing the problem in her study:

> Given the movie's backdrop of serious crime and retribution, Lee's persistent representations of sexy schoolgirls raise important interpretive questions: Why, in a somber film chronicling the last day of freedom for a convicted drug dealer, do we repeatedly find sexed-up schoolgirls? What relationships exist between these risqué Catholic prep schoolers and Lee's larger thematic concerns? Why does Lee present these icons of seductive adolescence in a story about a sentenced pusher in post-9/11 New York?

While Lauren chose to present the problem by stating her theoretical questions directly, you might decide to be less explicit, embedding your inquiries in declarative rather than interrogative forms. (In fact, your instructors may include this stipulation in a particular assignment.) If so, then you simply need to convert your questions into statements using phrases such as the following:

> This particular sign, then, prompts questions about . . .
> One of the central riddles of the text lies in how this sign . . .
> An enduring curiosity of this work resides in . . .
> This sign begs important questions related to . . .

An alternative articulation of Lauren's problem, rendered in the declarative mode, might read this way:

> Given the movie's backdrop of serious crime and retribution, Lee's persistent representations of sexy schoolgirls remain curious incongruities. One of the riddles of Lee's film, then, lies in why these sexed-up schoolgirls appear in a story

chronicling the last day of freedom for a convicted drug dealer. This essay seeks to explore the significances behind Lee's risqué Catholic prep schoolers in relation to his larger thematic concerns, and searches for meanings related to these seductive adolescents when placed inside a story about a sentenced pusher in post-9/11 New York.

Since Lauren had already generated a viable field of inquiry to drive her study, changing her questions into statements takes little effort. This flexibility in terms of posing the problem offers you a measure of freedom in staging your sign.

5. Staging from start to finish

Having isolated and studied the three parts of a successful staging, now consider two more examples in their entirety. We have inserted slash marks (//) between the key parts—(a) making the sign the star, (b) situating the sign, and (c) posing the problem—so that you can see clearly how both stagings manage each crucial step:

F. Scott Fitzgerald's *The Great Gatsby* brims with violence and bloodletting. The novel finds Tom Buchanan breaking the nose of his mistress after she merely mentions the name "Daisy"; it hints at the murder of Dan Cody by his gold-digging wife; it suggests secret snuff jobs by Meyer Wolfsheim and his underworld cronies; and it reaches narrative climax with the deadly mutilation of Myrtle Wilson by a speeding car and the shooting of Gatsby in his swimming pool. Repeatedly, the text presents characters in destructive, often fatal, contact with each other. Person-to-person violence runs rampant through this almost sadistic Jazz Age novel. Yet Fitzgerald's tale of anxious and aggressive class struggle also touches on another, less noticeable, form of life-ending brutality. On several occasions, the novel subtly introduces signs of suicide. Nick, for example, mentions in passing the sad plight of Henry L. Palmetto, who threw himself in front of a subway train. The character "Owl Eyes" emerges from a car wreck only to have a bystander ask if he was trying to kill himself. The title character, too, recalls the death wish he entertained while soldiering in World War I. Even George Wilson's suicide, coming at the climax of the novel, appears overshadowed by the murder of Gatsby. //

These side glances at self-erasure appear especially significant given the novel's interest in how individuals often ruthlessly pursue their own agendas at the expense of those around them. Fitzgerald's narrative, in other words, seems to center on the glorification of the self and its advancement at any cost. // Why, then, does the novel persistently, if quietly, portray signs of suicide? What complex significances underlie this predominantly social novel's treatment of individuals turning against themselves?

Recalling our discussions of sign selection, you may notice that this particular sign (suicides amid violent homicide) works by juxtaposition, adopting the "Little Sibling" formula. The sign, in other words, involves establishing a dominant system of meaning (violent killings) before splintering into a subcategory (killing of the self). Consequently, the first part of the staging—making the sign the star—highlights that heightened specificity in the sign. As the staging moves to the second part—situating the sign—it relates the phenomenon (self-erasure amid brutal murder) to a relevant narrative concern of the novel as a whole. Put simply, the example connects the sign to a particular and highly significant "situation" in the novel, namely, "the advancement of the self at any cost." Note how this situation adds depth and dimensionality to the study. The sign becomes almost "three-dimensional," when set against a well-designed and relevant backdrop. The spotlight on the sign has now widened to shed light on a larger thematic preoccupation in Fitzgerald's book. The mentions of suicide in the text no longer float free but are instead bound by context. The critical problem, then, seems straightforward enough: Why this incongruity between sign and situation? The point is, if you spend your time wisely in engineering a viable sign and effectively establishing its presence and situation, the interpretive problem often arises naturally.

For another example, consider student Shayna Harris's staging for a study of Lorraine Hansberry's play *A Raisin in the Sun*. Again, we have inserted slash marks (//) between the three parts of the staging process:

> In Act I of Lorraine Hansberry's *A Raisin in the Sun*, Beneatha voices a lengthy invective denying the existence of a supreme deity, vehemently stating, "I don't believe in God" (51). Beneatha's censure expounds upon the achievements of humanity, which, in her mind, deserves all the credit for its advancement. According to Beneatha, the successes of human culture spring not from any divine assistance but "through its own stubborn effort" (51). Even after enduring a reprimand and physical retribution from her mother Lena, Beneatha obstinately declares, "all the tyranny in the world will never put a God in the heavens!" (52).
>
> Despite her firm stance against the ideology of monotheism, however, Beneatha continually borrows lines from scripture when she finds herself embroiled in emotionally charged exchanges. For example, when chided for disrespecting the marital problems between Ruth and Walter, Beneatha saucily taunts her sister-in-law with a passage from Matthew 5:13: "Well—if the salt loses its savor" (46). Similarly, in defiance of Walter's vicious badgering about her chosen career choice, Beneatha acerbically and facetiously refers to him and other naysayers as "all those prophets who would lead us out of the wilderness" (38). Further, when Mr. Lindner visits and attempts to bribe the Youngers, Beneatha sarcastically

chimes in on the conversation, pronouncing the cost of her family's cooperation at "thirty pieces and not a coin less!" (118). And in defiance of Walter's
overbearing demand that she marry George Murchison, Beneatha lashes out
with "I wouldn't marry him if he was Adam and I was Eve!" (150). In quoting or
paraphrasing not only the Old Testament but also the Gospels, Beneatha displays
an astute knowledge of Judeo-Christian religious doctrine. Her curious use of
biblical wisdom, though, seems very much at odds with her rejection of God. //

Beneatha's odd "double-speak" calls particular attention to itself, given that the
other characters in the play mostly hold firm to their convictions and use language
in non-contradictory ways. They know and say what they want and mean. Lena,
for example, appears unshakeable in her absolute knowledge and policing of
Christian ideas when she demands that Beneatha repeat "in my mother's house,
there is still God" (52). Beneatha's suitors also exhibit verbal surety and subject
Beneatha to their decisive views. While Asagai reveals no ambivalence about the
place of women in the service of men, Murchison voices his certainty regarding
the backward nature of African culture as "a bunch of raggedy-assed spirituals
and some grass huts" (81). In addition, Walter seems supremely confident about
the exact profession to which Beneatha should aspire: nursing rather than doc-
toring. // One of the enduring riddles of Hansberry's text, then, lies in its careful
rendering of Beneatha's vacillating speech amid the firmly grounded rhetoric of
her dramatic counterparts.

Since Shayna's sign—warring tendencies within one character's speech—possesses a good deal of complication, the staging requires space. As she situates
her sign, widening the view to encompass the immediate surroundings, she
chooses a boldly contrastive backdrop. Whereas Beneatha is a linguistic waf-
fler, the play's other characters seem cemented to their verbal ground. This
inventive setup places Shayna's sign in an ironic relationship with its dramatic
context—the "Big Flip" of our earlier discussions regarding juxtaposition—
and leads nicely into a crisp one-sentence statement of her problem.

In closing out this chapter, we offer a few words of encouragement. Over
the years, we have watched students from a wide range of educational backgrounds become confident semiotic questioners and stagers, simply by following the steps laid out in this chapter. Just remember this: you are the director
of your analytical project. You choose the key player, or sign; you raise queries
about its meanings; and you set the stage for the interpretive work to follow. In the next chapter, we concentrate on the generation of claims. We look
closely at how to develop ideas about a chosen sign. If you have selected a sign
that passes the VOICE test, generated a viable field of inquiry, and staged
your study in an engaging way, then your analysis is far more likely to unfold
with greater incisiveness and ease. You will, in a manner of speaking, write a

"downhill" study, where the discovery of various meanings behind your sign is gradual and even potentially pleasant.

To help you toward that goal, we conclude with two additional examples of successful student stagings. We also include a professional model. (See if you can locate the three components described above.) After these staging examples, we present another student analysis in its entirety. Our hope is that these models offer a clear sense of the possibilities open to you as a committed analytical writer.

Staging for a study titled "'Termites in the House of the Mind': Internal Pestilence in *Red Azalea*," by student Christine Couvillon

Anchee Min's 1993 memoir *Red Azalea* presents a searing account of the Cultural Revolution overseen by Mao Zedong in communist China between 1966 and 1976. Some of the most shocking and memorable writing in the text details the awful conditions on Red Fire Farm, an unproductive rice-planting collective that Min joins at age seventeen. In addition to enduring poor nourishment, cramped sleeping quarters, and back-breaking work without pay, Min and her comrades must also contend with myriad pests that infest the farm. On Min's first day in the fields, for example, a fellow worker finds a leech on her leg. "When she tried to pull the leech out, it went deeper," writes Min, and "soon disappeared into the skin leaving a black dot on the surface" while the girl "screamed in horror" (49). Later, Min describes the voracious mosquitoes on the farm as "fat and clumsy after bloodsucking," and relates a time when she "played" with one mosquito, letting the insect bite her and "suck, suck to its satisfaction." Then she "pinched it with two fingers, firm, and watched its dark brown blood drip" (60). Much more threatening are the poisonous snakes that slither throughout the rice crop. These pests "horrified" Min, who recalls that "The grease on their tails made me paranoid" (91).

Vermin swarm and noxious creatures crawl all over Min's autobiographical narrative, lending an air of creepy foreboding to her tale of growing up under Mao's oppressive rule. Yet her memoir also references a different sort of pestilence—one far more menacing than anything caused by insects, rodents, or reptiles. Halfway through the text, Min speaks of "spiritual termites in the house of [the] mind" (112). This startling image of pests that invade the inner lives—the selves, souls, and psyches—of Min and her co-workers expands and deepens *Red Azalea*'s exposé of the plague-like agenda of Chairman Mao. While bloodsuckers such as leeches and mosquitoes attack the body and often spread disease, and while venomous snakes can lead to physical illness and sometimes even death, the threat of internal collapse suggested by termites eating at the mind's foundations raises subtler, more ambiguous issues including mental breakdown, internal destruction, and emotional ruin. Min has obviously chosen the metaphor with care, and its appearance in a text devoted to exposing the ideological manipulation of millions of people clearly calls for further investigation. This study explores the curious relationship between external and internal pests in *Red Azalea*, and seeks to situate Min's critique of Maoist China among other twentieth-century works that examine the invasive, contaminating effects of totalitarian ideologies and propaganda-wielding regimes.

Staging for a study titled "'Gag with Every Breath': Punk Rock and Toxic Chic," by student Jason Rains

Although many forms of popular music in the twentieth century were condemned as "noise pollution," none embraced an overt aesthetic of filth and toxicity more fervently than punk rock between the mid-1970s and early 1980s. Band names like The Germs, Poison Idea, The Plague, The Mutants, Fatal Microbes, Los Reactors, Toxic Reasons, The Urinals, and Black Flag (who shared their name with a household insecticide) explicitly conjured images of contamination, infection, and radiation. Furthermore, bands and audiences alike often adopted fashions that referenced urban grime and decay—unnatural, irradiated-looking hair colors; dirty and damaged clothing held together with safety pins. Sex Pistols manager and provocateur Malcolm McLaren occasionally even supplemented his business attire with a military-style gasmask.

Not surprisingly, toxicity permeated punk album and song titles, as well. X-Ray Spex—another group with a radiation-themed name—entitled their only album *Germ Free Adolescents*. Concert footage of the Dead Kennedys shows front man Jello Biafra clutching the microphone through heavy-duty protective gloves while belting out songs like "Kill the Poor" and "Chemical Warfare," both of which ironically celebrate the proliferation and imagined commercialization of neutron bombs and chemical weapons. Meanwhile, the always-irreverent Replacements gave their debut album the comparatively quaint but equally waste-minded title *Sorry Ma, Forgot to Take Out the Trash*. And above all, the sound of the music itself seemed trashy. Compared to the hyper-produced sheen of contemporary radio rock, most punk bands sounded disarmingly scuzzy, with sloppy performances, thick coats of amplifier distortion, and a far noisier production style.

For fans whose enthusiasm for the genre stemmed primarily from its abrasiveness and confrontational ethic, as well as for outsiders familiar only with punk's most sensationalist elements, the toxic aesthetic represented a hyperbolic and contrarian impulse toward anything valued by "safe" mainstream culture. Coming historically, as it did, on the heels of the pro-environmental hippie movement, however, punk's "fashion of contamination" appears to signal a whole lot more than mere adolescent rebellion. This study seeks to explore the complex meanings behind punk rock's toxic chic.

Staging for an essay titled "'Insurmountable Barriers to Our Union': Homosocial Male Bonding, Homosexual Panic, and Death on the Ice in *Frankenstein*," by James Holt McGavran, Professor of English, University of North Carolina, Charlotte.

At the end of his narrative on the alpine Sea of Ice, Victor Frankenstein's nameless creature demands no more than what most men say they want in life: love, a mate, a home. Realizing that Victor has rejected him because of his appearance, he continues, "But that cannot be; the human senses are insurmountable barriers to our union" (108). And he is right; pondering the creature's request, Victor thinks:

> His words had a strange effect upon me. I compassionated him, and
> sometimes felt a wish to console him; but when I looked upon him, when
> I saw the filthy mass that moved and talked, my heart sickened, and my
> feelings were altered to those of horror and hatred. (110)

This overwhelming revulsion has already led Victor to deny his creation love and care, others upon seeing him have tried to injure or kill him, and because of his loneliness and alienation he becomes a killer: "I am malicious because I am miserable" (108). By the end of Mary Shelley's novel, William, Justine, Clerval, Elizabeth, and Alphonse are all dead, while Victor and the creature are totally committed to their bizarre mutual pursuit, in effect a double suicide pact, in the Arctic seas of ice where Captain Walton finds them.

The barriers indeed prove insurmountable, but their shared obsession also bespeaks attraction, parodies courtship, constitutes union—no matter how weird, how negatively expressed, how destructive to both. Mary Shelley repeatedly uses the language of passionate attachment in their narratives; for instance, Victor tells Walton that when he saw his creature again after weeks of pursuit across the ice,

> I viewed the expanse before me with anguish, when suddenly my eye
> caught a dark speck upon the dusky plain. I strained my sight to discover
> what it could be, and uttered a wild cry of ecstacy [sic] when I distin-
> guished a sledge, and the distorted proportions of a well-known form
> within. Oh! with what a burning gush did hope revisit my heart! warm
> tears filled my eyes, which I hastily wiped away, that they might not
> intercept the view I had of the daemon; but still my sight was dimmed
> by the burning drops, until, giving way to the emotions that oppressed
> me, I wept aloud. (158)

Finding consolation for himself if not for the "well-known form," Victor cries the hot tears of a lover upon seeing his partner after long separation. Besides, the creature has not always revolted his creator: as Victor says earlier, "His limbs were in proportion, and I had selected his features as beautiful" (39). The great unexplained mystery in Mary Shelley's text lies precisely in the riddle of how Victor's "human senses" could have undergone so sudden and complete a change from the excited attraction that drove his creation, making him oblivious to both nature and his human family (38–9), to the utter revulsion which seizes him at the very moment of his success. "I had desired it," Victor says, "with an ardour that far exceeded moderation; but now that I had finished, the beauty of the dream vanished, and breathless horror and disgust filled my heart" (40).[7]

6. Student example

Creating Nature: Exotic Domestic Cats

Molly Sullivan

Increasing numbers of people are harboring wild cats in their homes, legally and safely. These animals—with leopard-spots, tiger stripes, and high-contrast markings—look best suited to jungles, savannahs, or the foregrounds of naturalist paintings, but their preferred habitat includes sofas, windowsills, and the laps of human companions. Some of these creatures were engineered by hybridization of domestic felines with actual wild cats such as the Serval, Margay, Jungle Cat, and Geoffrey's Cat, while others were created by carefully crossing and recrossing various domestic breeds to combine multiple desirable traits into one animal. Why, however, do people desire such a thing? We have domesticated cats for millennia, making them more and more adapted to human culture. We keep them indoors for the most part; we have them declawed; we feed them Fancy Feast entrees and special cat milk; we buy them toys. Why, then, should we turn around at this stage and attempt to make them more like wild animals?

One compelling reason for the recent creation and popularity of exotic breeds of cat is powerful nostalgia for an "authentic" relationship with the wild. Pet-keeping, as practiced today, is a relatively recent phenomenon. Only a century and a half ago, caring for domestic animals was satirized in European news journals and literature as an eccentricity either of the wealthy few—who had enough resources to waste their time and money however they pleased—or the numerous poor—who tended to ignore the dangers of letting filthy, disease-bearing, resource-consuming animals into their households (Ritvo 15–23). As of 2006, however, there are no fewer than 77 million household cats accounted for in American veterinary records, and 34% of American households contain at least one cat. This phenomenal increase in the keeping of felines strongly correlates to trends toward industrialization, urbanization, and the dissolution of subsistence-based agricultural lifestyles. Giving up farming or livestock husbandry for a factory job in the big city upset the interdependence with nature that pervaded human culture up to that time. Humans were now stripped of their accustomed, agrarian context; they were cut off from the land and its creatures.

A result of this shift was a loneliness borne of a need for environmental reconnection. By the mid-nineteenth century, municipal zoos proliferated, toys and books depicting animals became popular for children, and pet-keeping increased in all social strata. With the wide variety of media currently available, consumers now possess a privileged view into the lives of wild animals, and may even sense a close relationship with them. That sentiment, though, is artificially created and ultimately illusory. The beasts that appear in children's books, television programs, and feature films cannot authentically interact with and respond to us. Similarly, animals in zoos—confined as they are to unnatural spaces and deadened by the constant flow of people—ignore or look through us as if we did not exist (Berger 276–87). Just as the wild animals of our media and zoos fail to reestablish a genuine bond with wild nature, the same holds true for our common domestic cat breeds. These furry friends, whose primal tendencies have been diluted through domestication, are simply not wild enough. Ultimately, breeding an exotic cat may just be an attempt—albeit one fraught with irony—to reclaim an authentic relationship with wild animals and raw, unspoiled nature.

Another factor behind the popularity of exotic cats would seem to lie in our perceptions of the feline temperament, which differs markedly from that of the canine. Whereas dogs will gladly do their master's bidding—sitting on command, rolling over, "speaking," and catching Frisbees—the average domestic cat will have none of this. Most people would laugh, for example, at the suggestion that a cat could be trained to perform tasks in a similar manner to a dog. Even breeders and others with an intense love for the animals often characterize them as supercilious, fickle, unpredictable, and even unsympathetic. In short, cats constantly challenge our ideas about how a domestic animal is supposed to act. Many cat owners, however, appreciate that fiercely independent behavior. These feline enthusiasts would never think of training their cats to perform tricks or to fetch the morning paper. They want, in fact, a sign of nature less devoted to, and reliant on, humans. Exotic cats carry that characteristic to an even greater degree. Breeding a cat with high-contrast tiger stripes or leopard-like rosettes powerfully confirms the animal's autonomy and almost regal character. Imagine the psychological effect, for example, of a cat with the precise markings of a Bengal Tiger strutting through the kitchen. Owning an exotic cat, in other words, brings the zoo—in all its strangeness, power, and wonder—into one's home. This is a far cry from a miniature poodle in a pink sweater, or a Yorkie prancing at a dog show.

Still, there is no denying that these exotic cats—once welcomed into our homes—eat commercially prepared food from a dish, use automated litter boxes, and travel in cloth-lined carriers, facts which illustrate an interesting paradox. Like meticulously pruned bonsai or elaborate home swimming pools complete with grottoes, these semi-wild animals afford their owners a safe, simplified, and sanitized piece of the natural world. Nearly everyone has at some time harbored the fantasy of keeping company with a crocodile, an elephant, a lion, or a monkey. Most people, however, discard these ideas as dangerous or impractical. Furthermore, owning a wild animal without extensive certifications and permits is illegal in most locations; keeping a crocodile properly fed or supplying an elephant with a suitable enclosure would be financially ruinous; and corralling the often destructive and violent tendencies of a monkey would necessitate constant supervision. Nonetheless, the extremely wealthy and patently foolish often ignore these potential impediments and acquire wild "pets"—a scenario that typically ends in tragedy for the animal, the human, or both. The sheer number of rescue and shelter organizations full of "tame" wild animals, many of whom have been neglected or abused, is a testament to the problems of living with the wild. The case of Roy Horn of Siegfried and Roy—who was mauled and permanently paralyzed in 2003 by one of his many hand-raised tigers—illustrates the fact that no amount of resources, understanding, or experience can remove the factor of unpredictability and danger from working closely with undomesticated animals. With an exotic cat, however, a human can experience both the thrill of proximity to a "wild" creature and the feeling of control or dominion over it.

That positive experience of control over natural forces manifests itself not only as an internal affective state (giving us intrinsic pleasure as creator and dominator) but also as an external display of status and power. Keeping wild animals as symbols of one's authority and wealth, though, is nothing drastically new. Before the advent of public zoos, menageries of wild animals were the exclusive possessions of the ruling class. Kings and queens might maintain a collection of ostriches, giraffes, or panthers in the way that the modern elite may showcase collections of vintage automobiles and original paintings by Renaissance artists. Such extravagant displays conspicuously reveal the extent of the owner's disposable wealth. In a similar fashion, the ownership of an Ocicat or a Bengal not only displays one's mastery of nature (or a facsimile thereof) but also showcases his or her worldliness and material wealth. Since many of these exotic breeds are still relatively new and under intensive development, they are quite rare and fetch a hefty price. Chances are strong, then, that the cat yowling in the back alley is not a stray Serengeti. Similarly, those abandoned kittens under the bridge are probably not Chausies or Caracals. Purchasing even an adult female exotic (one unable to breed or be shown competitively) costs an average of $1,500, well out of the price range of the typical pet owner. A breeding or "show-quality" specimen, on the other hand, may sell for two to three times that amount. Younger male cats are considered the most valuable, and those that can be shown successfully command prices in the tens of thousands of dollars. With so many companion animals available for little or no money, ownership of an expensive animal like an exotic cat must also serve as a conspicuous display of status, one in which the natural world is rendered a commodity.

At the same time, the trend toward "wild" feline pets might also strangely serve a conservationist end. Many breeders, in fact, cite the need to raise awareness about conservation as their primary inspiration for engineering new domestic breeds. Nikki Horner, originator of the "Bombay," believed that if she were able to breed cats that resembled miniature panthers, people might better understand the plight of real black leopards. In a similar way, Paul Casey originated the "California Spangled Cat" after he visited Africa and was moved by the disappearance of the African Wild Cat from most of its original range. He hoped that if he made wild-looking spotted cats available as pets, no one would ever want to wear a leopard-spotted coat or attempt to keep a real endangered cat.

Initially, such a conservationist argument seems a bit self-serving. After all, the breeders of these animals stand to gain a staggering amount of money. There are, however, parallels that lend some validity to their arguments. Consider how many people from Western nations cringe at the thought of eating dog meat, even though dogs have been exploited as a food source by many cultures. (Several breeds, most notably the Chow Chow, were specifically developed as food-stock.) Dogs—at least for most of the Western world—are considered exclusively companion animals. We love them, but we don't eat them. Similarly, if we learn to love wild-looking domestic cats, we may be less inclined to allow cheetahs, tigers, and panthers to fall into peril. Owning exotic cats, then, might translate to greater sympathy toward their wild progenitors.

Fashioning "wild" domestic animals through intense processes of artificial selection and engineering demonstrates a striking paradox, where the road to wildness leads to the home. The line between the animal in its natural environment—stalking prey, raising its young—and the cuddly companion on one's lap oddly blurs. Yet when studied for their psychological effects, the new exotic cat breeds make curious sense: they fulfill a nostalgia for some primal bond with the natural world; accentuate the regal aloofness and autonomy of the feline; offer their owners a safe and sanitized form of wildness; serve as unique status symbols; and even function as emblems for the conservationist agenda. And even if most of us will never own a Chausie or a Bengal (and will remain quite content with our Calicos and Tabbies), the study of exotic cat breeds may suggest new ways of thinking about our human relationships with animals wild and domestic and somewhere in between.

Works Cited

Berger, John. "Why Look at Animals?" *Language of the Birds: Tales, Texts, and Poems of Interspecies Communication.* Ed. David M. Guss. New York: North Point, 1986. 276–87.

Ritvo, Harriet. "The Emergence of Modern Pet-Keeping." *Animals and People Sharing the World.* Ed. Andrew Rowan. Boston: UP of New England, 1988. 15–23.

4
Generating Ideas About Meaning

Chapter Outline

1. Becoming a deep diver

In a letter dated March 3, 1849, Herman Melville wrote, "I love all men who *dive*. Any fish can swim near the surface, but it takes a great whale to go down stairs five miles or more."[1] The author of *Moby Dick* applauds "the whole corps of thought-divers, that have been diving & coming up again with bloodshot eyes since the world began."[2] Similarly, in a journal entry written a decade earlier, Ralph Waldo Emerson insisted that one must dare to "plunge into the sublime seas, dive deep, & swim far."[3] According to Emerson, those who courageously travel to unseen depths will "come back with self-respect, with new power, with an advanced experience, that shall explain and overlook the old."[4] The importance with which these two celebrated writers imbue the concept of deep diving applies especially to cultural and literary analysis. Effective writing for university classes, as Melville and Emerson would no doubt argue, requires that you plunge below the waterline and explore the significances that underlie all sorts of semiotic phenomena. With that necessity in view, this chapter seeks to help you join the "corps of thought-divers" who go down "five miles or more" and come back with "self-respect," "new power," and lively, persuasive ideas about meaning.

2. The semiotic iceberg

The image of an iceberg—small at the top, gargantuan below—is one of the best ways we have found for conceptualizing the world of signs and the crucial dive into their multiple meanings. What lies above the waterline (the sign that is apparent in literature or culture) turns out to be a tiny piece of an invisible mass of significance. The visible sign, to borrow a familiar phrase, is just the tip of the iceberg. Its real size and magnitude—its expansive and important meanings—remain unseen, waiting for semioticians to penetrate the surface and make astute analytical discoveries. We can think of each sign, then, as connected to an enormous body of below-the-waterline concepts and forces, as suggested by the following graphic:

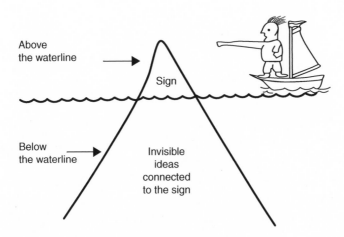

Above the waterline → Sign

Below the waterline → Invisible ideas connected to the sign

The task of the deep diver lies in offering theories about the connections between a chosen sign and a host of meaningful concepts and motivating factors hidden below the waterline. Each of our theoretical assertions—or "ideas about meaning"—must present a precise, unambiguous link between

1. the overt, above-the-waterline semiotic phenomenon, and
2. the covert, below-the-waterline causes for, reasons behind, and notions associated with the surface phenomenon

We want to make these links as specific as possible, in order to infuse our assertions with persuasiveness and point. We therefore need to identify particular ideologies and ideals, specific public opinions and historical factors, distinct biases and tendencies of thought that lend meaning to any sign under analysis. The expanded drawing below suggests the infinite possibilities that await our inspection in the underwater realm:

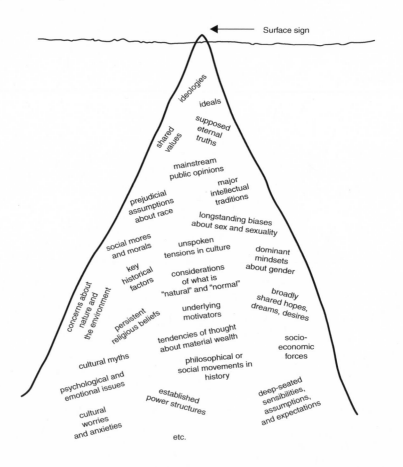

As we dive deep and probe individual concepts, searching for specificity, we want to locate examples that throw explanatory light on our chosen sign. For instance, under the heading "ideologies," we might list specific concepts that make up a particular culture's dominant outlooks—its mainstream, often unacknowledged beliefs. In America, for example, these might include the following notions, some of which may garner your approval, others which may strike you as wrongheaded or offensive:

"everyone must find a soul mate"
"individualism is paramount"
"people without 'normal' bodies or minds should be pitied"
"America rules the world"
"homosexuals are deviant, though acceptable"
"be fruitful and multiply"
"democracy is the best political system"
"racial groups should stick together"
"capitalism makes the most economic sense"
"the Christian God reigns supreme"
"the American dream is real"
"trust in the free market"
"follow the Puritan work ethic"
"believe in technology"
"protect the nuclear family"
"be practical and use common sense"
"hold on to the pioneer spirit"
"convenience is good"
"the accumulation of material is positive"
"one must locate his or her 'inner self'"
"men should seek to 'score' with many sex partners"
"humans are superior to animals and plants"
"America has a Manifest Destiny"
"the United States is the great melting pot of the world"

As stated above, you will likely agree with some of these assumptions and discount others as problematic. Be that as it may, you will probably accept that all of these ideas at least *circulate* widely in American culture at this time in history. Even if you find some of the thoughts abhorrent, would you concur that some Americans—vast numbers, in fact—consider many of them valid, perhaps even sacred? In large measure, one has to adopt an "anthropological" perspective in order to dive below the waterline and make convincing claims about the multiple meanings of any sign. This imperative stands behind the decision of most American universities to require students—in so-called core classes—to study sociology, psychology, anthropology, history, and other social sciences. These disciplines tend to reveal the rich varieties of "below-the-waterline" ideas and ideals that drive behaviors in various cultures and subcultures throughout time. As you plunge below the surface and explore the realm of invisible concepts and underlying causes, you will want to search for fruitful theoretical arenas (drawing on your "core" studies) and then describe them in great detail. The key, at this stage of analysis, is to allow yourself room to investigate the iceberg and to forge persuasive connections between your sign and the particular notions to which it seems to relate.

3. The semiotic simian

To put into action the process of deep diving, and to see the value of the semiotic iceberg as an analytical tool, consider a surprisingly enduring sign from popular culture: Bigfoot. More precisely, we will analyze "the persistent fascination with Bigfoot in an advanced scientific age that broadly discounts superstition." We have all seen representations of this hairy half-man, half-ape; we have glimpsed his shadowy form in "eyewitness" videos and TV shows devoted to the unbelievable. But while we might agree on Bigfoot's physical appearance, we may have a harder time trying to articulate ideas about his meanings as a cultural sign. Why, we might ask, does the legend of such a creature persist? The inquiry seems especially provocative during a time when science has already debunked countless hoaxes and unexplained mysteries—from the far-fetched claims of alchemists determined to transform lead into gold to the fantastical predictions of palm and tarot-card readers. We might ask: do reasonable people really believe in vampires, the Loch Ness monster, and alien abductions, in this day and age?

Studying the long-lived and seemingly unshakable legend of Bigfoot means setting the sign in its contemporary context, and therein lies the riddle that lends complexity and import to our investigation. Our rational, critical minds do not literally suppose that Bigfoot roams the distant hills, but as a culture, we curiously continue to imagine his potential existence, despite our better judgment. Waiting in the check-out line at the supermarket, we might find ourselves perusing a tabloid article about Sasquatch; or we might get momentarily sucked in to a television "documentary" devoted to our hirsute friend. Why, though? If we treat Bigfoot not as an actual life-form on the planet, to be studied by biologists and zoologists, but as a cultural sign full of varied significances that semioticians might persuasively unpack, then how do we develop ideas about his meanings in our modern timeframe? How do we "get at" the implications lurking beneath this specific cultural fantasy in our place and moment in history?

To initiate this process of generating ideas about meaning, we dive down and inspect the invisible realm underneath the iceberg's visible tip. When we begin our inspection process, particular areas below the waterline will prove more viable than others. In the case of the surprisingly persistent Bigfoot legend, for example, we would probably want to include "American assumptions about the environment," since we commonly associate Bigfoot with wilderness settings such as the Pacific Northwest and Northern California. Just as we did when we unpacked "American ideologies" above, we proceed by adding clarity and dimension, recording specific facets and illustrations of "American assumptions about the environment." Some of these might include:

> "we are the stewards of the natural realm"
> "nature is ours to use as we see fit"
> "nature is boundless"
> "nature is finite and in danger of being depleted"
> "our national character is historically bound up in land expansion"
> "Mother Nature can take care of herself"
> "nature is beautiful and must be preserved"
> "nature is fragile and must be protected"
> "nature is benevolent, like a mother who cares for us"
> "natural disasters are punishment for sinful behavior"
> "the ownership of land is our inalienable right"
> "endangered species deserve protection"
> "technology will save the environment"
> "nature exists to test our courage and prowess"
> "American culture possesses a frontier spirit"
> "being in nature refuels the soul"
> "nature is a guide to ethical behavior"
> "a benevolent spirit pervades the natural world"
> "nature is impartial and uncaring"
> "nature is a proper subject of art"
> "nature is dangerous and full of evil"
> "hunting allows us to tap into our primitive character"

Next, we locate and explore the ideas that appear most relevant to our sign. Take, for instance, the assumption that "nature is boundless." The easiest way to establish meaning is to link our above-the-waterline sign (the lingering belief in Bigfoot despite scientific skepticism) to a particular below-the-waterline notion such as "nature is boundless." In what ways might Bigfoot "signal" that particular, invisible belief? How could Bigfoot "mean" a boundless sense of the natural realm? With such inquiries in hand, we might note that in books, tabloid newspaper stories, and "unexplained mystery" television shows, Bigfoot always evades his hunters in expansive wilderness areas. The trackers who chase him remain merely foreign visitors in his immense natural domain, and they can never hope to capture him in such boundless lands. If Bigfoot seems always to escape human grasp—the argument might run— then the forests of the Pacific Northwest, the mountains and river valleys of the Sierras in California, must still be thriving and open.

We now have the beginnings of one claim about meaning ascribable to the legend of Bigfoot, which we might articulate in the following way:

> The lingering legend of Bigfoot signals notions of an uncharted natural realm where a gigantic half-human can roam undetected.

Because he constantly eludes us, he points to "the immensity of nature." The claim at this stage seems arguable, since we are clearly below the semiotic waterline, dealing with invisible notions and assumptions. In other words, while Bigfoot is visible—at least in the shaky, hand-held camera footage of documentaries, and in the blurry photos of the tabloids—the accepted wisdom that "nature is boundless" is not.

Next, we need to offer some sense of why that particular link is significant. In short, we need to "supply the why"—the deeper reason behind that particular connection between the above-the-waterline sign (the fantasy of Bigfoot in a scientific age) and the below-the-waterline concept (the alleged boundlessness of nature). Why might this link make sense at this particular historical moment? Why might we read Bigfoot as a sign of a limitless natural realm? Just turn on the news, and such an idea about meaning might make a bit more sense. We are constantly bombarded with the potential for ecological destruction of all kinds: the protective ozone layer is compromised, massive oil spills threaten our oceans, huge tracts of South American rain forest are leveled for new development. The looming threat of a complete collapse of our world—one specifically precipitated by our own species' expansion—is pervasive. Furthermore, many of us feel responsible. We want our consumer goods and creature comforts, even when we realize their effects on the ecosystem. We are torn, consequently, between our desires and our feelings of guilt.

Enter Bigfoot. If he still exists, healthy and free in the vast wildernesses of North America, constantly evading his captors, then whole expanses of untrammeled nature must remain. (Never mind that California is the most populous state in the union and continuing to grow; that the Pacific Northwest keeps losing forest areas, even as state and local groups attempt to defend them from overdevelopment; that arctic refuges in Alaska are constantly under the threat of oil-drilling and the attendant human settlements.) Bigfoot, in this way, becomes a kind of environmental savior, one who distracts us from our complicity in the difficult and potentially damaging processes of overdevelopment. Put another way, the legend promises us a boundless environment untouched by our own meddling hands.

At this point, we can formulate an interpretive idea about meaning that links the Bigfoot fantasy to a limitless ecosystem, which in turn frees us from apprehensions about environmental sustainability:

> The lingering legend of Bigfoot signals notions of an uncharted natural realm where a gigantic half-human can roam undetected, an idea that in turn assuages our sense of guilt over environmental destruction.

In this theoretical claim about the lingering legend of Bigfoot, we see exactly what invisible concept the sign points to (the "notion of an uncharted natural realm") and why that particular link seems significant (because it "assuages our sense of guilt over environmental destruction"). We draw a clear connection between the above-the-waterline sign and the below-the-waterline idea, and then show why that connection matters to a particular culture in a specific historical situation.

4. Sign, signals, significance

A successful idea about meaning contains three elements: the identification of the above-the-waterline sign; a highly specific below-the-waterline signal that the sign sends out; and a reason why that particular message matters, why it carries import in its unique cultural and historical circumstances. Each successful idea about meaning, in other words, needs to include a sign, a signal, and a statement about the significance of their union. With these key components in mind, we can delineate our Bigfoot claim in the following way:

(sign)	The lingering legend of Bigfoot
(signals)	signals notions of an uncharted natural realm where a gigantic half-human can roam undetected,
(significance)	an idea that in turn assuages our sense of guilt over environmental destruction.

In this example, we have utilized the verb "signals" in order to stress the semiotic link to a below-the-waterline concept. We can, however, easily use alternative verbs and phrases that function in similar ways. Signs can "point to," "indicate," "exemplify," "represent," "suggest," "imply," "critique," "connote," and "serve as reminders of" certain invisible forces and ideas. (The list is practically endless, and with time you will amass an archive of analytically dynamic verbs to deploy when needed.)

For practice, let's dive down again, this time to a different place on the semiotic iceberg. We begin, as we did before, with our sign: the legend of Bigfoot in an age of scientific skepticism. This time, however, let's examine the sign's relationship not to "American ideas about the environment" but to "deep-seated American assumptions regarding the self and the individual." If Bigfoot continues to captivate our imaginations with his lone wanderings, we might suggest, then he likely taps into some meaningful part of the American belief system related to the self. Just as before, we start by investigating that specific part of the semiotic iceberg, examining the blanket phrase "deep seated American assumptions regarding the self and the individual" in greater detail:

> "the individual should be self-reliant, as Emerson argued"
> "the self should be celebrated, as Whitman professed"
> "the self is a construction of God and, thus, subordinate to His will"
> "the individual is a vital part of a broader community"
> "the individual is designed to grow and self-actualize"
> "individualism for its own sake has helped make America great"
> "the self should be free from outside restraint"
> "too much focus on the individual can promote vanity"
> "the self is a unified whole with a central spiritual core"
> "the self should be tirelessly optimistic"

Again, you need not agree with all of these ideas about the self. Would you at least concur, however, that these sometimes competing notions about the status of one's inner identity continue to operate beneath the surface of American culture? We can assume, then, that they operate as ideologies—mostly invisible systems of thought that shape our lives, particularly when we are less than fully aware of how they do so.

We then want to select a likely candidate from our list—one specific American belief about the self that seems relevant to our sign. Again, some will appear more germane to the Bigfoot discussion than others. For instance, the extent to which Bigfoot signals a "tirelessly optimistic" self seems less viable than, say, the way in which he might reinforce a notion of the self ideally "free from outside restraint." Think about it: doesn't so-called eyewitness footage of the creature usually feature him in isolation, wandering the forests on his own? Don't the most popular conceptions of Bigfoot focus on his extreme solitude and distance from society? Doesn't the story usually center on lone individuals and not on entire Bigfoot families and social enclaves? Such observations trigger the first part of our formulation:

(sign)   The continued fascination with Bigfoot
(signals)   might also point to our powerful desires for autonomy.

Of course, we cannot prove beyond any doubt that a linkage exists between Bigfoot and a desire for autonomy. Still, we can persuade, argue, reason that the sign sends out this signal, since representations and narratives usually feature Bigfoot by himself. In this reading, as you can see, we are less concerned with Bigfoot's association to wilderness areas and more interested in his solitude and independence.

To extend our claim, we then need to ask ourselves: What might be the significance of such a link? Why might that particular signal—a desire for autonomy—hold import for us? Why might people unwittingly inscribe Bigfoot with their own dreams of unfettered movement and existence? Perhaps we could argue that present-day culture—at least in the common perception—can often feel a bit too "watchful," too "mindful" of our every action. Consider this: do you have a cell phone, a Facebook or Twitter account (or both), an email address (or, in fact, multiple addresses)? Don't all of these social utilities ensure that you can be reached (and in some sense "seen") at all times? The producers of these services sell us on the concept that our cell phones and social networks merely increase our freedom to move about, to work and interact whenever and wherever we like. As semiotics suggests, however, meaning is never singular. At the same time that these devices and services help to unite us—keeping us "in the loop" with family, friends, work, and even the world at large—they also confine us to a matrix of social relationships, weaving us further and further into the fabric of our culture.

In that particular context (an increasingly claustrophobic one) our belief in Bigfoot as an emissary of autonomy begins to make good sense. We look at him—perhaps through an internet browser that tracks each site we visit or a television that records our viewing preferences—and think, "There's the life: I'd be free of all social constraints; I could roam the wilds of the world, oblivious to all the commitments and responsibilities attendant on me as an active member of my community. Out there, it's all about me and me alone." With such suggestions, we could then add the third part of our sign-signals-significance formula:

(sign)	The continued fascination with Bigfoot
(signals)	might also point to our powerful desires for autonomy
(significance)	in a fiercely interdependent culture that can at times feel claustrophobic and constraining.

As in the environmental claim generated previously, we have both a "signal"—a below-the-waterline concept to which our sign points—as well as a reason why that signal might be "significant" in our present cultural moment. Often, in answering the "why?" question, our claims will include words such as the following, all of which drive us to explore the meaningfulness of the semiotic link that we have drawn between sign and signal:

because	given	thereby
since	in view of the fact that	thus revealing
due to	seeing as	considering that
while	due to	which suggests
for the sake of	during a time when	bearing in mind that

Our "significance" must, in other words, offer a rationale, a "because statement" about the associative link between the overt sign and the covert signal.

We don't have to stop, obviously, with just two potentially arguable ideas about the Bigfoot legend. We can arrive at additional ideas, all of which begin by forging a viable connection between the above-the-waterline sign and one particular below-the-waterline signal or message. Consider the ideas about meaning below, and see if you can identify the belief systems out of which we drew the particular signals:

(sign)	In addition, the persistent celebrity of this oddly peaceful wildman
(signals)	might lie in his transcendence of national boundaries and political divisions (in his myriad forms, Bigfoot is shared by many cultures worldwide),
(significance)	which invites cultural harmony and understanding at a time of disturbing racial and ethnic strife around the globe.

(sign)	The enduring fascination with Bigfoot
(signals)	simultaneously suggests a contemporary substitute for traditional religious assurances, a pointer to some shadowy world beyond our knowing
(significance)	in an age of increasing spiritual doubt and scientific objectivity.

(sign)	At the same time, our lasting fondness for Bigfoot
(signals)	appears to involve his status as an archetypal "gentle giant": a huge, apish male who poses no threat to others.
(significance)	As a result, he may ease fears of the male brutality that pervades our news reports, and also serve as counterpoint to the disturbing menagerie of larger-than-life despotic men who spread violence internationally.

As these additional ideas about meaning suggest, many interpretive opportunities lie behind every sign. Each idea highlights a different signal, probes a different area of significance, and offers a new angle on the same phenomenon. At this point, we might even begin to think about building a complete essay around our ideas about meaning, fleshing out paragraphs in support of our "sign-signals-significance" claims. But before we proceed to that work—the work of the next chapter—let's spend more time in the realm of idea generation.

5. A tilt of the cap

As a way to continue our study of the sign-signals-significance process (the very heart of semiotic analysis), consider a phenomenon from contemporary fashion: the baseball cap. When people choose to wear ball caps, they immediately face a range of choices, all of which inevitably send signals. What sort of logo will they select? A sports team, perhaps? What messages do they send when they wear a Yankees hat, and how might these statements differ, say, from a cap supporting the Dallas Mavericks (a basketball team) or the Arsenal (of English soccer fame)? What about the color? How do people modify the semiotic significances of their Yankees cap when they choose the color pink rather than the time-honored "Midnight Blue"?

Then ponder the myriad contexts—the situations and places in which people wear ball caps apart from the playing field. How does a Yankees hat signify when worn by a young girl drinking a Coke, holding her father's hand, and walking to her seat in Yankee Stadium? How do those significances change when the wearer is a tall, sharply dressed man climbing out of a limousine in front of a high-end restaurant like Le Cirque in Manhattan? Or what about someone wearing the cap in Boston, home of the Yankees' arch rivals, the Red Sox? As you can see, the particular (and sometimes peculiar) contexts in which we find ball caps are boundless, and since signs are relational in meaning, their significances are constantly shaped by the signs that surround them.

Finally, what about *how* people wear their baseball hats? What messages get sent when they position the bill forward, backward, or tilted to one side? For starters, we might plausibly suggest that "bill forward" (relative to the other two bill positions) connotes "traditionalism." After all, wearing a cap with its bill forward connects to its original purpose (to shade a player's eyes from sunlight), so we might feasibly theorize that such a link to the baseball cap's original utility bespeaks someone invested in the status quo, in things "as they should be." But then the question becomes, if a person wears a cap with the bill forward, does it automatically guarantee that he or she is, in reality, less rebellious? Is this individual necessarily an upstanding citizen interested in preserving mainstream values? Clearly, wearing a bill forward does not inevitably force a person to conform to any specific political or ethical doctrine. Still, we may legitimately posit that the sign "bill forward" (at least in our present cultural moment) *signals* "tradition" and "established ideals." It doesn't guarantee that the wearer *is* mainstream, but it *does* send that message, implying conventional assumptions, practices, and so on. And "bill forward" conveys these concepts because culture conditions us to decode this sign in terms of mainstream politics. Other signified concepts for "bill forward" might include "serious," "straight," "neat," "decent," "structured," "organized," "well-meaning," "nondisruptive," and so forth. We could list many associations—dozens of culture-specific codes—for this particular sign.

Since no perfect correspondence exists between any one sign and any one idea ("bill forward" can never *just* mean "nondisruptive"), we can make a variety of persuasive arguments about significance, especially as we study the specifics of the sign in place and time. Put simply, meaning constantly slips away from singularity, finality, and closure. This semiotic fact should come as very good news, since it opens many doors for you to test out your unique critical imagination in generating plausible and interesting ideas about meaning. You are not stuck, in other words, with one and only one way of understanding reality.

Recall, too, that the meanings of signs arise from their similarities to, and differences from, related signs in the same system. The material object itself (the sign "bill forward," for example) carries no intrinsic significance by the laws of logic or nature. Instead, each sign achieves its identity—its recognizable meanings in the world—by its relationships to other signs. How do we know that "bill forward" suggests "traditionalism"? Semioticians suggest that these bonds are produced culturally, through linguistic relations. "Bill forward" means "status quo" or "nice" or "compliant" because it is *not* "bill backward" or "bill sideways"—both of which carry different connotations and send alternative messages. As a culture, we have implicitly agreed (at this stage in history, in any case) on these connections. They are matters of often subtle and silent custom, unspoken social agreement and linguistic compact. Without "bill backwards" and "bill sideways" sending different signals, "bill forward" cannot suggest "mainstream" or "ordinary" or "middle-of-the-road." These signs play off of one another, in mutually informing ways. Their identities, in short, rely upon each other.

6. The historically shifty nature of signs

With meaning-making relationships in mind, let's now turn to the related sign "bill backwards" and recall another tenet of semiotics. In addition to their dependency on place and circumstance, signs can also change meanings over time. Their significances, in other words, are not just situationally but also historically specific. In the middle to late 1980s, for example, the sign "bill backwards" tended to connote "rebelliousness," "urban culture," "hard-edged toughness." It pointed to "solidarity in the face of oppression," "disruption of the established order," and so on. It also suggested the disenfranchised inner city as opposed to the moneyed suburbs, and signaled a "critique of racial and social injustice" (as represented by hip-hop stars who often wore their caps with the bills turned around, while rapping about inequalities in American culture). Furthermore, the sign suggested—by way of its oppositional relationship to the mainstream "bill forward"—the epitome of coolness. It conveyed all of these concepts for rap stars, disaffected inner-city youths, and a host of other readers of the sign, including many suburban white teens seeking to assume some of the grit and struggle associated with the "bill backwards" signal.

As you probably realize, though, these significations gradually shifted. When the sign "bill backward" became too pervasive and popular, it started to lose its countercultural connotations. The causes were many and varied, and it is these underlying factors that an effective semiotic study might analyze. When privileged, suburban white teens (many of whom had never set foot in an urban housing project) started turning around their hats, they dulled the edge—so to speak—of the original sign. And yet, "bill backwards" continues to carry the traces, the history, of its former identity. Surely, it still suggests a kind of "carefree nature," a "youthfulness," a "laid-back outlook" that—to a degree, at least—cuts against the "bill forward" position and, by extension, the established order. Nowadays, it seems to suggest, "I'm not uptight, or stuck up, or all that concerned about anything" (even while the wearer, ironically enough, may be deeply concerned about sending this particular "laid-back" message).

What is considered cool and gritty, in short, can transform over time. During the late 1980s and especially in the 1990s, hip-hop culture and urban fashion began emphasizing a sideways position for baseball caps, effectively offering a third pointer to significance in the "ballcap position" sign system. No longer would "bill backwards" mark the wearer as "cool," "tough," "urban," and so on. Those meanings shifted sideways and became the new signal of street-smart chic. Any glance at television shows or music videos in the 1990s and continuing to the present will affirm this fundamental change. For contemporary rappers like 50 Cent and Too Short, as well as for hip-hop impresarios such as Snoop Dogg and Jay Z, sideways appears to be the bill position of choice. In fact, because of the popularizing of "bill sideways" by such heavyweights in the music and television industries, the sign has also come to signify African-American culture and a particular aspect of black experience that emphasizes "nonconformism" of many kinds.

Given this system of related signs, we might now embark on interpretation by generating a field of inquiry—a unified group of theoretical questions that will prompt us to develop persuasive ideas about meaning. Focusing on a particular group that has adopted the sideways position, for instance, we might ask, "Why do many white teenage males from relatively privileged backgrounds wear their ball caps tipped to one side like inner-city black rappers? What meanings underlie this seemingly incongruous mimicry among white teens who live outside the urban ghettos that spawned the tilted ballcap fashion? Why, in short, have the suburbs gone sideways?" Drawing on the "sign-signals-significance" paradigm, we might now propose some theories. Note in these examples that we can vary the order in which the three elements occur—just as long as the sign is visible, the signal explores a specific message being communicated, and the significance explains why that message seems to carry importance in a given context:

(significance)	Under strong adolescent pressures to appear confident and trendy, as opposed to nerdy and out of touch,
(sign)	white suburban teens may turn their ball caps sideways
(signals)	to align themselves with cutting-edge black artists who have frequently defined coolness for American culture.

(signals)	With its roots in rough inner-city neighborhoods,
(sign)	the sideways ball cap carries an aura of gritty toughness,
(significance)	which may attract young white males worried about appearing weak or effeminate at an age when their masculinity comes under intense social scrutiny.

(sign)	By wearing caps with bills turned sideways, suburban white teens
(signals)	tap into the street smarts and survival savvy often associated with the challenges of poor urban life,
(significance)	thus making themselves appear less naïve and ignorant as they try to negotiate the transition from innocent boys to shrewd young men.

7. Becoming an idea machine

In 1957, Ben Hogan, one of the greatest golfers of all time, published an instructional book titled *Five Lessons: The Modern Fundamentals of Golf*, designed to show amateurs how to develop a reliable, repeatable swing.[5] Those of you who have ever tried to hit a golf ball understand that this is no easy task. It takes a lot of practice and requires a method that can produce trustworthy results. The same goes for developing ideas about the meanings of signs, and teasing out reasonable interpretations that will persuade readers that your ideas not only make sense but also illuminate reality. Improving as a semiotician—just like mastering golf or cooking or acting—takes persistence, patience, and practice.

As with sign selection, we want to explore a wide range of prospects in this stage of the process. Such ranginess and willingness to resist finality often leads to more persuasive and nuanced readings of the sign. By pursuing ever more sophisticated, yet still plausible, interpretations of your single phenomenon, you will avoid the trap of "the available reading," "the obvious interpretation," "the expected conclusion." You will also find yourself in the company of celebrated thinkers such as two-time Nobel laureate and scientist Linus Pauling, who declared, "The best way to have a good idea is to have lots of ideas."[6]

Still, the refusal to settle for the first—or even first three—ideas about meaning is one of the hardest facets of interpretive writing. Taking the first idea that comes to mind and moving toward the "finished project" can seem especially inviting. As accomplished writers of all kinds realize, however, this type of "product orientation"—where we view the act of writing simply as a means to a finished essay—can severely inhibit creativity and insight. Better to give yourself room to practice, to think in terms of processes rather than products, skills-building calisthenics rather than completed performances. That is why we strongly encourage you to become an "idea machine"—a thinker able to offer multiple, persuasive theories about a host of phenomena. To that end, let's consider some further ideas about the sideways ballcap position adopted by many suburban white males. In these additional examples, we once again include the three key parts—sign, signals, and significance—of a solid theory. The components may appear in any order within the idea, and the idea does not have to be presented in a single sentence:

(significance)	Because American culture tends to glorify personal autonomy and uniqueness,
(sign)	white teens may adopt the sideways bill position
(signals)	in order to call attention to themselves as "colorful" individuals instead of homogeneous followers obedient to the expectations of suburban experience.

(signals)	To suggest rebellious attitudes toward parents, teachers, and other authority figures,
(sign)	white adolescents may tilt their caps to one side on the model of black rappers.
(significance)	In effect, these teens channel the rage and frustration that many inner-city African-Americans feel toward established power, thereby authenticating their own cause against perceived injustices.

Now see if you can locate the sign, the signal, and the significance in the following claims:

- Compelled by their culture to act like so-called real men and prove themselves as attractive—if not irresistible—to women, many teenage males may seek to capitalize on the macho sexuality often associated with the sideways cap and black hip-hop culture.
- Since a connection exists between the sideways ball cap and a hip-hop call for racial equality, white teens may adopt this bill position in order to signify their progressive politics and awakening social consciousness.
- Teenaged suburban males who wear the sideways cap also fold the sign into white culture, where it no longer carries its original revolutionary fervor. Such a practice

may unconsciously serve a mainstream drive to contain dissent and diffuse social tensions that threaten the status quo. Unbeknownst to the white teens, in other words, their adoption of this fashion trend may actually temper the countercultural energies associated with the sign and its socially disenfranchised originators.

Working with an elastic formula such as sign-signals-significance helps writers avoid obscure and general claims that lack the argumentative specificity necessary to persuade university-level peers and professors. Arguing that the persistent popularity of Bigfoot speaks to our culture's love of the weird, for example, remains too broad. Bigfoot is a particular type of oddity, and we want to understand his nuances as a strange cultural production. The same goes for the sideways bill position. It will not do simply to suggest that "white teens copy black hip-hop fashion because it is stylish." If you can approach the act of interpretation more as a challenging game—an interactive puzzle that requires a great deal of ingenuity and creativity to solve—then you will likely earn higher marks for your critical prose and also enjoy the process more. With these goals in mind, we now introduce some specific ways in which to treat idea-generation as a fun and addictive game.

8. Games for generating ideas

When we watch children in a sandbox or toy room, we discover that they do not draw distinctions between work and play. Instead, kids inhabit an in-between world that simultaneously exhibits features of both play and work. They build castles out of sand, cities out of Legos; they imitate the duties of parents and homeowners when they "play house"; they mimic professionals such as doctors, nurses, astronauts, mail carriers, teachers, artists. Play is their work, work their play. But what about adults? Can we too embrace a childlike freedom that blends the presumably separate categories of work and play? Can we turn our challenging labors (such as studying and writing analytical papers) into activities that bring about joy, stimulation, and a pleasurable sense of achievement?

Many thinkers have stressed the importance of "in-between" mentalities for adults who take part in creative and critical enterprises. Flow theorist Mihaly Csikszentmihalyi, for example, calls this type of play-work "autotelic"—that is, a behavior performed first and foremost for its own sake.[7] The term "autotelic" also underpins our notions of a successful writing process. If you can begin to perceive interpretive writing as a creative activity worth doing for its own sake, if you can train yourself to enjoy the process without any particular aim other than the generation of interesting ideas and lively prose, then you will be much better served in your classes and will feel less anxious about deadlines and assessment. This is not to say that due dates and grades are unimportant, but our experiences have shown that students typically reach their greatest potential—and have more gratifying academic lives—when they concentrate more on the process of idea-generation than on the product of a final paper.

To help you approach cultural and literary analysis as a potentially enjoyable experience, here is a handful of "games"—tricks or playful moves designed to stretch your creativity and allow you room to experiment with the generation of plausible claims about meaning. You may not use all of these games each time you sit down to analyze a sign. Nevertheless, you will likely find at least one of them useful in your deep dives for meaning.

The association game

One effective way to generate ideas about a given phenomenon derives from the key semiotic tenet that meanings arise from *associations* between signs. Put another way, significance emerges through the *interactive relationships* between signs in specific contexts. We can, therefore, develop persuasive assertions about any sign's multiple meanings by closely studying its similarities to and differences from other signs in its midst. This "relativity principle" lends itself to a tool we call the association game.

To test out the game, first consider the following work by American poet Gary Gildner. The text depicts a group of school kids—seventh or eighth graders, it would seem—meeting their coach on the first day of football practice. In the opening two lines, the school physician administers the well-known "turn-your-head-and-cough test" to each of the boys, ensuring that none has a hernia; then the players follow their coach into a shelter beneath the school—a place designed for protection against tornadoes and hurricanes, and (even more threateningly) potential nuclear attacks during the Cold War. The coach voices his dog-eat-dog, kill-or-be-killed social philosophy, and proceeds to inform the kids of his violent military service, most likely during World War II (we can draw this inference about the coach once we realize that Gildner, who here relates an autobiographical adolescent experience, was born in 1938). As the poem unfolds, Coach Hill makes clear exactly what he expects of his players: manly aggression and the determination to win at any cost. The text concludes with the image of the boys beating on each other to prove their tenacity. As instructed, however, they avoid shots to the face, instead restricting their blows to areas of the body that will be covered by their clothing after practice. That way, parents and teachers will not notice the resulting bruises.

First Practice

After the doctor checked to see
we weren't ruptured,
the man with the short cigar took us
under the grade school,
where we went in case of attack
or storm, and said
he was Clifford Hill, he was
a man who believed dogs
ate dogs, he had once killed
for his country, and if
there were any girls present
for them to leave now.
                     No one
left. OK, he said, he said I take
that to mean you are hungry
men who hate to lose as much
as I do. OK. Then
he made two lines of us
facing each other,
and across the way, he said,
is the man you hate most
in the world,
and if we are to win
that title I want to see how.
But I don't want to see
any marks when you're dressed,
he said. He said, *Now*.[8]

Gildner's poem, needless to say, carries numerous signs on which we could train our analytical gaze. For our present purposes, let's keep matters relatively straightforward and concentrate on "the curious spatial gap in the middle of the poem." What associations can we draw to the "empty space" or "sudden void" falling between lines 12 and 13? In playing the game, we want to move from association to association, seeing how much relevant linguistic material we can generate. Then, after stringing out a long list of associative terms, we can then seek to compose theoretical claims about this spatial gap as a meaningful sign in the text.

Below you will find 60 associative terms, which we arrived at simply by asking ourselves, "What words, phrases, and ideas spring to mind when we think about an empty space, especially in the context of this poem?"

spatial gap	speechlessness	interruption
empty space	muteness	dearth
sudden void	suppression of sound	scarcity
fissure	stifling of voice	shortage
rift	lifelessness	suspension of time
cleaving	utter quiet	abyss
break	gaping	hollowness
openness	whiteness	unknown
erasure	lack of speech	indefinite
vacancy	something missing	unfamiliar
blankness	absence	wordless
unfilled	nonexistence	voiceless
evacuation	nothingness	unfathomable
clearing out	vacuum	cancellation
bareness	oblivion	negation
unoccupied place	stupor	loss
expressionless	trance	wasteland
silence	daze	desert
nullify	pause	lack of movement
stillness	hiatus	paralysis
removal	annihilation	strip away

The association game produces a vast collection of words and notes that may serve as guides in the formulation of convincing claims. Our list might lead us, for example, to ideas such as the following:

(sign)   Gildner's careful placement of a <u>gap</u> in the center of his poem
(signals)   suggests the <u>negation</u> of innocence in the boys and
(significance) underscores one of the text's central concerns: the problem of young American males being <u>stripped</u> of their adolescence and driven toward manhood long before they can cope with its pressures or shoulder its often violent expectations.

(sign)	The <u>white space</u> in the middle of the text
(signals)	also points to the forced <u>silence</u> of the boys and the swift <u>nullification</u> of dissent on their part,
(significance)	which strengthens the poem's critique of dictatorial leaders who expect <u>mute</u> submission from the individuals they command.

(signals)	With its suggestion of the young players' <u>stupefied</u>—almost <u>para-lyzed</u>—response to their war-mongering coach,
(sign)	the calculated <u>blankness</u> in this poem published in 1969
(significance)	may additionally recall the anti-war attitudes of the Vietnam era, when many writers took activist stances against a culture they considered either <u>oblivious</u> to the American military machine or too dis-empowered and frightened (like the boys in the text) to speak out against forceful political rhetoric.

As you can see from the underlined words above, our list of associations has come in handy at every stage of claim development. That is not to say, of course, that the association game forces you to incorporate terms from your catalog throughout your claims. Rather, we hope the examples we have presented reveal some of the theoretical possibilities of this tool.

Playing with verbs game

Powerful and specific verbs not only lend muscle to your writing but also very often lead you toward nuanced ideas about meaning. An effective verb *connects* the sign to an invisible idea below the semiotic waterline, but it also *describes* the relationship between the two. Consider, for example, the following verbs and their potential usefulness in claim generation:

echoes	summons	reveals	escalates
mitigates	softens	intensifies	palliates
critiques	exposes	undermines	erases
exploits	calls attention to	interrogates	underscores
destabilizes	demystifies	reinforces	encapsulates
parodies	mocks	ironizes	ridicules
dramatizes	invalidates	subverts	rejects
quells	obscures	sanitizes	sanctifies
foregrounds	marginalizes	privileges	and so on

Given a strong sign and a list of highly specific verbs, we can generate ideas simply by "mixing and matching." As a way of practicing this verb-centered game, let's look at poem 712 by Emily Dickinson (who, as you may already know, did not title her works):

> Because I could not stop for Death—
> He kindly stopped for me—
> The Carriage held but just Ourselves—
> And Immortality.
>
> We slowly drove—He knew no haste
> And I had put away
> My labor and my leisure too,
> For His Civility—
>
> We passed the School, where Children strove
> At Recess—in the Ring—
> We passed the Fields of Gazing Grain—
> We passed the Setting Sun—
>
> Or rather—He passed Us—
> The Dews drew quivering and chill—
> For only Gossamer, my Gown—
> My Tippet—only Tulle—
>
> We paused before a House that seemed
> A Swelling of the Ground—
> The Roof was scarcely visible—
> The Cornice—in the Ground—
>
> Since then—'tis Centuries—and yet
> Feels shorter than the Day
> I first surmised the Horses' Heads
> Were toward Eternity—[9]

One of the more interesting facets of Dickinson's text lies in her radical "familiarizing" of the infamous grim reaper. If the Western imagination often conjures Death as a black-clad, corpse-like wraith, then Dickinson's version appears more akin to a prim, gentleman caller, a dapper and available fellow taking his date on a romantic ride. And if our common rendering highlights Death's function as a gruff, agricultural laborer, an insensitive field worker with cold scythe in hand, Dickinson elevates his status to gentry: he is now a carriage-owning, "kindly" man who seems to hold particular promise for an unmarried woman.

Dickinson's version of Death, in other words, jars against the commonly held correspondence between his physical manifestation and the concepts he symbolizes: decay, loss, cruelty, pain, sorrow, and so on. She cuts strikingly against the grain of expectation—which should come as little surprise. Even a cursory look into Dickinson's biography reveals her penchant for being the proverbial fly in the ointment of mainstream New England during the nineteenth century. This is the same writer who, at the age of 15, declared, "I was almost persuaded to be a christian . . . But I soon forgot my morning prayer or else it was irksome to me. One by one my old habits returned and I cared less for religion than ever";[10] and who, a year before her death, at the age of 54, still called herself "but a Pagan."[11] We know, through the slightest of background information then, that our interest in Dickinson's iconoclastic version of Death not only represents a viable phenomenon for analysis but also carries import with respect to Dickinson's unique brand of theology.

Having identified our sign as "Dickinson's odd rendering of Death as a kindly gentleman caller," we can start to formulate ideas about meaning by mixing and matching our chosen sign with any number of strong, analytical verbs. For example, what particular, below-the-waterline belief might Dickinson *mitigate* by painting Death as a genteel visitor? Which hidden predispositions might Dickinson's gentlemanly Death *critique*? What kinds of associations might Dickinson *summon* with her "prim reaper," and to what ends? From there, we allow the verbs themselves to suggest avenues for analytical exploration:

(sign)	Dickinson's portrayal of Death as genteel rather than dominating, inviting rather than annihilating,
(signals)	mitigates fears of the self's complete erasure,
(significance)	a terror made all the more potent by the poet's unconventional agnosticism in the Christian-dominated culture of nineteenth-century New England.
(sign)	Dickinson's "dapper Death"
(signals)	at the same time critiques the Western cultural predisposition to demonize natural processes such as the end of life.
(significance)	Such an ironic reversal situates her squarely in a Romantic tradition devoted to testing custom and challenging mainstream outlooks.
(sign)	The prim reaper of Dickinson's "712"—with his refined manners and fleet, roomy carriage—
(signals)	also summons images of pleasant liberation
(significance)	from the claustrophobic pressures of small-town New England life, which emphasized strict social mores and constraining roles, particularly for unmarried women.

In each of these three claims about Dickinson's "gentlemanly Death," we trust the verb to suggest a particular relationship between the above-the-water-line sign and a specific below-the-waterline signal. The verbs stir the critical imagination. They serve as theoretical prompts. With patience and effort (along with some research, if necessary), our minds make strong connections and delve into plausible meanings. Time and again, our students have suggested that this game works wonders. So the next time you get stuck in generating ideas, pull out the list above (or better yet, construct your own catalog by opening a thesaurus or mining the work of professional writers), and let verbs help you dive below the waterline.

Trafficking in ideas game

When we steer our cars around town, we see constant reminders of how to behave behind the wheel. Such cues appear in the form of directional signals and road signs. All of these pointers and markers form an intricate system that, in its entirety, comprises the culture of the road. We enter that culture, that sign system, whenever we step on the gas and pull out into traffic. As noted in this textbook's introduction, however, we can approach any organized cultural practice—an art form such as poetry writing or pottery making, a sport like lacrosse or motocross, an everyday social activity such as shoe shopping or attending the cinema—as a system of signs. Each of these social enterprises presumes knowledge of specific rules and regulations, various codes of conduct, and particular properties of order and value. Each assumes training and expects participants to possess an awareness of—and an ability to read—the signs that comprise the system.

Often, we can formulate interesting ideas about a sign in one system by studying the meaning-filled markers in another. In the trafficking in ideas game, ask yourself how your chosen phenomenon operates in ways similar to signs in the driving world. For example:

1. How and why is my sign a command to obey specific rules (like the traffic laws that must be mastered for a driver's test)? What are these rules, and what invisible beliefs and unspoken values created and maintain them?
2. How might my sign function as a marker of status, wealth, and success (like a Mercedes or BMW)?
3. How and why is my sign a means to safety, protection, and the common good (like road signs designed to prevent collisions)? Whose best interests does my sign especially protect, and whose might it tend to overlook? Why?

4. How is my sign an indicator of exuberance and sexiness (like a flashy sports car)?

5. How and why might my sign function as an invitation to transgress (like a speed limit sign on the highway), even though such behavior may endanger the self and others? What deep-seated mindsets feed the temptations and potentially harmful pleasures inscribed within my sign?

6. How might my sign point to ideas about modernity, industrialization, and technology (like the complex roadways and traffic management systems of highly developed nations)?

7. How might my sign serve as a symbol of power and dominance (like a Hummer or hot rod)?

8. How might my chosen sign point toward dominant attitudes about the environment and the use of natural resources (the way an automobile culture assumes that land may be cleared for roads and petroleum processed for readily available fuel)?

9. In what ways might my sign indicate a specific intention or plan for the future (like a turn signal)?

10. What else do cars and roadways signify, and how might these suggestions trigger interpretive thoughts about my sign?

As a way of modeling the ways in which we can "traffic in ideas," consider the popularity of baseball great Derek Jeter or English footballer Tom Huddlestone. How, for instance, might their celebrity function like a "merge" sign, which manages traffic flow and helps to minimize crashes? What or whom might their fame serve to bring together in a safe and orderly way, and why? Here is one possible response:

(sign)	The enormous popularity of premier athletes like Derek Jeter and Tom Huddlestone, aside from their skills as players,
(signals)	lies partially in their racial ambiguity,
(significance)	which subtly encourages equality in cultures saddled with long histories of marginalizing groups of people based on skin color.

The devotion we pay to a Jeter or a Huddlestone, then, may have as much to do with their skills as cultural unifiers as with their prowess on the diamond or pitch.

Or what about a sign from the classic *Star Wars* films, namely, the way in which the series depicts evil as polished and uniform (the pristine blackness of Darth Vader's shiny outfit alongside the gleaming sameness of the storm troopers), while the "good guys" seem diverse and ragtag (from clumsy, nonhuman "droids" and illiterate simians, to gunrunners and farm boys). In what ways might this peculiar opposition—homogeneous evil versus heterogeneous good—behave like a sign in our car culture? After contemplating the variety of American cars, and comparing them to automobiles made in other countries during the 1970s, we arrived at this claim:

(sign)   The fact that the original Star Wars films portray evil as pristine, uniform, and orderly, while depicting the noble "rebels" as ragtag and assorted,

(signals)   highlights the dangers of homogeneity

(significance)   in a late twentieth-century context that pitted American individualism and democratic diversity against collectivizing ideologies such as fascism and communism.

Here, the perceived diversity of American autos (with their seemingly endless makes and models, and their numerous color choices) appears in contrast to the presumably uniform vehicles manufactured in the "evil empires" that arose directly before, during, and after World War II. These cars might include the Nazi-era Volkswagen, the fascist-sponsored Fiat, the East German Trabant, and the Soviet-made Zaporozhets (or "Zapor," for short).

As a final example, consider the rather recent phenomenon in the music industry of recording artists who offer their music to the public at no charge or at drastically reduced prices. Radiohead, for instance, initially released *In Rainbows* in 2008 at any price the consumer was willing to pay, from one cent on up. How might this interesting business model—where artists essentially give away their music—function as a sign of rebellion, an invitation to transgress, in much the way that a "speed limit" sign both commands us to obey but also entices us to misbehave?

(sign)   The "donation model" of music distribution (where artists such as Radiohead, Madonna, and The Charlatans offer their work to the public at little or no cost)

(signals)   represents a new kind of legitimacy, coolness, and unconventionality—the latest innovation in rock rebelliousness and independence. In other words, the sign serves as the marker of a perceived freedom from music moguls and big recording companies

(significance)   in an entertainment arena where one's popularity and reputation is increasingly linked to the avoidance of corporate enterprise and the threat of being branded as a sell-out.

As these examples make clear, using traffic signs and phenomena from the system of our driving culture often leads to new avenues of interpretation. We need not stop, however, with road signs. If we tap into the signs that comprise professional sports culture, we could ask how our chosen phenomenon functions as a "site of contest" or—like a Sunday football game—"a pleasant distraction from the pressures of daily responsibility." If we home in on the semiotic matrix of organized religion, we might wonder how our sign behaves as "a mechanism of communion"—like the Catholic Mass—or as "a source of comfort in a turbulent world." And if we pitch our sign through the system of avant-garde music, we might ponder how it functions as "a call for political action" or "a challenge to authority." The point of this game is simply to borrow from other sign systems as a way to trigger unexpected and persuasive thoughts.

Making it strange game

In "A Martian Sends a Postcard Home"—a poem by British author Craig Raine—we read in wonder as a Martian catalogs some of the oddities of earthly life. To this intergalactic visitor, even the simplest of artifacts seems weird, literally from another world. A book, through the eyes of Raine's narrator from outer space, transforms into a "mechanical bird with many wings";[12] a telephone becomes an infant wakened by "tickling [it] with a finger";[13] and a bathroom transforms into the gulag image of "a punishment room / with water but nothing to eat."[14] Raine's poem, with its alien vantage point, offers perceptive, comic, and at times horrific takes on everyday objects, reminding us of how oblivious we often become to our surroundings. Over time, through habit, we stop seeing the phenomena of our world as imbued with uniqueness. By assuming the role of alien observer, the writer intervenes in this predicament, reviving objects that have become inert to us through familiarity.

As a generator of plausible claims about signs, you too can adopt a "Martian perspective." By approaching your sign through a series of "alien" comparisons, you set the stage to discover uncanny relationships, fresh ways of reading your chosen phenomena that lend depth and interest to your study. With an alien approach in mind, consider again the expanded popularity of tattoos in mainstream culture. Now look around your room and choose some objects at random. In implementing the Martian's point of view, you test out a range of odd comparisons by asking how your sign is "like" those objects, how it might (weirdly enough) resemble them:

How is my sign similar to jewelry?
What connections might exist between my sign and a blanket?
How could I argue for likeness between my sign and a barbell?
In what ways might my sign resemble a textbook?
How is my sign like a family photo?
What possible links could I draw between my sign and a house plant?
How might I argue that my sign is like an alarm clock?
Under what conditions might I liken my sign to an iPod?

As you can see through these examples, varying degrees of strangeness exist. Likening the mainstream appeal of tattoos in present-day culture to jewelry, for example, probably seems less bizarre than comparing them to house plants. And while all of these alien similes might produce good results, the most provocative discoveries typically come when the comparison is especially strange or counterintuitive.

How might we follow through, then, with a few of these alien comparisons? If we liken the mainstreaming of tattoos to jewelry, then we might note that both behave as accessories, adornments to the body. That association seems clear enough. If we think through that simile further, though, then tattoos seem to represent a special case. With so many choices in contemporary culture for adorning the self, at some point we push past the changeable accessory (worn one day but not the next) and desire something more lasting. Getting a tattoo, it might be argued, marks us as people who scoff at the flitting desires of a fickle consumer culture, who instead desire permanent representations of our core attitudes and personalities. Such a notion might lead to an idea about meaning such as the following:

(sign)	The recent rise of tattoos in mainstream culture
(signals)	may stem from a sense that each individual needs to advertise a trustworthy core identity
(significance)	in a culture where surface images appear to lack deep substance and reliable truth value.

Or consider a slightly more alien simile: the contemporary tattoo fad as similar to barbells. In this particular comparison, we might begin by brainstorming how both are related to the "personal manufacture of beauty." Like the barbell, the tattoo says, "We can overthrow nature. We individualists have the power to expand the parameters of the body." Therein lies the uniqueness of the tattoo—it not only becomes part of the body, but also literally enlarges the scope of a person's physical form. It signals expansion—a reshaping or repicturing of the original. In this way, the tattoo seems more like bodybuilding than fashion accessorizing. In fact, the tattoo is even more permanent than bodybuilding (since our muscles eventually go lax and shrink). In other words, the increasing popularity of the tattoo reflects a contemporary view that the body is what a person makes of it—that one can mold and shape the body to suit individual desires, and can expand and enlarge its significances. With these observations in hand, we can proceed again to claim-building:

(sign)	Additionally, the mainstreaming of tattoos
(signals)	signals a widespread belief that the body is a place of almost inexhaustible possibility and change.
(significance)	The sign, therefore, represents a trendy expansion of a deeply embedded ideal of the self-made individual, who possesses the power not simply to improve his or her standing as established by culture, but even to move beyond the form and limitations of the body as set by nature.

As a final example (one perhaps even stranger in terms of its simile), let's compare our sign to an alarm clock. Some might argue, for example, that both function to wake people up. The alarm clock stirs a sleeper from deep slumbers. Similarly, the tattoo—once it enters the mainstream—arguably rouses the culture from its complacencies and collective stupor. When worn by the everyday stock broker, librarian, and check-out clerk, the tattoo may function to disturb the established system of expectations regarding the body and its proper display.

(significance)	In a culture of increasing sameness, where each town resembles the next with its mandatory mall, fast-food restaurants, and warehouse superstores, the desire to escape monotony carries particular significance.
(sign)	Enter the recent tattoo trend,
(signals)	whose participants signal their desire to shock the system, to wake culture from its homogeneous trance.

While the examples above test out similes of increasing strangeness, all three produce arguable claims about the meanings behind the mainstream tattoo. By exploring the sign through a "Martian mentality"—by playing with similes that stretch our powers of imagination and argumentation—we expand our options for manufacturing plausible, insightful interpretations.

The frame game

This final game encourages you to place your chosen sign in a variety of social, historical, and academic "frames" that may trigger viable ideas about meaning. These frames of reference are, as you might imagine, practically infinite in number and scope, but you can begin to get a grasp on your options simply by looking at the different departments of study at your institution. Since universities organize themselves around discrete categories of knowledge, you can exploit that classification when searching for meaningful frames that might throw new light on your sign and spark your analytical imagination.

With respect to the physical sciences, for instance, you might consider the frames of biology, chemistry, and physics, paying special attention to the ways in which these fields have fueled controversies, solved problems, and changed attitudes throughout the centuries. Then there are the social sciences such as psychology, sociology, anthropology, political science, and economics. In what ways might these disciplines open windows of discovery about the multiple meanings of your chosen sign? In addition, you can consider the humanities, including history and philosophy, literature and languages. These academic arenas present countless theoretical prospects, as well. By remaining eclectic in your studies and making connections across a range of disciplines—as the frame game encourages you to do—you position yourself to approach your sign from a host of scholastic angles. You also guide yourself to potentially relevant paths of research.

What's in a name?

As a way of showing the frame game in action, consider again a sign from Mary Shelley's *Frankenstein*: the namelessness of Victor's monster. (You may recall that we referenced this sign in Chapter 2.) Shelley's classic 1818 novel—which she completed before her twentieth birthday—narrates the tale of a rebellious young scientist named Victor Frankenstein, who defies the conventional wisdom of his profession and shockingly succeeds in stitching together and bringing to life the body parts of various corpses that he has pilfered from cemeteries and morgues. Determined to fashion, as he puts it, "a being like myself,"[15] Victor fantasizes that "A new species would bless me as its creator and source; many happy and excellent natures would owe their being to me. No father could claim the gratitude of his child so completely as I should deserve theirs."[16] After two years of laborious study and experimentation, he finally gives birth, in effect, to a "beautiful" man-child "about eight feet in height, and proportionably large."

Yet despite the strange attractiveness and impressive physique of his creation, Victor panics when he sees "the dull yellow eye of the creature open."[17] As he tells his friend Robert Walton, "I rushed out of the room."

Abandoned by his maker, the "creature" receives none of the care typically provided to newborns—attention, affection, nourishment, shelter, clothing. Left to fend for himself, Victor's "child" garners no nurturance, no love, no support of any kind from his "father." Neither does he receive a name. While recollecting the horrific events that subsequently unfold, Victor refers to his offspring strictly in negative and general terms such as "creature," "being," and "monster." Never does Victor consider giving his creation a first name, and it seems utterly unthinkable that he would pass on to such a "Wretched devil"[18] the noble surname of "Frankenstein." What's more, the creature never adopts a name for himself, even after he learns to read literature and philosophy and to deploy language with great fluidity and argumentative force.

The monster's namelessness catches our attention as semioticians, in no small part because the novel places considerable emphasis on names. (Think back to our discussion of import in the VOICE test, and how we search for signs that seem especially germane to the texts in which we find them.) The title of Shelley's work provides the most glaring evidence of the importance of a name. But consider, too, Victor's own first words in the novel:

> I am by birth a Genevese; and my family is one of the most distinguished of that republic. My ancestors had been for many years counsellors and syndics; and my father had filled several public situations with honour and reputation. He was respected by all who knew him for his integrity and indefatigable attention to public business.[19]

Lineage clearly matters to Victor Frankenstein. His opening sentiments highlight the value that he places on paternity and a respected family name. His name, it would appear, cannot be passed down to just anybody, least of all a "fiend."[20]

With additional regard to names and naming, Shelley's work is an epistolary novel (a story told through letters). As such, the book contains its fair share of signatures, with correspondents regularly signing their names to written communications (which are themselves "creations" of a kind). It seems plausible to state, then, that *Frankenstein* calls noteworthy attention to its characters' names, even while the "monster"—one of the arguable heroes of this famous gothic tale—never receives a specific moniker of any sort. That is curious because, on the most fundamental level, we can hardly fathom a major character in any novel (one who converses and comes in dramatic conflict with others; one who performs a range of actions both good and evil; and one who expresses complex emotions and outlooks on life) without a distinct, memorable name. We therefore find ourselves on safe argumentative ground in assuming that the creature's namelessness is not an oversight on Shelley's part, that the invention of a main character who lacks a name carries meanings and purposes about which we may offer reasonable speculations. "What could Shelley's narrative be suggesting," we might ask, "by leaving Victor's creation nameless? Why does this key figure in the work never receive a personal identifier, a name of his own?" With our sign and theoretical questions firmly in place, we can now test out the frame game. Though we may not know of any relevant frames right away, we can experiment, test various options, and behave (interestingly enough) much like Victor when he fuses one body part to another in fashioning his creation.

A few prospective frames

To begin the process of finding meaning within a particular discipline or field of study, consider the frame of psychology. Shelley's book contains a host of emotional extremes, from wild hopes to terrible fears to vengeful expressions of rage. There are even suggestions of madness. Consequently, this field seems like a good fit. But how can we deploy the frame of psychology in relation to our specific sign concerning the monster's lack of a name? One possibility might involve a concept from the so-called father of psychoanalysis, Sigmund Freud. In an introduction to psychology class, you may have encountered the Freudian notion of the "Id"—an uncontrollable (and unnamable) constituent of the human psyche. This notion seems particularly fruitful when applied to Victor's unnamed creation, since "Id" is simply the Latin word for "It." The monster's namelessness, we might say, aligns him with this deep-seated, animalistic, and nonverbal part of Freud's psychic model. Whereas the Freudian ego and superego are distinctly linguistic, connected to language and culture, the unruly "Id" remains beyond language. Consequently, we might speculate that the monster represents some form of Victor's own psychological makeup, a ghastly manifestation of his unarticulated fantasies and desires. No wonder the novel keeps this "It" unnamed, for that withholding may signal both Victor's exercise of power over his "hideous enemy"[21] and a manifestation of his fear that this "other being"[22] might wreak unspeakable havoc.

Another likely "framing" candidate belongs to the physical sciences. Since Victor is a scientist himself, we can sensibly begin with the areas that interest him most: chemistry, biology, and anatomy. With these frames in mind, we can explore developments in these fields during the late eighteenth and early nineteenth centuries, wondering how the information might prove valuable in our quest for meanings. For example, in 1761, Giovanni Battista Morgagni published a comprehensive treatise on postmortem dissections, which dramatically expanded the fields of anatomy and pathology; by 1764, William Smellie had lent scientific scrutiny to the previously mysterious processes of labor and childbirth; and in 1771, Luigi Galvani began experiments into bioelectricity by feeding electrical currents into the legs of dead frogs. Though all three of these avenues seem worthy of pursuit, the last appears especially fruitful, since Victor is also driven by the prospect of reanimating flesh. With that in mind, we could then ask in what ways "galvanism"—the use of electrical currents to stimulate muscle—might "frame" a discussion of meaning about the monster's namelessness? How might historical attempts to reanimate lifeless tissues with jolts of electricity offer a way to read the creature's lack of a name?

When we place our sign inside the frame of galvanism, we see a curious and potentially useful discrepancy. The experiments of Galvani and others were performed on dead animals, not dead humans, and especially not the cobbled together parts of corpses. Ironically, though Victor performs his experiments at the human level, he does not allow his successful creation to enter fully into the human sphere. The creature's namelessness, in other words, aligns him more clearly with Galvani's dead frogs—lowly forms of life that do not receive personal names. In fact, Victor himself wonders whether he should produce a human-like creature or just one of "simpler organization."[23] Already we see an interesting idea about meaning as it emerges from the relationship between our sign (the withholding of a name for the monster) and a particular frame (the history of galvanism). Keeping the creature nameless sequesters him in a subhuman category, more closely related to lower animal life. (Victor even refers to the creature as a "vile insect"[24] and "animal."[25]) In a way, Victor exercises a particular form of scientific power over a physically more powerful being, and he does so simply by keeping his creation nameless.

From there, we could dive deeper, searching for other relevant clues to galvanism's importance in contouring our sign within Shelley's novel. We could also, however, reclaim some of the other frames dealing with biology—the increased interest in cadaver dissections, the new wealth of knowledge regarding labor and childbirth. In fact, we could potentially root an entire study in the monster's namelessness and the various scientific frames afforded by the text's historical surroundings. For the purposes of our discussion of the frame game, however, let's move toward other viable contexts.

What about economics? How might the study of the socioeconomic divisions of class in late eighteenth- and early nineteenth-century Europe shape our sense of the monster's namelessness? Shelley's moneyed protagonist—a student who possesses the time and privilege to run complex experiments in his university apartment—appears in stark contrast to the "Wretched devil" with a "dull yellow eye."[26] Especially when considering Victor's description of his family as "most distinguished," and of his father serving the public "with honour and reputation," we gradually understand the class dynamics at work between the elite scientist and his lowly offspring. For if Victor originally desired "a being like [him]self"—in other words, another privileged and "honourable" gentleman— what he ends up producing more closely approximates the underclass, jaundiced and rough. When placed in the frame of socioeconomic struggle (particularly one that harks back to the French Revolution even as it anticipates the mid-nineteenth-century socialist theories of Karl Marx and others), this nameless creature might signal some uniform and homogenous "proletariat," the embodiment of revolutionary rabble. Victor, it would appear, has given birth to a powerful, if nameless, "working class" that threatens his very privilege.

We could also extend this frame—one rooted in ideas about the distribution of wealth and capital—by incorporating the fact that both of Shelley's parents were philosophers engaged in questions of class imbalance. In *An Enquiry Concerning Political Justice* (1793), her father, William Godwin, offers a vigorous critique of aristocratic power, declaring, "The thing really to be desired is the removing as much as possible of arbitrary distinctions, and leaving to talents and virtue the field of exertion unimpaired."[27] Meanwhile, in the 1792 manifesto *A Vindication of the Rights of Woman*, Shelley's mother—the founding feminist thinker and author Mary Wollstonecraft—frequently condemns inequalities between the social classes in Britain. For the outspoken Wollstonecraft, "The preposterous distinctions of rank, which render civilisation a curse, by dividing the world between voluptuous tyrants, and cunning envious dependents, corrupt, almost equally, every class of people."[28] Although Wollstonecraft died ten days after giving birth to Mary, the thinking preserved in her books and philosophical treatises would powerfully influence the teenage author of *Frankenstein*.

Sticking with a single frame

To exemplify an extended treatment of the frame game, we now turn to sociology. Just as we did with the frames of psychology, biology, and economics, we can scan the field of sociology for factors that bear on our sign. As one example, consider this: when Victor refrains from bestowing a name on his creature, he effectively disowns him. Victor's "child" essentially becomes an orphan, a being bereft of parents, a name, and a legitimate cultural identity. From there, we might pursue some research into issues related to orphaned children in the years surrounding the publication of Shelley's book. Take, for instance, this passage from Naomi Tadmor's 2001 study, *Family and Friends in Eighteenth-Century England: Household, Kinship, and Patronage*:

> At a time in which about one marriage in three was broken by the death of a partner before the end of the wife's fecund period there could be a considerable fluidity in household composition. Illness and widowhood could bring about new household arrangements, re-marriage could lead to the creation of families with half-relations and step-relations, and orphanhood could necessitate various forms of boarding and fostering.[29]

Tadmor goes on to suggest:

> This, for instance, may have been the lot of at least some of the 16 percent of late eighteenth-century children who were motherless by the age of eleven, the 20 percent who were fatherless, and the 4 percent who were total orphans by the age of fifteen. By the time they reached their first marriage, 45 percent were motherless and 49 percent fatherless.[30]

With Tadmor's statistics in mind, we might try to formulate an idea about meaning, one situated within the frame of British orphanhood:

(sign)	Shelley's novel arguably leaves Victor's creation anonymous
(signals)	in order to signal the largely unnamed and unaddressed problem of orphanhood in late eighteenth- and early nineteenth-century England.
(significance)	The nameless monster would seem, therefore, to represent the troubling numbers of nearly invisible orphans that British culture, in Shelley's view, had doubly abandoned.

In addition, we could gesture toward other literary texts that treat the profound social problem of orphanhood around the same time. Our claim about the meaning behind Shelley's nameless monster, it turns out, anticipates a treatment of the orphan problem by Charles Dickens in *Oliver Twist*:

> [T]he parish authorities magnanimously and humanely resolved, that Oliver should be "farmed," or, in other words, that he should be despatched to a branch-workhouse some three miles off, where twenty or thirty other juvenile offenders against the poor-laws, rolled about the floor all day, without the inconvenience of too much food or too much clothing.[31]

The bitter ironies embedded in Dickens's text suggest the later writer's own scathing critique of the system governing orphaned children, and could easily serve as evidence to add to our *Frankenstein* argument.

We needn't stop there, however. A frame devoted to issues of orphanhood in eighteenth- and nineteenth-century Britain seems capable of offering even more ideas regarding the significance of our chosen sign. We could, for example, also discuss the ways in which the creature's namelessness becomes a manifestation of the shock and pain associated with such abandonment. The psychological trauma of being torn from one's family and left to the vagaries of failing social institutions, we might suggest, seems frightful, intensely painful, and even beyond language. In fact, to theorists such as Judith Herman, one of the foremost characteristics of trauma lies precisely in its resistance to being understood and named by its victims. It remains, according to Herman and many other trauma theorists, unspeakable and unfathomable; it slips free of representation, escapes full comprehension.[32]

Paradoxically, though, language—in the form of testimony—paves the way to recovery. Ultimately, trauma theory recognizes the restorative power of speaking about the horrors that have passed. Recovery from trauma (which is never absolute, since residues cling, shadowy remembrances rise) demands expression in words. Shelley's book, then, may be read as a narrative of the trauma associated with parental neglect and desertion. The monster's namelessness captures the loss and unutterable pain that he carries at all times. His identity is one of orphaned absence, and we come to understand this horrible void when the creature describes his pitiful lot: "I, the miserable and the abandoned, am an abortion, to be spurned at, and kicked, and trampled on."[33] At the same time, however, we see Victor's monster struggling to use language as a way to cope with his traumatizing rejection—all of which suggests a viable idea about meaning:

(sign)	The withholding of the creature's name
(signals)	might also signal the nameless pain associated with orphanhood and abandonment,

(significance) which inaugurates *Frankenstein's* exploration of the relationship between language and psychological trauma.

Such a reading proves even more persuasive when buttressed by the fact that Shelley herself was orphaned and, thus, had presumably experienced this precise form of trauma. Indeed, noted Romanticism scholar Anne Mellor argues that a "desire for a loving and supportive parent defined [Shelley's] character, shaped her fantasies, and produced her fictional idealizations of the bourgeois family."[34]

For good measure, let's examine one more way to generate meaning in this particular "sign and frame" relationship rooted in sociology. Victor, recall, "creates" the monster, is its "father." But where, we might ask, is the mother? Victor's "unhallowed" offspring, it appears, exists outside the culturally sanctioned means of reproduction (namely, wedlock). In many ways, the monster's "secret" birth curiously approximates the bastard child of an adulterous affair, an illegitimate threat to the father's reputation. Treating the creature literally as the unnamed bastard son of Frankenstein accrues even more import when we consider other prominent orphans in the text: Caroline Beaufort Frankenstein (Victor's mother) and Elizabeth Lavenza (whom Victor's parents adopt as a girl and whom Victor makes not only his childhood playmate but also, eventually, his wife). In both cases, the role of the noble family is one of benefactor. Victor's father provides for, rather than produces, these two orphans. Shelley's book seems to suggest, however, that this *noblesse oblige*—the perceived obligation of the rich to provide for the poor and outcast—is just one side of the story. The empowered man of means may just as easily produce, as provide for, orphans, and it is he who ultimately decides the fate of the illegitimate children. The monster born of Victor's "profane" activities is disowned and cast into anonymity, and this decidedly different treatment of the orphan question might yield the following idea about meaning:

(sign)   The monster, in some sense, cannot receive a name in Shelley's novel
(signals)   because he is illegitimate in the eyes of Victor and wider British
               culture—the mysterious offspring of a moneyed gentleman secretly
               engaged in "unhallowed" acts of reproduction.
(significance) As a result, Victor's anonymous bastard—produced outside of any
               cultural sanction—serves as a critique of patriarchal privilege, one
               that can provide for or discard its illegitimate offspring at will.

From there, we could enlist the help of scholars who have tackled the troubling issue of illegitimacy and privilege in British history. Lisa Zunshine's *Bastards and Foundlings: Illegitimacy in Eighteenth-Century England* or Wolfram Schmidgen's *Illegitimacy and Social Observation: The Bastard in the Eighteenth-Century Novel* would no doubt provide helpful support and historical context for a reading of Victor's monster as a threatening orphan-bastard.

As this final section illustrates, a single frame can often engender multiple ideas about a given sign. When we strike those analytical goldmines, we might even choose to organize an entire paper around them. At other times, certain frames do not lend themselves as easily to our chosen phenomenon. We are compelled, at those moments, to cast about for other meaningful contexts, other viable discourses relative to our semiotic project. Yet even when a particular frame does not help our interpretive endeavors right away, our efforts still pay dividends, simply because the information dredged up in possible service of one analysis may prove useful in a future semiotic project.

9. Wrap up

In this chapter, we have focused on developing ideas about the divergent meanings of individual signs. Up to this point, we have largely remained "horizontal" with regard to ideas. That is, we have deferred thinking about the finished product of our analysis (the final paper to be submitted for a grade) and have instead privileged restlessness and multiplicity in generating claims about each phenomena under analysis. Staying rangy—lateral and widespread in idea formation—helps to keep the writing process from falling prematurely into a "vertical" orientation, by which we mean a tendency to latch on to an initial theory and begin writing the paper straight down the page. Our experiences as writers and teachers have suggested that the process of making the most persuasive and provocative essays tends to be nonlinear, nonvertical—especially in the early stages of production. Part of the challenge lies with the fact that many people try to "write the way they read." In reading an argumentative essay, we start at the beginning of the analysis and follow its logic to conclusion. In *writing* such essays, however, we do not typically proceed from start to finish with a clear-cut beginning, middle, and end. Some critical studies do arrive this way, but these tend to be exceptions. More frequently, strong analyses are pieced together (in Frankenstein fashion) from disparate ideas about significance. In our next chapter, we turn to structuring essays based on those assertions about meaning.

10. Student example

The Apparition Condition: Virgil as Half-Shade, Half-Man in the *Inferno*

MacKenzie Regier

Dante's *Inferno* contains several instances in which Virgil, the pilgrim's famous guide through the underworld, embodies a puzzling contradiction. When first encountering the renowned Roman poet, Dante questions his master's form, wondering whether he is "a shade" or "a man" (I.66). Virgil replies, "Not man; I once was man," thus confirming his status as an apparition (I.67). Further support of Virgil's understandably ghostly condition comes during an episode in Canto VIII. When the two travelers board Phlegyas's boat to cross the River Styx, "there seem[s] to be no weight until [Dante] board[s]" (VIII.27). The text then describes "the ancient prow [. . .] cutting water / more deeply than it does when bearing others," which supplies additional evidence of Dante's solidity in relation to Virgil's immateriality. These statements offer explicit proof of the pilgrim's physical presence and the guide's lack thereof. The living poet possesses bodily substance, the dead one does not. What could be more logical?

Yet strangely, the *Inferno* challenges this commonsensical contrast in Canto III, when Virgil "place[s] / his hand upon [Dante's]" (III.19–20). Later, after the Furies threaten Dante with the presence of Medusa, Virgil turns Dante around and, "not content with just [Dante's] hands, / use[s] his own as well to cover up [Dante's] eyes," thus shielding his ward from Medusa's dangerous gaze (IX.58–60). Virgil manages to do with ease what might seem an exercise in futility—he, an incorporeal shade, makes bodily contact with a member of the living. At one point, he even "[bears Dante] with him upon [his] chest" like a mother who "lift[s] her son and run[s] without stop" (XXIII.50, 40). Furthermore, a being with no physical presence, like the long dead Virgil, should not be able to "lift [Dante]" or "thrust [him] forward" or "lovingly [take him] by the hand" (XXIV.27, XXIV.24, XXXI.28).

In these clashing examples, Dante's legendary guide oscillates between a being dispossessed of corporeal form and the opposite—an individual able to engage Dante physically. In a work devoted to verisimilitude—the exact number of turrets on Limbo's castle, the precise punishments for evildoers, the gory details of each sinner's castigation—this blurring of bodily demarcations seems decidedly odd. What possible import might Virgil's hybrid bodily status carry in Dante's text? Why portray the Roman poet in this particularly dichotomous way? How might Virgil's curiously "hyphenated" existence (somehow between the living and the dead) speak to Dante's larger epic goals?

Perhaps most available is a reading of Virgil's unusual physicality as signifying a vitality and permanence in life that the Roman poet maintains after death. The shade's curious ability to touch and to carry in turn emphasizes the poetic influence that he exerts over Dante, a power that reaches beyond life. In his very first meeting with Virgil, Dante exclaims, "You are my master and my author" (I.85), a phrase that captures how completely Dante emulates his Roman precursor, from whom he learned to hone his passion for writing into a viable craft. Dante, we know, closely studied Virgil's own version of Hell in the *Aeneid*, and based much of his own underworld on Virgil's inventive architecture. Without Virgil's writing, the *Inferno* might not exist at all. No other person, dead or alive, shaped Dante's writing as powerfully. In their fictional afterlife encounter, then, that immense influence transforms into physical contact, a reaffirmation of their connection that crosses generations and mortality. Virgil may have been long dead when Dante wrote the *Inferno*, but—as exhibited by his noteworthy status as somehow more substantive, more palpable than any other shade—his ability to mold Dante still thrives.

The *Inferno*'s depiction of Virgil as a half-man, half-spirit might also function as a way for Dante to offer his master a tacit apology for having to write him into "THE CITY OF WOE" with its "EVERLASTING PAIN" (III.1–2). Because Virgil lived long before Christianity's rise to state-sanctioned power, Dante is compelled to place in the Christian Hell a man whom he deeply admires. Dante scholar Thomas Bergin sums up how completely Catholicism enveloped not just Florence but most of medieval Europe: "Throughout all of Christendom, which was all the western world, one faith, one corpus of philosophical concepts [. . .] maintained a cohesiveness" that lasted until the Reformation (28). Subtly working around Catholic doctrine, Dante favors Virgil over all the other condemned residents of the *Inferno*. This special treatment is also apparent in his placement of the Roman poet in Limbo, the first and most lenient circle of Dante's underworld, where the pilgrim observes "a meadow of green flowering plants" (IV.111) and "an exalted castle," "defended [. . .] by a fair stream" (IV.106, 108). The inhabitants of Limbo can never touch the perfection of paradise, but neither do they wallow in a fecal lake or boil in a river of blood. In a startling nuance to this privileged status of the virtuous pagans, then, Virgil may occasionally even know the luxury of human touch. Combine these two advantages, and the Roman poet becomes singularly prized in the abyss, a status befitting a figure whom Dante describes as his personal "author," and therefore one deserving of an apology.

Dante's representation of Virgil as a shade capable of making physical contact additionally recalls—and in fact surpasses—similar interactions in the two texts that most influenced the Italian poet: Homer's *Odyssey* and Virgil's *Aeneid*. Dante's unstable division between the states of body and shade in his mentor, then, might also signal how the Italian poet seeks to update the two previous tales, helping to solidify the *Inferno*'s place among the classic epics. In the *Odyssey*, for example, when Odysseus visits the Greek version of the underworld, he encounters the spirit of his mother. Three times he attempts to embrace her, but "she [goes] sifting through [Odysseus's] hands, impalpable /

as shadows are, and wavering like a dream" (XI.231–2). Similarly, in the *Aeneid*, when Aeneas finds the ghost of his father among the dead, he encounters the same problem: "the shade untouched [slips] through his hands, / Weightless as wind and fugitive as dream" (VI.941–2). While much of Dante's epic still glorifies and emulates these previous works, his blurring of the lines between shade and man positions the *Inferno* as a unique achievement, one particularly inflected by Christian thought. In a way, Dante's own faith makes it possible for Virgil to move past the possibilities offered by paganism. Dante's curious portrayal of Virgil—a shade who physically aids and protects the religiously devout Dante—possesses more power, more potential to act, than even the noblest of shades in the pagan underworlds of the *Odyssey* and *Aeneid*.

Dante's puzzling portrait of a half-dead, half-living Roman guide, however, does not just add nuance to classical archetypes. In his rendering of Virgil, Dante also illustrates how his version of Christianity is more inventive than dogmatic, more dynamic than static. Virgil's hybrid form—a dead soul able to touch the Italian poet—may signify Dante's willingness to deviate from early fourteenth-century Catholic doctrine and to "play God," as it were, in his own textual universe. What appears at first a clear-cut reaffirmation of Dante's traditional theology—namely, the subordination of his great pagan mentor to a Christian paradigm—also appears as an exercise of imaginative freedom within that seemingly unshakeable orthodoxy. The hybrid vision of Virgil in the *Inferno* thus becomes a kind of paradox: Dante himself has written his poetic father into Hell as a pagan, but the Roman remains privileged through Dante's maneuvering. Here, as in other subtly transgressive areas in the epic, Dante assumes the role of divine creator. Consequently, while Dante claims Christian humility, he also manipulates religious dogma in ways that border at times on iconoclasm. Dante's seemingly idolatrous treatment of Beatrice, for example, supports the idea that his Christianity is itself a hybrid. As Joseph Gallagher points out, "Beatrice's [name] is too holy to be directly mentioned in Hell," a fact that borders on idolatry when considering that "Even God is usually mentioned [by Dante] in paraphrase" (10). Considering as well Dante's "predictions" of self-salvation—particularly in a Christian framework that condemns both soothsayers and the prideful—it seems that Dante's religious beliefs are at best inventive and expansive and at worst heretical and self-centered. Virgil's dichotomous representation, then, belongs among these acts of near "imaginative heresy."

The curious construction of a ghostly yet at times tangible Virgil thus allows Dante some poetic leeway without inciting the full wrath of the Catholic Church. In fact, the text often tests the boundary between Dante's fondness for Rome and Virgil, and the requisite allegiance to Christian orthodoxy. In constructing the entire underworld as viewed through a Christian lens, Dante takes great pains to tread carefully, since medieval Catholicism warns against the sins of hubris and the glorifications of institutions other than the church. Through his uncanny portrayal of the Roman poet as one able to transcend the boundary of death, then, Dante simultaneously signals his great love for the old magnificence of Rome without overtly overstepping his place as a dutiful Christian in fiercely devout early fourteenth-century Florence. By endowing the Roman Virgil with an ability that no other shade shares, Dante cleverly gives rise to a vision of a glorious and newly unified Roman empire. This makes sense given the context of Dante's political allegiances. Whereas the so-called Black Guelphs in Florence tended to support mercantile expansions and high-church policy, the "White Guelphs" (to which Dante belonged) were, in the words of scholar Tom Simone, "more moderate and somewhat sympathetic to the need for new political unity that might come about through the Holy Roman emperor" (5). It seems arguable, therefore, that Virgil's hybrid form comes to embody Dante's own blendings of the political and theological debates of his day.

If Virgil enjoys brief moments of near embodiment, however—fleeting instances of the power to touch his pupil—they are just that: ephemeral and rare. In this way, Dante's choice to render his poetic father in curiously ambiguous form ultimately emphasizes and further reinforces Christian power and Dante's allegiance to it. The in-between state that Virgil embodies—while arguably superior to the shade-only and tortured existences of others, and emblematic of the power bestowed upon the Roman—still resides far from Dante's ideal of the saved soul. What may be understood as a celebration of Virgil oddly enough also underscores the awesome distance between the Roman poet and Dante's ideal conception of salvation. If the devout Christian Dante will one day enjoy the touch of God, the best Virgil can hope for remains the touch of an adoring literary disciple.

Instead of glorifying Virgil, then, the text might construct a Christian warning, a stark portrait of a soul caught between the tantalizing freedom of life and the cold confinement of death. Shortly after Virgil declares himself "not man," thereby confirming his existence as a shade, Dante addresses him as "O poet—by that God / whom you had never come to know," offering explanation for Virgil's presence in Hell (I.130–1). The only real sin Virgil has committed is that of never knowing the Christian deity, since he lived during "the season of false and lying gods" (I.72). In this vein, two points in the text which previously supported Virgil's privilege now appear to reverse. Instead of a merciful gift, Virgil's afterlife on Limbo's "enameled green" and his fleeting corporeality become a cruel imitation of life—a counterfeit Earth and a fickle physical presence, neither sufficient to satisfy (IV.118). Virgil, as an innocent man and yet one who never knew the Christian God, remains trapped between the palpable presence and satisfaction of the living and the impermanence of the damned. In this reading, Virgil functions as a lesson to all Christians: in Hell, even the least punishable of sinners—indeed, even the most acclaimed Roman poet—still must endure an eternity without God. What may seem like a lenient fate and even a challenge to Christian orthodoxy also serves to reaffirm and further inscribe the reigning religious forces of medieval Europe.

Works Cited

Alighieri, Dante. *Inferno*. Trans. Allen Mandelbaum. New York: Bantam Classics, 1982.

Bergin, Thomas, G. *Dante*. New York: Orion, 1965.

Gallagher, Joseph. *A Modern Reader's Guide to Dante's* The Divine Comedy. Liguori, MO: Liguori Publications, 2000.

Homer. *The Odyssey*. Trans. Edward Fitzgerald. New York: Farrar, Straus and Giroux, 1998.

Simone, Tom. *Introduction to Dante's* Inferno. Newburgport, MA: Focus, 2007.

Virgil. *The Aeneid*. Trans. Edward Fitzgerald. New York: Vintage, 1990.

5
Building Essays Around Your Ideas

Chapter Outline

1. Drafting your essay

In the previous chapter, we discussed the all-important generation of ideas about meaning. We looked at several examples of the "sign-signals-signif-icance" model, and we examined various strategies designed to help in the construction of persuasive theoretical claims. These assertions about mean-ing, as we will now see, form the backbone of any strong interpretive study. As we work on the last major phase of the analytical process—structuring essays around our ideas—we strive to flesh out our claims with supportive evidence and logical, in-depth argumentation. We enter the arena of research, when applicable, and test our reasoning powers. We seek to edify, enlighten, and even entertain our readers.

2. The Three-"I"ed Monster

With our sign selected and staged, and multiple ideas about meaning in hand, we can start to amass the support that will persuade our readers of the validity of our theories. As a way to build bulk and substance around each theoretical assertion, we now turn to a trusted friend—the Three-"I"ed Monster:

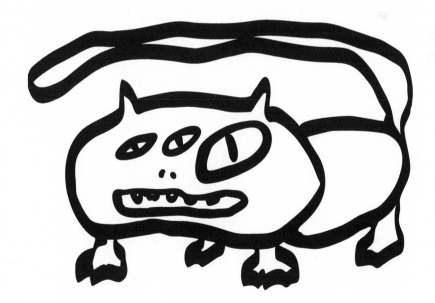

Note that our helpful beast possesses three "I"s, which stand for:

- *Idea*: Our theoretical claim about meaning that we intend to substantiate. (This portion draws on the work discussed in Chapter 4.)
- *Illustration*: Our catalog of hard evidence in support of the idea about meaning. (This section offers concrete examples and factual data that confirm the link we have forged between the visible, above-the-waterline sign and the invisible, below-the-waterline concept, motivator, or theme.)
- *Interpretation*: Our in-depth, persuasive reasoning as to why we think our idea and illustration make sense. (In this part, we unpack our idea about meaning in the light of our evidentiary support. We make our full-blown case, in other words, for the theoretical assertion that we have proposed.)

As you can see from the drawing, the monster's final "I" is several times larger than the "I" of idea or illustration. That is because we want to spend the most time and effort providing interpretation designed to convince readers that our idea deserves attention and carries import.

To watch the monster in action, consider the following interpretive response, which attempts to unpack one particular meaning attributable to the enduring appeal of official university apparel such as sweatshirts, t-shirts, and hats. No doubt you have seen such clothing items, available in a vast array of colors and styles: the classic, the retro, the one featuring the school mascot, and so on. As the argument below unfolds, see if you can identify the three "I"s of the monster: look for the direct declaration of the "Idea" (or claim about the sign's meaning), the "Illustration" (or specific pieces of evidence that support the claim), and the "Interpretation" (or complex argument that confirms the persuasiveness of the claim).

> The purchase and display of university gear, it might be argued, helps to placate fears of isolation in a culture that has traditionally glorified—and perhaps overemphasized—the self and its independence. An official school sweatshirt or ballcap, in other words, may alleviate the threat of feeling cut off or outcast, allowing its wearer to signal membership in an exclusive club. At the team game, a sea of sameness washes over the stands, with energized fans sporting their team colors—an enormous collective bonded around a single cause: to show the power and unity of their winning institution. And of course, university attire does not appear strictly in athletic and campus settings: people don this often pricey apparel while traveling, going out on the town, and so on. No matter the social situation, school paraphernalia broadcasts the idea of belonging, of possessing membership in an admirable group.
>
> What looks simply like cheerful rallying around the good ol' alma mater, though, may also signal the wearer's fight to stave off solitude—especially given

America's longstanding ethic of intrepid self-reliance. Celebrated nineteenth-century author Henry David Thoreau provides ample support for this deep-seated idea of the rugged individual amid the clamor of the masses. "If a man does not keep pace with his companions," Thoreau claims in *Walden*, "perhaps it is because he hears a different drummer."[1] Similarly, he states that he "would rather sit on a pumpkin and have it all to [himself] than be crowded on a velvet cushion."[2] Thoreau followed his own counsel and sought solitude at Walden Pond, on the outskirts of Boston, for more than two years. How many of us, however, would even desire such radical isolation, let alone actively seek it out? Nevertheless, calls for unwavering individualism still inform our behaviors and choices, even in the clothing we wear. As a result, university attire can be read as a psychological balm, a means of escaping social pressures to be original and to go it alone. In fact, it might be said that school gear finds a comfy middle ground between outright autonomy and bland conformity. Because these clothing items promote an individual's particular choice of academic institution—his or her unique educational family—they honor singularity while simultaneously providing community. What could be more comfortable (on the body) and comforting (to the psyche)? One gets to sit, as it were, on both a pumpkin and a velvet cushion.

After declaring the idea in the first sentence (and then restating it in the second), the response quickly moves to illustrations: examples, proof, evidence to buttress the idea. The second paragraph then devotes itself to interpretation—the largest of the monster's three "I"s. In this case, our interpretation brought to the surface evidence about the presence of self-reliance as a dominant force in American culture, and it raised the concern of psychological anxiety, particularly the need to belong.

For practice, let's try another Three-"I"ed Monster response, one focused on a sign in the hit television series *Gilmore Girls*. This family comedy, which ran for seven seasons starting in 2000, centers on Lorelai Gilmore—a sassy, quick-witted single mother—raising her only daughter, Rory, in a quaint Connecticut town. The series picks up with Lorelai as a woman of about 30 and Rory as a 15-year-old girl. Quickly, a tense back-story comes into view: Lorelai became pregnant with Rory during high school, dropped out and ran away from home, and separated herself from her scandalized parents. These actions on Lorelai's part created lasting tensions with her mother and father, who play key roles in the show as they seek to establish a relationship with (and to dote on) their bright and beautiful young granddaughter. For our purposes here, we are interested in how the show—one devoted to the complex bonds between a single mother, who bears numerous adult responsibilities, and her teenage daughter—often presents Lorelai acting in particularly "girlish" or juvenile ways. In short, we want to use the Three-"I"ed Monster to unpack one possible reading of why the series often portrays the *adult* protagonist performing patently *adolescent* behaviors. In the following example, we insert double slash marks to indicate the divisions between the monster's three "I"s:

> By regularly depicting Lorelai as an adult who acts in decidedly juvenile ways, the show's writers capture the perpetual wound that Lorelai and her parents—Emily and Richard—share with regard to Lorelai's past teen pregnancy. That is to say, every time Lorelai acts like a wise-cracking, back-talking teen—particularly in defiance of her parents—the writers explore the residual effects of her traumatized teenage experiences. As a girl, the pregnant Lorelai felt rejected and outcast by her parents, and the show seeks to underscore the persistent pain of that history by often portraying her as a kind of "perpetual teen." // In "Emily in Wonderland," for instance—an episode from the second season—Lorelai and Emily bicker over the fact that Lorelai ran away from home after giving birth to Rory. Refusing any assistance from her wealthy parents, she moved with her daughter into a tiny place with no amenities. "You hated us that much?" rails Emily. "You had to take that little girl away, that was bad enough. But to that? To live there in a shed like a hobo?" In her surly, teenaged fashion, Lorelai cuttingly jokes, "Who uses the word 'hobo' anymore?"[3] In this case, a quarrel between two mature women— one in her fifties, the other in her thirties—sounds a great deal like a spat between a mother and her adolescent child. //
>
> In this scene and many like it, *Gilmore Girls* reveals that the damages of childhood and adolescence cannot be boxed away, suppressed, or waved off with a casual joke about hobos. Instead, the show suggests that early trauma must be treated with patience and persistence. Every time Lorelai "acts out" in the manner of a defiant "girl" against Emily and Richard's authority, the writers remind us that the Gilmore family ties remain frayed, and that both daughter and parents suffer by constantly postponing the necessary work of psychological repair. Everyone knows—even the Gilmores themselves—that the family members need to admit past wrongs, make apologies, and directly voice their love for one another. And yet, the old wounds always seem to prevent these honest expressions. Past bitterness rules the day, and the historical pain (from back when Lorelai literally *was* a girl) remains submerged—only to resurface problematically, time and again, through Lorelai's persistently juvenile actions.
>
> Ultimately, by transposing into the adult sphere the typical ways in which teenage girls defy their parents, the show dramatizes a kind of "girl stasis" in Lorelai. She seems trapped, the writers suggest, inside her former life as a teen rejected because of her early pregnancy. In this way, *Gilmore Girls* appears to send subtle cautionary signals to viewers regarding the dangers of such suppressions. Through the "girlish" Lorelai and her psychologically "young" parents, the show demonstrates what can happen if families avoid honest speech and direct acknowledgment of prior mistakes.

As with our university-attire example, this Three-"I"ed Monster argument directs readers below the surface of the sign and into the semiotic waters of invisible ideas. The response moves from idea to illustration to interpretation, linking the visible sign of Lorelai's girlishness to deep-seated psychological struggles and unexamined familial pain.

3. The monster has teeth

The monster in our drawing clearly possesses three "I"s, but notice that it also bears teeth. These sharp incisors remind you to sink into the political and social realities of the time period and culture in which your chosen sign appears. All signs, whether part of literature or popular culture, participate in the turbulent debates of their day. They suggest specific ideas and ideals; they champion various mores and expectations; they reject certain biases and assumptions. As a savvy interpreter, you want to discuss the facets of public consciousness and social experience that inform and lend significance to your sign—even when these details are troubling. This ensures that your arguments carry import. Ultimately, semiotics asks you to explore the unspoken tensions, histories, and power struggles that underlie such critical categories as follows:

- social class and distributions of wealth
- race and ethnicity
- gender and sexuality
- mental and physical health and disability
- nature and the environment
- education
- crime, punishment, and law
- national identity and globalization
- capitalism and consumerism
- labor and unemployment
- housing, land development, and homelessness

Put simply, the "bite" of the Three-"I"ed Monster helps writers avoid "toothless" essays—analyses that amount to mere academic exercises without real-world importance and social value.

As an example of an argument that bites into issues of politics and ideology, let's return to a sign that we explored in Chapter 4. You will recall that we generated several assertions about the cultural phenomenon of suburban white teens who turn their ballcap bills sideways in emulation of inner-city rap artists. One of our theories focused on the "macho sexuality" associated with the sideways bill position. In the following interpretation—which you might think of as a compact legal case—consider the amount of writing devoted to each "I" of the Three-"I"ed Monster. Also notice how the monster's "teeth" confront complex issues of power, prejudice, and historically oppressive notions about African-American males. With its references to various mythologies about blackness; its evocation of a recognized philosopher who has closely studied the intersections of race and sexuality; and its fleshed-out discussion of the specific sign under analysis, the following interpretation seeks to model several expectations of mature, university-level composition. Once again, we supply double slash marks to indicate the separate parts of the Three-"I"ed Monster approach.

> Urged by their culture to behave like so-called real men and to prove themselves attractive—if not irresistible—to women, many young white males may seek to capitalize on the macho sexuality often associated with the sideways cap and black hip-hop culture. // In books and magazines, and especially on television and the big screen, white teens receive repeated messages that urban black males exude sexual potency and easily attract gorgeous, uninhibited women. 50 Cent's video for "In Da Club," for instance, initially presents the rapper bare-chested and riddled with tattoos, before cutting to him—ballcap turned sideways—entering a club with his entourage. 50 Cent's lyrics reinforce the dangerous machismo and illicit activities often associated with club scenes generally and with the African-American "players" who frequent them. He raps, for example, of having "the X if you into taking drugs," and also declares that he is "into having sex," not "making love." Meanwhile, enticing woman of all races crowd around him. They gyrate to his music and whisper in his ears—proof that he enjoys "plenty of groupie love."[4] The women seem insistently drawn to 50 Cent's music and, by extension, his virility. Countless signs in the video, then, point toward black male sexual prowess and potency. //
>
> Such suggestive imagery comes as little surprise, given that Western culture has a long and complex history of regarding black males as sexual dynamos. As Cornel West asserts in "On Black Sexuality," black men have for centuries been hypersexualized by the white majority. According to West, a professor in the Center for African-American Studies at Princeton, "Americans are obsessed with sex and fearful of black sexuality."[5] Noting that "the fear is rooted in visceral feelings about black bodies fueled by sexual myths of black women and men," West points to a pervasive superstition that imagines black men as "threatening creatures who have the potential for sexual power over whites."[6] In the eyes of theorists such as West, this widespread assumption of sexual power derives at least in part from the flawed notion that black men possess libidos that are

"naturally" wild and uncontrollable. Through these racist linguistic associations, black males are alleged to be full of virility, force, and potential danger.

Whether aware of it or not, the vast majority of young white males in the American suburbs have been deeply conditioned by these cultural illusions about race and masculinity. Smack in the middle of their adolescent development, filled with apprehensions about dating, physical appearance, and sex, white teens who tilt their ballcaps sideways get to "play" at being "players" by sending the sign that they too—like the black male in the traditional Western imagination—possess some kind of supercharged sex drive and dangerous power. In effect, by turning their bills to one side, they "perform" blackness—an act that arguably helps them compensate for fears about their lack of sexual attractiveness and success. The white teen feels empowered, rather than emasculated, strong and wild rather than weak and domesticated. Thus, he soothes his anxieties and makes himself feel potent, more of a "man," by drawing on a system of signs that continues to degrade African-Americans. In such a racist paradigm, built up over centuries, the suburban teen can signal "macho sexuality" and empower himself, simply by borrowing concepts historically used to disenfranchise black men.

University-level analysis, as you can see, often locates troubling material, which can trigger feelings of vexation, fear, frustration, and grief. Frequently, as we delve into cultural history, we dredge up information and ideas that make us profoundly uncomfortable. Learning to respect but also manage our emotions—especially those of shock and outrage—within an interpretive-writing environment presents one of the greatest challenges of an advanced education. Yet the maturing writer cannot sidestep complex and difficult issues that lie below the surface of everyday reality. To ignore these disturbing parts of culture is to treat them uncritically and to fuel their perpetuation. Instead, we want to remain as level-headed and "scientific" as possible (knowing that absolute impartiality can never be achieved) as we analyze our world's often problematic beliefs, tensions, and exercises of power both past and present.

With all that said, though, let's not forget that some of our ideas related to the tilted ballcap involved celebrations of African-American culture. White teens can, with the tip of a cap, show solidarity, communion, a sincere desire for social equality and racial harmony. We can easily imagine, for example, a white teenager declaring, "I have no interest in macho sexuality. That's not why I wear my ballcap sideways. I don't think of black men as powerful sexual animals. I'm showing my respect for them as artists." And that may very well be the case. Yet, as we have noted, we cannot suppress the multiplicity of meanings in any given sign. Meaning, according to contemporary semiotics, is inherently shifty, contestable, and rife with contradictions. Furthermore, we cannot cordon off difficult facts of history, even if particular events informing the sign remain out of our control or part of an earlier era. Becoming sensitive to the complex function of even the most innocent-looking signs will inevitably lead you toward a greater understanding of the world around you. Is Barbie, for instance, *merely* an innocent doll for young girls to play with—ignoring the fact that the toy encourages unrealistic standards of female beauty and embodiment? Is Thanksgiving *simply* and *unequivocally* an occasion to share the bounty of the land in a way that commemorates the cooperation between Native Americans and pilgrims—despite the troubling history surrounding the formation of the United States? Are lawns *just* beautiful and harmless spaces on which to cavort—never mind the environmental costs of maintaining their uniformity? The point is this: no matter what the apparent innocence of the sign, close analysis will often expose difficult hidden truths and require the monster to show its teeth.

4. Anatomy of a monster

In this section, we examine the constituent parts of the Three-"I"ed Monster in greater detail. Here we look at how to build an interpretive response from start to finish. To do so, we turn once more to Bigfoot. In Chapter 4, we analyzed the lingering fascination with Sasquatch in an advanced scientific age that broadly discounts superstition and magical thinking. You might remember that our first analytical idea about the sign's meaning ran as follows:

> The lingering legend of Bigfoot signals notions of an uncharted natural realm where a gigantic half-human can roam undetected, an idea that in turn assuages our sense of guilt over environmental destruction.

In this idea, the sign functions as a psychological remedy, soothing the shame we might feel about our role in damaging the natural world. Still, we will need to supply more than just that raw idea if we hope to persuade our readers of this claim. Since we already have the first "I" of the monster (the all-important idea), we now need illustrations—or verifiable data—to articulate how a potential environmental collapse weighs heavily on our minds. Such concrete facts might include:

- the devastation of rain forests worldwide
- detonations of radiation-producing atomic bombs, and meltdowns at nuclear power facilities such as Three Mile Island (1979), Chernobyl (1986), and Fukushima Dai-ichi (2011)

- ruinous oil spills such as the Exxon Valdez disaster in 1989 and the British Petroleum catastrophe in 2010
- receding polar ice caps

From there, we move to interpretation, and develop arguments that explore why this particular reading of the Bigfoot mystique carries significance. Such argumentation might include notions that the enduring Bigfoot fantasy:

- renders scientific doomsdays less threatening
- taps into comforting ideas of an unspoiled Edenic realm
- promises a healthy and clean environment—the reverse of guilt-riddled fears about the destruction of the natural world
- imagines a creature who inhabits huge expanses of "virgin forest" without human detection
- highlights some of the world's most hotly contested tracts of land, thus suggesting their pristine status in light of battles over developing them

Next, we need to integrate (a) our idea about meaning, (b) our illustrations, and (c) our interpretive argumentation. In so doing, we will want to emphasize the fundamentals of strong critical writing, including crisp verbs cast in the active voice (underlined here for your inspection) and the liberal use of highly detailed nouns. Once again, we have inserted slash marks to indicate the shifts between the monster's three "I"s:

> The lingering legend of Bigfoot <u>signals</u> notions of an uncharted natural realm where a gigantic half-human <u>can roam</u> undetected, an idea that in turn <u>assuages</u> our sense of guilt over environmental destruction. Put another way, the Bigfoot fantasy would seem to <u>placate</u> our anxieties about the human devastation of nature, because if such a creature still <u>exists</u> in our vast wilderness areas, constantly <u>evading</u> his captors, then whole expanses of nature must <u>remain</u> wild, healthy, and beautifully untamed. // With the detonation of radiation-spewing atomic bombs, the damaging accidents at multiple nuclear sites, the obliteration of vast sections of the tropical rain forests in South and Central America, and the massive oil spills in Alaska and the Gulf of Mexico, recent history <u>has witnessed</u> many ruinous environmental calamities. Hurriedly, scientists <u>flock</u> to <u>warn</u> against greenhouse gases and the receding polar ice caps. Meanwhile, cultures <u>work</u> to <u>reintroduce</u> falcons and other endangered species to their native environments with special shelters and assisted matings. //
>
> Such anxiety seems to <u>underscore</u> a deep concern that we, one species, might be guilty of <u>destroying</u> the Earth for all living creatures. <u>Read</u> through the lens of ecology and the green movement, the seemingly unshakable Bigfoot legend <u>represents</u> our need to <u>feel</u> exculpated from the horrors that we <u>have visited</u> on the planet. For, the

reasoning might <u>run</u>, if such wide expanses of forest <u>continue</u> to thrive "out there" (whether in Southeast Asia, Tibet, or the Pacific Northwest of the United States), <u>allowing</u> a rangy giant like Bigfoot to <u>survive</u> undetected, then surely the Earth is not as ravaged as modern science <u>purports</u>. The hills, valleys, and woods <u>remain</u> healthy, with Bigfoot as their vigorous (if evasive) emissary. This vision <u>calms</u> our worries, <u>mitigates</u> our guilt. In his blissful Eden, our imaginary Bigfoot <u>finds</u> all he needs and wants, and <u>suffers</u> no harm from pollutants and habitat destruction. Earth is alive and well, Bigfoot <u>assures</u> us—even if, deep down, we <u>realize</u> that our own large (and damaging) footprints not only <u>mark</u> but often <u>mar</u> the planet's surface.

Here, our illustrations—pieces of factual data—demand more space than our claim, while our interpretive section clearly represents the largest "I." In this third portion of the writing, we dwell in analysis, supplying plausible reasons why the Bigfoot legend carries import in our cultural and historical moment. In addition, we use the teeth of the Three-"I"ed Monster to bite down into important issues of the environment and our collective role in its damage.

5. The "five ideas about meaning" model of essay construction

Now that you have seen several examples of how to support and unpack ideas using the Three-"I"ed Monster method, you can start to think about structuring an entire essay around a collection of strong theoretical claims. In a semiotic study based on this model, you construct your essay around multiple ideas about meaning (we suggest five), and use the Three-"I"ed Monster method to build a persuasive argument for each of the five key assertions about your chosen sign. In our "five ideas about meaning" approach, it often makes sense to move from your most obvious to your most sophisticated ideas and interpretations: this sequence tends to be effective in terms of logic, coherence, and persuasiveness. As a matter of fact, all of the student essays that we have reproduced so far in this textbook follow this model. The Bigfoot example below does, as well. Slash marks once again show the shifts between the monster's three "I"s. We have also underlined the five main ideas about meaning, so that you can clearly view the essay's architecture.

The Feat of Bigfoot:
Reading the Persistent Legend of Our Famous Hairy Giant

With his gargantuan body, gorilla gait, fetid smell, and, of course, enormous feet, Bigfoot continues to capture the world's collective imagination, as well as a portion of its collective checking account. For a mere 30 dollars, one may not only purchase a resin replica of his foot mold but also choose the particular site of the original print. (The "Bluff Creek" cast is still the classic.) And though the official Bigfoot Museum outside Santa Cruz, California, offers free admission—as does the annual Bigfoot Festival in Honobia, Oklahoma—a "Bigfoot Crossing" sign at either venue costs 15 dollars. In fact, Bigfoot's big, lucrative feet have crossed much of our culture, colonizing not just pop territory such as the television series *The Six Million Dollar Man* and the film *Harry and the Hendersons*, but also infiltrating contemporary fiction and poetry. (See Nobel laureate Wisława Szymborska's poem "Calling Out the Yeti" or Ron Carlson's story "Bigfoot Stole My Wife.") And if a quick search for Bigfoot-related books on amazon.com yields a staggering 991 hits—including *Bigfoot: I Not Dead* and *In Me Own Words: The Autobiography of Bigfoot*—perhaps even more staggering remains our gigantic appetite for all things Bigfoot in a scientific age of skepticism. For while science might demote puny Pluto to a mere icy rock or render the Bermuda Triangle obsolete with Global Positioning Systems, it appears helpless to stop the relentless spread and global feat of Bigfoot. Why, though? Why does the legend of such a creature persist, during a time when science has already disproved countless hoaxes and unexplained mysteries? What hopes and desires, fears and anxieties, might Bigfoot represent in an age of skepticism rooted in the objective discoveries of science?

<u>One way to explain the persistence of Bigfoot in our cultural imagination involves reading him as a manifestation of our desires for autonomy. Such a powerful yearning for self-sufficiency makes sense given our fiercely interdependent culture, which can at times feel claustrophobic and constraining.</u> // Amid our busy days of work and social responsibility, we might catch his solitary form traipsing through internet browsers that simultaneously capture our every movement; we pause momentarily on his lone image in a television that records our viewing preferences, tracks where we have been; we flip casually to his likeness in the pages of a tabloid, while waiting in line in a crowded supermarket. No matter the setting in which he appears, however—a rugged forest, a snow-covered pass, a quickly running river—he comes to us as an embodiment of solitude. With no family, no social group, no responsibilities to others, he ranges inside the radical individualism that we have imagined for him and that we ourselves desire. //

Such a yearning for autonomy holds particular import in American culture, which has historically placed a huge premium on the individual. We have been taught over centuries how important it is to stand on one's own, to be—as Emerson argued in 1847—"self-reliant." What is Thoreau's retreat to Walden Pond, for instance, if not a return to this deeply held American ideal of the individual powerful enough to exist apart from the herd? And yet, we find the notion of a proud outsider increasingly difficult to maintain. We depend not just on our supermarkets and movie theaters and gasoline stations but also on the entire social infrastructure around which we plan our lives. "Living off the grid," for most of us, is almost as big of a fantasy as Bigfoot himself. Still, we require some representative from that realm of complete self-sufficiency. As Joshua Blu Buhs argues, Bigfoot embodies just this "older tradition" of the rugged individual, "gritty as a cowboy, self-reliant, [and] living on [his] own terms" (108). And even if, deep down, we know no Bigfoot exists, we sustain the illusion, one rooted in the psyche's deep and abiding love of the individual. Ultimately, Bigfoot allows us to have our proverbial cake (or, in the case of Bigfoot, foraged mushroom?) and eat it, too.

In addition, the persistent celebrity of this oddly peaceful wildman might lie in his transcendence of national boundaries and political divisions. In his myriad forms, he is shared by many cultures worldwide, thereby inviting cultural harmony at a time of racial and ethnic strife around the globe. // Bigfoot, Sasquatch, Yeti, Abominable Snowman—many diverse cultures retain some version of this creature. Hardly just an American fancy, Bigfoot traipses through the woodlands and snow-covered passes of the world's geography. The "big" in Bigfoot points to his massive global presence, and no matter what we name him, he is shared by all. No single culture may claim him as its own. Hence, he becomes the very incarnation of all that lies outside the bounds of specific political and cultural boundaries. // Bigfoot therefore signifies, it would seem, the wish for unity—certainly between us and the fascinating creatures of nature, but perhaps more so between ourselves, a collection of diverse peoples that frequently fear each other and often respond cruelly to differences.

Even the hunt for this large, apelike humanoid embodies international harmony. When recalling the Yeti Himalayan expedition of 1954 in which he participated, for example, Ralph Izzard claims that "the total colour effect [of the diverse people in the group] is, happily, that of the United Nations flag." He even declares that his team—with its claim to international unity amid growing Cold War fears—"can be taken as symbolic," since they all worked "in perfect harmony" (qtd. in Buhs 38). If we have tended toward ethnic and racial strife, and at times seem a species destined to destroy itself from within, then the shared belief in, and collaborative search for, a peaceful ape-man might appear to work against those discouraging prospects. Even though we know he is a harmless bit of fraud, Bigfoot still occupies an important role on the world stage. He becomes a primitive version of a goodwill ambassador, one who promises appreciation and respect for diverse cultures.

At the same time, our lasting fondness for Bigfoot appears to involve his status as an archetypal "gentle giant": a huge, apish male who poses no threat to others. As a result, he may ease fears of the male brutality that pervades our news reports, and also serve as counterpoint to the disturbing menagerie of larger-than-life despotic men who spread violence internationally. // Surveying history over the past century offers an inventory of imposing tyrants capable of unspeakable destruction and persecution. Hitler and Stalin, Mussolini and Mao, Saddam Hussein and Muammar Gaddafi: these overbearing despots teach us that big men often equal big trouble. The scariest part of this story, however, lies in the possibility that we may just be fated to damage each other. In their 1996 book *Demonic Males*, noted primatologist Richard Wrangham and science journalist Dale Peterson link the human male's propensity for violence to the chimpanzee—our closest relative in the animal kingdom—suggesting that "our warring tendencies go back into our prehuman past" (22). Wrangham and Peterson argue that "very few animals live in patrilineal, male-bonded communities" that exhibit "intense, male-initiated territorial aggression" (24). In fact, "[o]ut of four thousand mammals and ten million or more other animal species, this suite of behaviors is known only among chimpanzees and humans." The barbarism of males, in other words, might just be genetically encoded. //

Countless references to Bigfoot's gentleness suggest a radical alternative to the typical power-hungry, violent male. Bigfoot wears his wildness on the outside (recall that many eye witnesses note a strong odor) so that he remains peaceful on the inside. And even if a few sketchy reports suggest that he is capable of throwing an occasional stone at his pursuers, such actions appear more defensive than aggressive. As such, he embodies the hope for a male who—though hulking and powerful—remains no physical threat. Does the preservation of the Bigfoot legend mean that we have deluded ourselves in terms of our propensity toward violence? Certainly not. Still, our gentle giant offers a psychological safe haven, given the overwhelming evidence of male leaders and their brutish armies who often force their will on others.

Another fear may lurk behind Bigfoot: that of ecological ruin. The lingering legend, in other words, might also signal notions of an uncharted natural realm where a gigantic half-human can roam undetected, an idea that in turn assuages our sense of guilt over environmental destruction. The Bigfoot fantasy would seem to placate our anxieties about the human devastation of nature, because if such a creature still exists in our wilderness areas, constantly evading his captors, then whole expanses of nature must remain beautiful, healthy, and untamed. // With the detonation of radiation-spewing atomic bombs, the damaging accidents at multiple nuclear sites, the waste of vast sections of the tropical rain forests in South and Central America, and the massive oil spills in Alaska and the Gulf of Mexico, recent history has witnessed many environmental calamities. Hurriedly, scientists flock to warn against greenhouse gases and the receding polar ice caps. Meanwhile, cultures scramble to reintroduce endangered species to their native environments with special shelters and assisted matings. //

Such anxiety seems to underscore a profound concern that we, one species, might be guilty of destroying the Earth for all living creatures. Read through the lens of ecology and the green movement, the seemingly unshakable Bigfoot legend represents our need to feel exculpated from the horrors that we have visited on the planet. For, the reasoning might run, if such wide expanses of forest continue to thrive "out there" (whether in Southeast Asia, Tibet, or the Pacific Northwest of the United States), allowing a rangy giant like Bigfoot to survive undetected, then surely the Earth is not as ravaged as modern science purports. The hills, valleys, and woods remain healthy, with Bigfoot as their vigorous (if evasive) emissary. This vision calms our worries, mitigates our guilt. In his blissful Eden, our imaginary friend finds all he needs and wants, and suffers no harm from pollutants and habitat destruction. Earth is alive and well, Bigfoot assures us—even if, deep down, we realize that our own large (and damaging) footprints not only mark but often mar the planet's surface.

What's more, the enduring fascination with Bigfoot might also suggest a contemporary substitute for traditional religious assurances, a pointer to some shadowy world beyond our knowing in an age of increasing scientific objectivity and spiritual skepticism. // Even though 80 percent of Americans still identify themselves as Christian—an overwhelming majority of the populace professing belief in a higher power—our contemporary world remains a site of constant theological challenge. From Darwin's discoveries in evolutionary biology to the now accepted theory in astrophysics of a universe created by the "Big Bang," an uncontested belief in a god-ordained or spiritually infused world seems increasingly difficult to find. // Enter Bigfoot, who represents a more tangible substitute for these transcendental mysteries.

The endurance of Bigfoot seems, then, little more than the persistent desire for the unexplained, some option beyond the purview of science. In *The God Gene*, Harvard-trained geneticist and author Dean Hamer argues that our yen for the ineffable, a realm beyond the everyday, "is among the most ubiquitous and powerful forces in human life." What's more, our desire for religious mystery "has been evident throughout recorded history in every civilization and culture, in every nook and cranny of the globe" (4). Simultaneously, however, religious faith seems constantly put to the objectivity test. How can we believe in such a realm, science continually asks, if we cannot empirically measure it? Placed in this scientific context, Bigfoot helps to preserve a sense of the unknown in a world of increasing knowns. Ironically, then, his high visibility helps to maintain that most special of invisible realms: the spiritual domain beyond this life.

Surrogate deity, environmental emissary, gentle giant, goodwill ambassador, rugged individual: all these readings seem at odds with the ghostly image receding into California scrub and pine in the Paterson super-8 film. And though scientists have all but laughed at the zipper-lined torso, Bigfoot continues to haunt our collective imagination. Maybe, however, "haunt" misses the mark, since he appears on closer inspection to act more like a nurturing spirit or, at the very least, an encouraging friend. Perhaps, finally, the actual feat of Bigfoot is just that: for all his wildness, his untamed, missing-link aura, his powerful smell and bestial howls, he seems just an oversized stuffed animal. And like a toddler's teddy bear or favorite blanket, Bigfoot remains at our side, assuring our security and safety. The advanced society to which we belong, he seems to suggest, will not strip us of our autonomy; the world that threatens to fracture into nationalistic standoffs is more unified than we imagine; powerful males do not necessarily lead to cruelty and peril; the environment remains healthy; and even our spiritual well-being—in the light of a twenty-first-century scientific skepticism—is being, well, coddled by our hirsute hero. One might even argue that we depend on those enormous feet, or, put more precisely, on the signs they leave in the mud. Without them, our world seems darker, lonelier, smaller.

Works cited

Buhs, Joshua Blu. *Bigfoot: The Life and Times of a Legend*. Chicago: U of Chicago P, 2009.

Hamer, Dean. *The God Gene: How Faith is Hardwired into Our Genes*. New York: Anchor, 1995.

Wrangham, Richard, and Dale Peterson. *Demonic Males: Apes and the Origins of Human Violence*. New York: Houghton Mifflin, 1996.

As you can see, the essay above structures itself on the "fives ideas about meaning" model and seeks to model strong university writing in the following ways:

- it focuses on ideas about the sign's meanings
- it ensures that interpretation remains the largest "I" in each of its five argumentative sections
- it "dwells in analysis"—diving below the semiotic waterline into culture, ideology, history, and so forth
- it marshals substantiating factual evidence and quotations, and
- it attempts, in lawyerly fashion, to persuade readers of the various significances of the chosen phenomenon

In addition, the study offers a lively introduction and conclusion while also forging real-world connections between the sign and often troubling particulars of our time. Finally, it gestures toward research from a broad range of disciplines, and reflects a flexible analytical mind at work and at play.

6. Responding to a literary sign

We now move from a contemporary pop-culture phenomenon to a literary text from the early Victorian era: Robert Browning's 1842 poem "My Last Duchess." The work belongs to a particular category of verse known as "dramatic monologue," about which we will offer more information. First, consider this supremely disturbing poem:

My Last Duchess

Ferrara

That's my last Duchess painted on the wall,
Looking as if she were alive. I call
That piece a wonder, now: Frà Pandolf's hands
Worked busily a day, and there she stands.
Will 't please you sit and look at her? I said
"Frà Pandolf" by design, for never read
Strangers like you that pictured countenance,
The depth and passion of its earnest glance,
But to myself they turned (since none puts by
The curtain I have drawn for you, but I)   10
And seemed as they would ask me, if they durst,
How such a glance came there; so, not the first
Are you to turn and ask thus. Sir, 't was not

Her husband's presence only, called that spot
Of joy into the Duchess' cheek: perhaps
Frà Pandolf chanced to say, "Her mantle laps
Over my lady's wrist too much," or "Paint
Must never hope to reproduce the faint
Half-flush that dies along her throat": such stuff
Was courtesy, she thought, and cause enough   20
For calling up that spot of joy. She had
A heart—how shall I say?—too soon made glad,
Too easily impressed; she liked whate'er
She looked on, and her looks went everywhere.
Sir, 't was all one! My favor at her breast,
The dropping of the daylight in the West,
The bough of cherries some officious fool
Broke in the orchard for her, the white mule
She rode with round the terrace—all and each
Would draw from her alike the approving speech,   30
Or blush, at least. She thanked men,—good! but thanked
Somehow—I know not how—as if she ranked
My gift of a nine-hundred-years-old name
With anybody's gift. Who'd stoop to blame
This sort of trifling? Even had you skill
In speech—(which I have not)—to make your will
Quite clear to such an one, and say, "Just this
Or that in you disgusts me; here you miss,
Or there exceed the mark"—and if she let
Herself be lessoned so, nor plainly set   40
Her wits to yours, forsooth, and made excuse,
—E'en then would be some stooping; and I choose
Never to stoop. Oh sir, she smiled, no doubt,
Whene'er I passed her; but who passed without
Much the same smile? This grew; I gave commands;
Then all smiles stopped together. There she stands
As if alive. Will 't please you rise? We'll meet
The company below, then. I repeat,
The Count your master's known munificence
Is ample warrant that no just pretence   50
Of mine for dowry will be disallowed;
Though his fair daughter's self, as I avowed
At starting, is my object. Nay, we'll go
Together down, sir. Notice Neptune, though,
Taming a sea-horse, thought a rarity,
Which Claus of Innsbruck cast in bronze for me![7]

7. The drama of (and in) "My Last Duchess"

Readers often assume that poetry expresses the deep feelings, private thoughts, and personal experiences of the writer, and with lyrical works such as sonnets and odes, this may often be the case. The dramatic monologue, however, operates by different rules. As its name implies, this type of poem borrows key features from the stage play. The speaker is a character invented by the poet—a separate identity entirely—whose attitudes and values cannot be directly associated with the author. In reading such poems, we first have to disconnect the narrator from the poet, just as we detach the views and actions of Lady Macbeth, Iago, and Malvolio from those of the playwright William Shakespeare.

As with a theatrical work, the dramatic monologue also implies an audience (usually a single, silent listener to whom the speech is addressed), and the utterance typically comes at a pivotal moment in the speaker's life. In "My Last Duchess," for example, the narrator is an Italian nobleman: the Duke of Ferrara. Given his rank, we know that he presides over a duchy, or dukedom, a territory that would typically include several cities and towns. (Indeed, the duchy of Ferrara encompassed an area about the size of Connecticut when it dissolved in 1597.) Following the dramatic monologue form, the duke's speech is addressed to a silent envoy (a go-between or agent) who represents the interests of another European aristocrat—specifically a count (whose rank falls one rung lower than a duke on the traditional noble hierarchy). Prior to the start of his monologue, the duke has greeted his guests—the count, the count's daughter (to whom the duke will soon be married, if everything unfolds according to plan), and the intermediary who represents the count in negotiations regarding the future marriage and the daughter's dowry, to be paid to the duke once the men seal the deal. The duke has led the envoy upstairs in his palace to show off a particular "wonder" in his collection—a painting of the "last Duchess" who shared his home, wealth, and family name. In addition, we learn through not-so-subtle innuendo that the duke has had his former wife secretly executed because she failed to follow what he takes to be proper decorum for an aristocrat's spouse. The duke "gave commands," he explains, "Then all smiles stopped together." In other words, he instructed one of his henchmen to do away with the duchess. The duke would never "stoop," needless to say, to do the job himself (he leaves the dirty work of assassination to a hired hand), yet the suggestion of murder performs a key function in the monologue, indicating to the envoy precisely what the next duchess better understand about her behavior in the duke's court. Here again, the comparison to drama makes sense, given that Shakespeare and many other playwrights at times seek to portray the twisted psychologies and murderous machinations of powerful lords.

Dramatic monologues additionally offer complex insights into the speaker's personality and disposition, frequently by supplying healthy doses of dramatic irony. In other words, these poems often reveal aspects of the narrator's character that he or she may not fully recognize or comprehend. A link to theater once again helps clarify the point. In a play, dramatic irony operates by giving the audience or reader an insider's perspective on the characters' lives. The author sets the scene so that the audience has inside knowledge about the fortunes of particular characters, while those characters themselves remain in the dark about their circumstances and fates. Shakespeare deploys dramatic irony in a tragic context, for instance, when Romeo discovers his beloved and mistakes her for dead. The audience knows that Juliet has merely swallowed a potion that causes her to appear dead, and when Romeo speaks the following passage to the seemingly deceased Juliet, we feel the full force of dramatic irony:

> Death, that hath suck'd the honey of thy breath,
> Hath had no power yet upon thy beauty:
> Thou art not conquer'd, beauty's ensign yet
> Is crimson in thy lips and in thy cheeks,
> And death's pale flag is not advanced there.[8]

Romeo's statement that death has "no power" and has "not conquer'd" Juliet is in fact the truth: she is still alive. His words are literally true, but he fails to realize this. Romeo becomes, in the end, the tragic sufferer in a piece of dramatic irony that the playwright has carefully engineered and that we grasp in our roles as textual insiders. In true Shakespearean fashion, furthermore, the irony becomes increasingly dreadful—first, when Romeo commits suicide out of despair, and next, when Juliet (waking from her death-like slumber and discovering that Romeo has poisoned himself) takes her own life. Our references to Shakespeare in this section are not accidental. As Kenneth Maclean asserts, "However special his use of the dramatic speaker, Browning obviously learned from Shakespeare and identified himself in a number of particular instances with Shakespeare's art."[9] As we begin to grasp the personality of Browning's Italian duke, we need to keep our ears pricked for potential "Shakespearean" dramatic ironies in his speech. In that way, we will sense the power of the dramatic monologue as a poetic form, and also stir our analytical minds to interesting and plausible interpretations.

8. The history of (and in) "My Last Duchess"

Written over 170 years ago and spoken by an Italian Renaissance monarch, Browning's poem tests our skill and patience as close readers. The references can seem alien, the phrasings archaic, the shifting tones hard to pin down. But whatever our present-day difficulties with Browning's style, we may take comfort in the fact that his Victorian contemporaries had their own troubles following his dense and highly suggestive works. Indeed, as Laurence Lerner notes in "Browning's Painters," many Victorian critics "thought that what Browning wrote was not poetry."[10] Similarly, when Browning received an honorary degree from Oxford University in 1882, the ceremony included the unveiling of "a very funny caricature of [him] with a great head [. . .] and a reader on his knees before him begging him, 'Oh, Mr. Browning, do tell us the meaning of your poems.'"[11] Within his long list of difficult literary productions, however, "My Last Duchess" remains one of Browning's more approachable and successful poems. It continues to be introduced to students worldwide and boasts a reputation as one of the masterpieces of British literature. Nonetheless, appreciating and comprehending the poem requires genuine scrutiny and slow, repeated reading.

For Browning, the arts served critical social functions. He condemned the notion that poetry should merely please or entertain, noting in an 1868 letter, for example, that verse is not "a substitute for a cigar, or a game of dominoes, to an idle man."[12] As a result, we might characterize his work as consciously multifaceted, deliberately rigorous, and studiously historical. That is not to say that Browning's poems remain mere servants of historical fact. Much in the manner of Shakespeare again, who at times fictionalized history—basing entire plays, for example, on the political aspirations and struggles of long-dead monarchs such as Richard II and Henry V—Browning takes great poetic license in speculating about the life of Renaissance nobleman Alfonso II, who ruled the northern Italian duchy of Ferrara from 1559 to 1597. The last of five reigning dukes from the illustrious Este family, Alfonso married the 14-year-old Lucrezia di Cosimo de' Medici in 1558. Daughter of the Duke of Florence,

Cosimo I the Great, and a member of one of the richest, most influential families in European history, Lucrezia died suddenly only a few years after becoming Alfonso's wife. While historians suspect tuberculosis as the likely cause of death, initial suspicions of foul play (Lucrezia was rumored to be poisoned) no doubt stand behind Browning's portrayal. As Louis S. Friedland notes in his important 1936 study "Ferrara and *My Last Duchess*," Browning was "widely read in [Ferrara's] history and legends,"[13] and he certainly knew of this marriage uniting two dominant and rival Italian families—both known for their extravagant patronage of the arts.

Alfonso remarried in 1565, this time to Barbara of Austria. Like Alfonso's "last duchess," Barbara hailed from prominent lineage—in her case, the Austrian royal House of Habsburg. Her father, Ferdinand I, ruled the Holy Roman Empire from 1558 to 1564, and two of her brothers later held the emperorship: Maximilian II from 1564 to 1576 and Ferdinand II from 1619 to 1637. It is this second brother who factors into Browning's historically based, if highly fictionalized, text. At the time of Barbara's marriage, Ferdinand ruled a large state of the empire known as the Tyrol, which comprised parts of present-day Austria and Italy, and kept its capital in Innsbruck. As Friedland explains, Count Ferdinand of Tyrol, along with his older brother Maximilian and younger brother Charles, sanctioned the betrothal of Barbara to Alfonso, and their diplomatic intermediary—a man named Nikolaus Madruz—most likely expedited the negotiations.[14] According to Friedland's research, then, Ferdinand would be the real-life counterpart of Browning's "Count," making Madruz the envoy and, thus, auditor of the duke's sinister monologue.

Even the wall painting in the poem retains a degree of historical verisimilitude. Again according to Friedland, "In 1559, shortly after his assumption of the dukedom, Alfonso ordered his court-painter, Bartolommeo Faccini, to cover the walls of the castle with lifesize portraits of the princely ancestors."[15] He also notes that "Unfortunately, there is no statement to the effect that Faccini painted an al fresco panel of Alfonso II and Lucrezia. Nevertheless, we may think that Browning knew of these murals in the famous Castello of Ferrara and that Faccini's frescoes came readily to his mind when he was meditating on Alfonso and the sad fate of the young Lucrezia."[16] These, then, are the facts and actual aristocrats on whom Browning bases his poem. And yet, we need to remember that the biographies of Alfonso, Lucrezia, Barbara, and Ferdinand—as well as the information about the castle's fresco wall paintings—serve merely as starting points for the poet, springboards for his imagination to leap from the literal to the literary. Poet-critic Anthony Hecht explains it this way:

Browning allowed himself some latitude in creating his psychological portrait. But he was a keen student of history, and he would have known all about the moral vagaries of Italian Renaissance princes, a topic Shakespeare himself was acquainted with. [The duke] feels no more *guilt* than Shakespeare's Antonio in *The Tempest*, who plots the murder of his brother, Prospero. [. . .] Doubtless this is chilling, even monstrous; yet there have been such men.[17]

Thus, while the historical Alfonso II probably never spoke anything close to the words that Browning conjures, the sociopolitical backdrop of the text deserves mention, if only because Browning's impulse to embellish facts of the past may be worth considering in an analysis of the poem's multiple meanings.

9. Selecting and staging a sign

Once we possess a clear understanding of Browning's poem, as well as a solid grounding in the historical references with which the poet tinkers and toys, we can move on to selecting a sign to analyze. Obviously, choosing as a sign "the full-length portrait of the duke's last duchess" would never pass the VOICE test. For one, the duke spends the majority of his monologue discussing the fresco of his former wife. The portrait, therefore, seems far too visible and obvious as a marker of significance in the poem. That does not mean, however, that we must discount the painting altogether as a semiotic prospect; it only suggests that we will need to build in greater complexity, more engineering. With such a necessity in mind, we might note that the duke devotes most of his speech to detailing the specifics of the wall painting, but suddenly references an entirely different artwork at the end of the poem:

> Nay, we'll go
> Together down, sir. Notice Neptune, though,
> Taming a sea-horse, thought a rarity,
> Which Claus of Innsbruck cast in bronze for me!

What might first appear to be the animated small talk of an art connoisseur—idle banter by the duke, as he and the envoy make their way back to the castle's ground floor—becomes charged with significance when set in relation to the portrait of the duchess. Why, we might wonder, does Browning filter the duke's words through descriptions of two pieces of art? What might these relational references to "wonders" and "rarities" of the art world signify about the duke and, by extension, the aristocracy to which he belongs? How might these seemingly disparate artworks—one a full-length fresco portrait on a wall, the other a freestanding bronze sculpture—inform one another and create meaning together?

The sign of "the two conversant artworks" seems more likely to pass our VOICE test, since it carries juxtapositional energy and tension. While focusing on the portrait of the duchess alone seems too expected an act, reading it in tandem with the sculpture at the end—which receives scant attention from the duke—carries interesting potential. Curiously, the two artworks appear drastically dissimilar: they differ in form (two-dimensional fresco and three-dimensional statue), disclosure (one concealed and the other in plain sight), subject (one personal and the other mythological), coverage (one discussed throughout the poem and the other addressed in merely a few lines), and likely even value (one a quickly rendered portrait, the other a time-consuming bronze cast). What's more, bringing the two artworks together situates the portrait of the duchess in a semiotic system, which helps us see how she served as an "object," a "collectible," to the duke. We might also begin to think of the ways in which the sculpture—one that depicts a mighty, masculine god taming a wild horse—speaks to the fate of the duchess, another apparently "wild" being in need of "taming."

Before we proceed too far with unpacking the sign, however, let us first formulate a staging that will help us to concentrate on our chosen phenomenon:

> Robert Browning's 1842 dramatic monologue "My Last Duchess" begins and ends with references to works of art that could not appear—at least at first glance—more dissimilar. The two pieces differ, for example, in form and medium (the one a richly colored fresco, the other a monochromatic bronze statue); they vary in manner of display (the one concealed behind a curtain, the other in open view); and they diverge in subject matter (the one depicting a young noblewoman in courtly attire, standing alone and still, the other capturing a dynamic episode from Roman mythology, as the god of the sea breaks a wild horse to help draw his divine chariot). The painting, too, is an individualized family portrait, while the statue portrays a scene from broader classical culture. In addition, the fresco took much less time to produce, and its commission no doubt cost the duke far less than the sculpture. Perhaps most importantly, the two artworks contrast in their descriptive coverage (the one enjoying in-depth discussion for most of the poem, the other mentioned more as an aside, while the duke and the count's envoy return to the ground floor of the castle). The extent to which the duke devotes time and language to the artworks, in other words, is decidedly different: the

portrait of his former wife receives comprehensive treatment, while the statue of Neptune surfaces only in the poem's final three lines.

Though differences prevail, however, close inspection reveals that the wall painting by the skillful and speedy friar Pandolf and the sculpture cast by the reputable Claus of Innsbruck form a curious bond, echoing one another in ways that underscore several of the poem's key thematic concerns. Browning's poetry, as is well known, regularly incorporates material from the art world: "Fra Lippo Lippi," "Andrea del Sarto," and "Youth and Art" represent only a sample of texts that center on artists, their craft, and their productions. Yet "My Last Duchess" appears unique in its formation of a complex, mutually defining relationship between two disparate artworks in a single poem. That the monologue focuses not on an artist but on an art collector—a sinister connoisseur—adds further interest to the connections between the two differing "rarities" in the duke's collection. Why, the question becomes, does the poem link these contrastive aesthetic objects? What significances underlie their juxtapositional relationship in the text?

Notice that this staging follows the model outlined in Chapter 3, which suggests establishing the presence of the sign in the text, situating the phenomenon within a particular context, and posing an interpretive "problem" through a set of related theoretical questions. In addition, the staging employs a "yes, but" approach. That is, it first discusses the vast differences between the two artworks before establishing their potential similarities. With our sign and staging in hand, we can proceed to unpacking significance and formulating ideas.

10. Generating ideas about the sign

Just as with the Bigfoot analysis above, we seek to build our ideas around the "sign-signals-significance" paradigm, which ensures that we dive below the semiotic waterline into the realms of ideology, history, and culture. Since we have already gestured toward a possible link between the taming of the wild horse and the killing of the duchess, we might begin with constructing an idea about the violent mastery at which both artworks hint:

(sign)   The conversant artworks in "My Last Duchess"
(signals)   establish the duke as a refined, moneyed aristocrat, a patron of
            the arts, all of which runs counter to the cold-blooded murder he

masterminds. In effect, his role as an art connoisseur serves as a screen to conceal his far less noble activities.

From there, we must dive deeper below the waterline and ask why that particular signal might interest Browning and what it might suggest about the nobility from which the duke descends:

(significance) Such a curious gap between the refined art and the despicable art collector allows Browning to expose how signs of elite culture and civility often mask savage expressions of power.

This initial theoretical gambit might then lead us to consider how the works of art function in the poem—not merely as aesthetic objects but also as means of enforcing behavior. Both the fresco and the sculpture, in other words, send messages to the envoy, which he will then convey to the count and his daughter, the next duchess. In this way, the art works in tandem to indicate the duke's ulterior motives. They are hardly just beautiful masterpieces to appreciate, which might suggest the following idea about meaning:

(sign) By paralleling these two impressive works,

(signals) Browning underscores the duke's propagandistic attitude toward art, which functions for him not only to represent beauty but—more importantly—to advance his agendas of power.

(significance) Through the monstrous duke and his use of art for political and personal gain, Browning critiques utilitarian notions of aesthetics. Instead of "art for art's sake," in other words, it is "art for power's sake" in the duke's mind and in the minds of others like him.

Or consider the way in which both artworks point—in a suggestive way—toward a third and unspoken masterpiece: the duke himself. In his mind, art is timeless, just as he should be. Indeed, the "wonder" of the fresco and the "rarity" of the sculpture help Browning to nuance his portrait of the duke as a self-aggrandizing monomaniac:

(sign) At the same time, the two precious pieces of aesthetic wonder

(signals) point toward a third, if less obvious, "work of art" in Browning's poem: the duke himself. The relational artworks serve, in a sense, to illuminate the duke as the crowning glory, the one timeless work of art above all others.

(significance) This embedded "third masterpiece" in turn allows Browning to explore the self-aggrandizing motives behind the duke's art collection. Furthermore, the conversant artworks illuminate the corruption and decadence of the aristocracy, and reveal the vice and egomania that exists among the nobility.

From there, we might widen our lens and include issues of gender. In so doing, we could ask a more pointed question: "What do these two conversant artworks—one a fresco of a young and unfortunate duchess, the other of a Roman god in the act of breaking a wild horse—suggest about the patriarchal tradition to which the duke belongs?"

(sign) In its clever correlation of the two artworks,

(signals) "My Last Duchess" aligns the domineering, egotistical duke with a superhuman domesticator, a mythic breaker of wild energies.

(significance) Consequently, the poem offers a biting satire of men whose traditional patriarchal views sanction the containment and mistreatment of women. Browning's duke, in other words, represents a villainous portrait of the reactionary male who believes in his own superiority over women as natural and even divinely authorized.

We could also consider other embedded hierarchies that the duke assumes to be the natural consequences of his rank, privilege, and "nine-hundred-years-old name." That is, just like his assumptions regarding male superiority, his sense of class supremacy also seems to emanate from these works of art. We could read the wild horse, in this respect, as inflected not only by gender but also by class. And if the horse becomes representative of how the aristocracy assumes its mastery over the lower classes—the rich have the god-given right to "tame" the workers—then so too does the duchess come to represent a laborer in service of the duke. She remains, ultimately, a mere pawn in the duke's class-based machinations and political strategizing. One false move, and she can easily be replaced by another worker, and another after that:

(sign) The poem's two interconnected works of art

(signals) represent innocent, culturally subordinate figures overcome by powerful, aristocratic men. The duke, as part of the ruling class, assumes his right to own and "tame" both the horse and, by juxta-positional relationship, the duchess.

(significance) Browning's poem, then, subtly indicts unjust exercises of power by the wealthy and powerful. The two conversant, mutually informing artworks center on huge patriarchal forces wrestling down and taming unruly and "lower-order" energies, and this arrangement serves as an emblem of the battles that rage along class lines.

With assertions such as these, we could go ahead and construct an essay on the "five ideas about meaning" model. As in the Bigfoot example, our full-scale analysis would require us to elaborate on each of our five key assertions. In doing so, we would deploy the Three-"I"ed Monster method, relying on its "idea-illustration-interpretation" format to help unpack our sign and lend persuasiveness to our project. We would also order our responses so that they moved from the least to the most theoretically complex. We are confident that—following the tools and procedures mapped out so far in this textbook—you could compose such an essay based on the five ideas detailed above, surprising yourself (and your readers) with the richness of your analysis. At this point, though, we want to add to your writing repertoire by showing you a second major model of essay construction, one based on a single overarching idea.

11. The single-idea model

In an 1822 letter to his publisher about the epic poem *Don Juan*, Lord Byron wrote the following: "You ask me for the plan of Donny Johnny—I *have* no plan—I *had* no plan—but I had or have materials."[18] In the interpretive arena, it often makes good sense to follow Byron's lead, postponing any unified idea or thesis, and working instead to unpack the "material" of the sign—to turn the sign like a prism and inspect it from a variety of angles. We advocate, in other words, an initial "planlessness" with respect to the analysis of meaning. Our students have discovered that it is often better to explore multiple readings and arguments at the outset, to delay the drive toward an overarching theory about the sign. The common question "What is your thesis?" typically leads to premature conclusions and closes down the play of analysis. Nonetheless, many classes will require you to write a single-claim or "thesis-driven" essay, and we want to explore that model now. Our reason for discussing the single-idea paper late in this textbook should be clear. It is our fundamental belief that without the rangy searching for multiple meanings first, without the restless inquiry up front, such a project will often fall short of its full potential. When we begin by developing five ideas about meaning, however, we dramatically increase our chances of locating one powerful assertion capable of steering an entire study. In the following pages, we explore two effective strategies for creating a single-thesis study, both of which presume the generation of multiple ideas beforehand.

12. The "umbrella approach" of thesis generation

In this approach to thesis formation, we ask some fairly routine questions about our five ideas. Under what heading or "umbrella" might they fit? What statement could unify the five separate assertions? What "common denominator" factors into each of the interpretive claims about the sign? As we examine our five ideas about the conversant artworks in "My Last Duchess," for example, we might notice that each stresses an "ulterior motive" related to art. For Browning's duke, the painting and sculpture are not simply aesthetic objects, artifacts to appreciate for their beauty and skillful execution. Rather, both pieces become charged with purpose. The poem offers the portrait of a duke who expects his art to *work* for him, just as he assumes that his duchess should serve his desires, and just as the horse must labor for Neptune. All five readings, then, suggest how art carries ideological force—private and political meanings that transcend mere beauty and craft. With this observation in mind, we could formulate the following umbrella thesis:

> Through its juxtaposition of the painting and bronze sculpture, "My Last Duchess" questions the widespread notion that art offers a purified expression of beauty, untarnished by the gritty facts of politics and power-mongering. The poem reveals, in other words, that art cannot simply be appreciated for its aesthetic value, divorced from clashes of ideology and struggles for social dominance.

We would then simply reorient our five ideas to stress this overarching thesis, which ties together our original five readings and highlights the ideological forces embedded in each idea. In this way, the thesis deals less with the duke, per se, and more with prevailing notions about the "purity" of art. And since we uncovered Browning's own claim regarding the complexity and social value of art—that it is not simply "a substitute for a cigar, or a game of dominoes, to an idle man"—our thesis already appears germane to this particular poet.

As you probably realize already, we can mine our five interpretive claims for a variety of umbrella theses. Out of *one* grouping of ideas about the sign, in other words, comes a *range* of umbrella prospects. In fashioning a different overarching thesis based on the same five claims, for instance, we could create an umbrella that addresses the "static form" of each artwork. Both the fresco of the duchess and the sculpture of Neptune, that is, reinforce immobility and fixity. Even though the duke calls the portrait of his deceased wife a "wonder" and claims that she looks "as if she were alive," the fresco form has nonetheless fused her—literally—to a wall upstairs in his castle. Likewise, though the sculpture depicts a wild animal struggling for freedom, its being "cast in bronze" also suggests weight and immovability. The life-size fresco of the duchess as part of the duke's domain, the muscular horse tamed by a god and forged out of a heavy metal alloy: both stress the duke's wish for stasis. We could, therefore, argue that all five readings point to his obsession with securing an elevated social status, which might lead to a thesis such as this:

> The parallels between the two artworks in "My Last Duchess" underscore the duke's wish to fix his position atop the social hierarchy and to master potentially disruptive energies. Both the fresco (literally painted onto a castle wall) and the sculpture (cast in weighty bronze) serve as stabilizing forces, markers of a timeless and conservative status quo that the duke seeks to preserve and the poem seeks to question.

Again, we would then have to modify our five original ideas to ensure that they all fit logically underneath the umbrella claim. In this case, for instance, our initial interpretations might be adjusted in the following ways:

- Both artworks reinforce the notion of the duke as a refined, moneyed aristocrat. His role as an art connoisseur serves, in effect, as a screen to conceal his far less noble activities, which he can perform with impunity, as long as his elevated status remains secure.
- Both artworks also reveal the duke's propagandistic attitude toward art, which functions for him not so much to represent beauty but to advance his agenda of power and maintain his status. As a social elite, secure in his privilege, he may define and use art however he sees fit.
- Both artworks point toward a third and less obvious masterpiece in Browning's poem: the duke himself. The art, in a sense, illuminates the duke's sense of himself as the crowning glory, the one timeless work of art above all others, worthy of perpetual adoration and obedience in his perch high on the social order.

- Both artworks additionally underscore the way in which fixed social hierarchies often sanction the containment and mistreatment of women. The two pieces of art thus call attention to the patriarchal elite who believe their superiority over women to be natural, timeless, and even divinely authorized.
- Both artworks feature huge forces wrestling down and taming unruly, "lower-order" energies. This arrangement serves as an emblem of the battles that rage along class lines and the need for the duke to remain on top of the social ranks. In order to preserve his status, he must quash any rebellious behavior, any threat to his prestige.

We need not stop with these two umbrella options, however. For good measure, consider this third example in which we attempt to cut against the grain of expectation by offering a thesis that employs some lively irony. If, until now, we have stressed how the artworks function in unison, with equal import given to each, we might have some fun in this third approach by asserting that the sculpture is actually the more significant of the two masterpieces in the text. This rather unexpected, "turn the tables" thesis might assume the form of an exposé, where we work against common perception to suggest the following:

> While Browning's poem devotes itself primarily to the portrait of the duke's former wife, mentioning the Neptune sculpture only in the last few lines, it is this second, almost ancillary work of art that holds the keys to meaning in the text. When read in relation to the spotlighted fresco of the duchess, the apparently less significant bronze statue actually carries greater import, since it serves as an integral blueprint to understanding not just the portrait but also the duke's maniacal obsessions and, by extension, Browning's critique of them.

Having composed this somewhat counterintuitive thesis, we would then edit our five ideas to suggest how the bronze statue functions as a "code breaker," a clever means of revealing the significances behind the painting. In this example, we hold all of the readings together with a reversal of common assumption. Readers expect that a poem titled "My Last Duchess" will give great weight to the portrait. And yet, as we might argue, the bronze sculpture—about which the duke offers only a sketchy outline—becomes the means with which to understand the fresco and, in turn, the duke. Ironically, the casual reference to Neptune assumes the significant role of decoder for the entire monologue.

All three of these potential umbrella claims still rely on our five previous interpretations. The basis, then, for a strong analytical paper (whether you choose the five-idea or the single-thesis model) begins with restlessness and multiple readings. Once you possess convincing and rangy ideas about your chosen sign, you can package them in various formats. In the next section, we look at another single-thesis approach, this one involving a so-called big frame.

13. The "big frame" approach to thesis generation

In Chapter 4, we deployed several frames to help generate ideas about the nameless monster in Mary Shelley's *Frankenstein*. We placed the novel's unnamed creature, for example, inside the frame of scientific experiments such as galvanism—the notion of reanimating dead tissue by way of electrical current—and fashioned an idea about the monster's namelessness and its connection to lower-order animals. We next positioned the sign within the frame of social problems—specifically orphanhood in early nineteenth-century Britain—and forged a link between the creature's absence of a name and the pressing concern of orphaned children. In each case, we asked how our sign reacted to the frame in which we situated it, what energies it accrued through its relationship to larger historical and cultural conditions. We can now test out framing once again—not, this time, to help create ideas about the sign, but to provide the broader context for a single-idea essay format. Basing an entire paper on one idea or "thesis" typically necessitates this kind of comprehensive treatment of context, where the chosen frame factors into the study from start to finish.

Having already developed five ideas about the two conversant artworks in Browning's poem, we can now select one of these and construct our analysis using a "big frame" (or extended coverage of context). Consider, for example, our fourth idea about meaning, which deals with gender inequalities. Since the poem's speaker has eradicated his wife for failing to meet his strict expectations, exploring gender frictions in nineteenth-century England appears especially relevant. While Browning's narrator is a sixteenth-century Italian rather than a nineteenth-century British husband, we would argue that "My Last Duchess" speaks just as powerfully about the early Victorian period as it does about the late Renaissance. The poem looks back into history, in other words, as a clever way of addressing issues of its own time—in much the way that a twenty-first-century film, say, about the American Civil War might subtly comment on race relations in the contemporary United States.

Even some preliminary research into Browning's era and its gender politics yields a good deal of information potentially useful in our analysis. Take, for example, the 1825 treatise *Appeal of One Half the Human Race*, in which William Thompson and Anna Wheeler exclaim, "Women of England! women, in whatever country ye breathe—wherever ye breathe, degraded—awake!" Such a passionate cry against gender injustices was no anomaly in the decades directly preceding the publication of "My Last Duchess" in 1842. Women's rights advocacy was undeniably in the air, with campaigners marshalling scandalous evidence in their efforts to bring about change. On March 24, 1826, for instance, a writer identified only by the initials "S. E." published an essay in the *Liverpool Mercury* newspaper condemning the abuses enacted by husbands on their wives. The article describes one particular woman who was pummeled with "the butt end of a [carriage] whip, till the great part of her body was beaten to a jelly." She was also robbed of her fortune and only child. "None but the unprincipled and unfeeling," writes S. E., "would desire to keep wives in the state of abject submission, dependence, fear and trembling."[19] Furthermore, in the 1840 treatise *Woman and Her Master*, Sydney Owenson, Lady Morgan, laments the fact that women remain "the victim of man's physical superiority."[20] And Browning's own future wife—the poet and women's-rights activist Elizabeth Barrett—referred to herself as one of the "militants" who "foam with rage" over Victorian prejudices against women.[21]

These thinkers and writers, along with many others in the second half of the century including Barbara Leigh Smith Bodichon, Harriet Taylor, and John Stuart Mill, railed against established ideologies of gender and the feminine ideal of the time, which centered on devotion to husband and home; charitable works rather than waged labor; and acceptance of a woman's place outside the university and the voting booth. Would-be reformers also questioned the notion of "separate spheres," where women were relegated to the private domestic space, while men participated in the public worlds of business and politics. With its murdered duchess who comes under the policing eye of her husband, Browning's poem—although set in Renaissance Italy—seems equally to capture the domestic lives of many Victorian women in legal and economic subjugation to their husbands.

Given this divisive history, the poem's apparently disparate works of art—one of a duchess whose smiles have been "stopped," the other of Neptune taming a horse—seem to have a good deal in common. The "breaking" action by the god, in other words, presents an explicit analogy to the implicit and nefarious "taming" of the duchess. The two artworks subsequently allow the poem to explore rising resistance to certain lingering ideas about women held by Victorian patriarchy: that women are simply objects for men to manipulate and even discard when necessary; that they belong to a lower order of being—more of the body than the mind—and, therefore, require the direct control of their "masters"; and that they possess unruly energies that need to be curtailed by men, with violence if needed. Through the related signs of the painting and the sculpture, the text thus illustrates the duke's sexist notions about women (as animal, as requiring restraint, as dangerous to a civilized man). And if our original claim about sexism suggested that, together, the two artworks "offer a biting satire of men whose traditional patriarchal views sanctioned the containment and mistreatment of women," new to the argument is the big frame, which seeks to contextualize the poem within its historical place in nineteenth-century British gender politics. In other words, we will now be interested in how our sign helps to expose the objectification of women by men in Renaissance Italy but, more importantly, in nineteenth-century Britain.

14. The thesis about the artworks

With some preliminary research and a dominant frame roughly intact, we can proceed to thesis formation. If, in this model of essay construction, the frame must grow in size and nuance, then so too must the main idea. We want to create an overarching assertion that will introduce our contextual material. Still, we need to remember that building a sizable and complex thesis requires several smaller initial steps. Note that we have already arrived at five different interpretations of our sign; we have staged it; we have selected one avenue of theoretical approach; and we have completed some introductory research on women's rights in early Victorian Britain. Such groundwork remains necessary, for it sets the stage for strong single-thesis construction.

Above, we suggest that the conversant artworks allow the poem to explore rising resistance to lingering ideas about women held by Victorian patriarchy, which seems like the germ of a comprehensive thesis. From there, we need only apply more specificity and depth:

In its clever correlation of the two artworks, "My Last Duchess" aligns the domineering, egotistical Duke of Ferrara with a superhuman domesticator, a mythic
breaker of wild energies, and consequently offers a biting satire of Victorian
men whose traditional views sanctioned the containment of women based on
erroneous ideas about their lower and even animal status. Browning's deliberate correlation of Neptune and the duke—an empowered noble who tames his
unruly duchess—calls to mind reactionary British males who sought to corral the
reformist activities of feminists in the early decades of the nineteenth century.
The poem consequently enters one of the liveliest debates of its day and seeks
to curtail the abuses of women by men who regard themselves as godlike and
omnipotent.

Notice two distinct features of this longer, more involved thesis: it establishes
the historical link between the poem's Renaissance Italian speaker and its
nineteenth-century British audience, and it deploys a useful "in other words"
statement that positions the sign and poem more squarely in its social milieu.
Our thesis now seems forceful and complex enough to support an entire
paper. We may then turn toward building a defense of the proposition. To do
so, we will need a set of supportable reasons as to why we believe this dominant assertion makes good interpretive sense.

If we look at the thesis again, we will notice certain particulars upon which
we may expand. The sign, by our reading, functions as a criticism of the following patriarchal beliefs, to which many nineteenth-century British men
subscribed:

- men are superior—even godlike—in relation to women
- men may treat women as objects
- men may think of women as lower-order animals
- men must master the female body, since it can be dangerous
- men may resort to violence in order to achieve that containment

All of these assumptions regarding women, we argue, come embedded in
the sign. The two artworks expose the duke's anxieties over femininity
and, by extension, similar concerns among many British men at the time
of the poem's production. We reason that the sign addresses the patriarchal
practice of objectifying and dominating women, since Browning's poem
invites us to side with, and feel sympathy for, not only the late duchess
but women in general under the rule of abusive husbands. If in building
our initial "big frame" we uncovered some disturbing information about

male dominance over women in Victorian England, we can now take our research even further, bringing not only the general era but also the actual poet into sharper relief.

15. Tapping into criticism

Consider, in this regard, the work of Ashby Bland Crowder, who extensively studied Browning's personal correspondence. While acknowledging that Browning shared some of his culture's prejudices against women, Crowder also argues that the poet resisted several commonplace notions such as "the worship of women as the source of moral and spiritual good"[22] and the placement of them inside the "Victorian ethic of purity."[23] According to Crowder's work, Browning also "aligned himself with Florence Nightingale's cousin Barbara Leigh Smith, who in 1855 was to campaign for a law that allowed married women to retain their earnings for their own use."[24] Furthermore, the poet "held that women had the 'originating, creative minds' and that men were some simply practical in their abilities."[25] Ultimately, Crowder suggests that "Browning seems, at least at times, to have been an advocate for equality between the sexes"[26] and that "he transcended the Victorian ethos in insisting that women be treated with the respect that all human beings owe to each other."[27] As Crowder observes, "any attitudes about the relationship of the sexes that subjected wives to the haughty wills of domineering husbands Browning strongly rejected."[28]

Similarly, in "Women without Meaning: Browning's Feminism," Judith Weissman suggests that "Unlike the women in almost all other English poetry written by men, [Browning's] do not embody types, values, ideals, beauties, or sources of inspiration."[29] Instead, his "female characters [. . .] transcend type and become individuals," and do not act as "keepers of domestic peace [or] providers of moral guidance."[30] According to Weissman, Browning successfully avoids the tendency among canonical male poets to turn women into "insentient things that exist for men's pleasure";[31] Weissman also argues that the poet remained a stern critic of the male "egocentric need to dominate women."[32] Both of these scholars support our theory that "My Last Duchess"—through the conversant artworks—questions mainstream Victorian gender codes and debilitating assumptions about femininity.

In the light of Browning's own criticism of patriarchal prerogative, the poem's portrayal of the two artworks also seems slightly more ironic. That is, despite all his talk of never stooping to instruct an underling, Browning's duke ironically offers a monologue that primarily serves an educational function. His upstairs art gallery is, in effect, a classroom, with the painting and statue serving as the prime means of conveying his lesson. Together, the artworks send a clear message to the envoy (to be carried to the count, to be passed on to his daughter) about proper comportment in the duke's court. In his pedagogical role, the duke conveys up front what the new duchess needs to know—that if she behaves like a wild animal rather than a civilized duchess, then she will be "tamed" by the duke's godlike force and added to his stable of dead wives. The duke's villainous lecture thus works as a warning, with emphasis on his ability to corral, to domesticate, to punish. And yet, given Browning's own thoughts and declarations on women—and his poetic portrayals of them in general—we can reasonably argue that the duke's sense of his power remains something of a myth, just like the subject of his commissioned sculpture. Only in his imagination can the duke fully control the duchess. While he can order her execution, he cannot contain or eradicate her completely (just as Victorian patriarchy could not ignore or erase passionate demands for women's rights).

Here, too, scholarship helps with substantiation. In "Male Authority and Female Subversion in 'My Last Duchess,'" for instance, Shifra Hochberg explores the destructive misogyny of Browning's duke. For Hochberg, the poem's careful dramatic ironies reveal a nobleman who is strangely haunted by his former wife: he cannot seem to put her out of his mind, to the point where *she* essentially controls *his* psyche, even after death. Although the painting of the duchess initially appears "to signify the pre-eminence of male desire and male-authorized culture," writes Hochberg, it simultaneously "resists and subverts the Duke's attempt to textualize and interpret the Duchess after her death."[33] By ironically placing the duchess's counter-story in the duke's mouth—by cleverly making the murderous nobleman reveal the respectable (rather than condemnable) facts of his young wife's life—"My Last Duchess" invites us to sympathize with the plight of women subjected to sadistic husbands. Not surprisingly, Hochberg notes that the sea-horse is "a creature not yet bent to [Neptune's] will and still in the process of resistance."[34] Such an argument about the duke's latent anxieties also corresponds to Ulrich Knoepflmacher's claim that "the reader of 'My Last Duchess' becomes a detective who wrests away the control the Duke desires."[35] Ultimately, Knoepflmacher argues for the poet's feminism, suggesting that "Browning permits the reader to free the Duchess from the Duke's possessive 'My.'"[36]

In constructing this "big frame" based on gender frictions, we might look further into Victorian attitudes about male power in relation to women. One piece of valuable research along these lines comes from Melissa Valiska Gregory, who suggests that poems such as "My Last Duchess" "shed new light on a domestic problem of considerable importance to the Victorian period: the psychology of sexual violence."[37] In Gregory's view, "Browning at once intervenes in a Victorian debate about domestic violence (a debate which struck at the heart of nineteenth-century domestic ideology and heterosexual norms), and, moreover, implicitly argues that this cultural problem is best explored through poetic representation."[38] She goes on to assert that

> Throughout his career, Browning persistently portrays the dynamics of the home as deeply painful for both men and women, and focuses especially on the various forms of masculine violence occurring in the struggle for sexual dominance between husbands and wives. His poetry explores the psychology of domestic strife with unrelenting fierceness, luring his readers into intimate contact with speakers whose transgressive sexual fantasies and disruptive familiar behavior profoundly violated nineteenth-century domestic norms and intensely troubled his contemporaries. [Browning's work, in short, often explores] the theme of sexual brutality and intimate violence, giving a voice to the inner secrets of sexual dominance.[39]

At this point, we have convinced ourselves of our sign's significance in relation to the frame of early Victorian-era gender relations. We have concluded that the two artworks reflect Browning's relatively progressive thinking about women and their oppression in rigid patriarchal societies. We now need to consider how best to package and present the essay—how to outline our analysis so that we proceed clearly and confidently with our argument.

- We already possess our staging, which establishes the sign's presence in the text, poses a particular interpretive problem, and establishes a unified field of inquiry.
- We have also built our dominant frame. Since we are asking readers to consider our sign in the light of (or "framed by") gender inequalities in mid-nineteenth-century Britain, and since these facts are not common knowledge, we will need to establish the context—the specific social, historical, and scholarly arena in which we have placed our sign—before presenting the thesis. (Note that the order of the staging and framing is not fixed. We may start with the staging and then present the frame, or vice versa.)

- We then state the main idea (or "thesis") of our study, which arises out of the relationship between our sign and the specific frame we have chosen.

Once we have developed these three elements of the single-idea model, the packaging of our supportive evidence becomes relatively straightforward—especially when we rely on the Three-"I"ed Monster.

16. Return of the Three-"I"ed Monster

In the five-idea essay format, as exemplified by the Bigfoot study presented earlier in this chapter and by all of the student examples printed so far in this book, all three "I"s of the monster come into play in each section of the paper. We adopt the "idea-illustration-interpretation" pattern, in other words, in *each* of the five movements of our analysis. The architecture of such an essay thus takes the following form:

Five-Idea Structure

- Staging
- Idea 1
  Illustration 1
  Interpretation 1

- Idea 2
  Illustration 2
  Interpretation 2

- Idea 3
  Illustration 3
  Interpretation 3

- Idea 4
  Illustration 4
  Interpretation 4

- Idea 5
  Illustration 5
  Interpretation 5

- Conclusion

In the single-thesis essay format, however, the Three-"I"ed Monster plays a slightly different role. On this model, we offer one main idea (the first "I"), followed by several sections that include only illustration and interpretation (the second and third "I"s). This type of essay patterns itself on this blueprint:

Single-Thesis Structure

- Staging
- Framing
- Idea (Overarching Thesis)
- Illustration 1
  Interpretation 1

- Illustration 2
  Interpretation 2

- Illustration 3
  Interpretation 3

- Illustration 4
  Interpretation 4

- Illustration 5
  Interpretation 5

- Conclusion

In presenting this type of essay, we put forward one key assertion (the first "I") and then offer five illustrations (or proofs), each of which is accompanied by persuasive, in-depth interpretation. The second "I" of illustration, however, must perform some expanded work in this format. Each illustration functions as support for the main idea, like evidence in a court case. As before, we stress the number five to encourage you to seek out multiple interpretations that build an air-tight case about your chosen sign. Often times, you may include only four or even three argumentative sections, but the important point is to seek multiplicity in meaning and to offer enough material to solidify your persuasion.

Applying this second Three-"I"ed Monster pattern to our analysis of nineteenth-century British gender politics and the relational artworks in "My Last Duchess," we arrive at the arrangement below:

- Stage the sign (establish the presence of the sign in the text and pose the interpretive problem)
- Build the "big frame" (invite the reader to consider one dominant historical or theoretical context in relation to the sign)

- State the thesis (synthesize the sign and the frame)
- Marshal illustrative evidence that supports the points embedded in the thesis, followed by in-depth interpretations:
    o belief that men are superior—even godlike—in relation to women
    o belief that men may treat women as objects
    o belief that men may think of women as lower-order animals
    o belief that men must master the female body, since it can be dangerous
    o belief that men may resort to violence in order to achieve that containment
- Write conclusion

17. Outlining the single-thesis essay

We now possess a viable staging, frame, and thesis, and have also generated stripped-down versions of each of our pieces of supportive evidence (the "beliefs" articulated above). Rather than offer a finished version of the single-thesis essay for "My Last Duchess," however, we turn to an outline that details each illustration and interpretation for the study. Outlining at this late juncture in the composition process might seem counterintuitive, since we often think of such exercises as part of the planning stage—actions one takes at the outset of a writing project. Our experiences, however, suggest that such outlines prove more beneficial at a later phase of the analytical process. In fact, they seem to serve students better than rough drafts, particularly when dealing with large historical framing and copious research. The effort of engineering a sign and developing multiple readings, then forming a single thesis related to a historical frame, renders the actual building of the essay much easier. The remaining work is primarily one of organization, of keeping our various pieces of supportive evidence discrete and logically ordered. For that purpose, a comprehensive—or "full sentence"—outline appears ideal.

Each movement of a full-sentence outline details one of the five illustration-interpretation sections that will supply argumentative support for the thesis. For example, we would present each "belief" above as an illustration, and then develop our interpretation with specific reference to early Victorian England, so as to confirm and lend depth to our main idea. Each illustration, as you will see, generally remains within the text itself, while the interpretation incorporates textual evidence but also reads the sign through the lens of Victorian-era gender tensions. Note, as well, that it makes good sense to include specific notations and action items in each section of your outline (these remarks often come in handy as you draft your paper). Here, then, is an example of a full-sentence outline:

Thesis

In its clever correlation of the two artworks, "My Last Duchess" aligns the domineering, egotistical Duke of Ferrara with a superhuman domesticator, a mythic breaker of wild energies, and consequently offers a biting satire of Victorian men whose traditional views sanctioned the containment of women based on erroneous ideas about their lower and even animal status. Browning's deliberate correlation of Neptune and the duke—an empowered noble who tames his unruly duchess—calls to mind reactionary British males who sought to corral the reformist activities of feminists in the early decades of the nineteenth century. The poem consequently enters one of the liveliest debates of its day and seeks to curtail the abuses of women by men who regard themselves as godlike and omnipotent.

Illustration 1

- The two artworks testify to the duke's sense of himself as godlike, omnipotent, and free to act with impunity.

Interpretation 1

- In his mind, the duke remains so far above women and lower animals that he finds it inconceivable to "stoop" to their level.
- The godlike mentality of the duke sanctions whatever action he sees fit, particularly concerning the maintenance of his status within his domain.
- The poem continually stresses the duke's elite power:
  o "none puts by / The curtain I have drawn for you, but I" (9–10)
  o "My gift of a nine-hundred-years-old name" (33)
  o "no just pretence / Of mine for dowry will be disallowed" (50–1)
- Browning establishes an implicit connection between his nefarious duke and early Victorian patriarchal attitudes about male superiority.
- Men who ascribed to this code of behavior believed it was not simply their privilege but also their cultural duty "never to stoop."
- Quote Crowder: "any attitudes about the relationship of the sexes that subjected wives to the haughty wills of domineering husbands Browning strongly rejected."
- Look up statistics on English laws and customs favoring males as "superior."

Illustration 2

- By paralleling the fresco and sculpture, the poem also illustrates how the duke thinks of the duchess as an object, a possession to be disposed of at his discretion.

Interpretation 2

- The two artworks reveal the duchess as nothing more than another art object—a beautiful "rarity" and a sign of the duke's status and wealth.
- An emphasis on "my"—with that simple word's possessive power—permeates the poem.
  - first word of poem "My"; last word "me"
  - "My favor" (25); "My gift" (33); "my object" (53)
  - curiously puts the word in Frà Pandolf's mouth: "my Lady's wrist" (sign of paranoia over competition?)
- Knoepflmacher: "Browning permits the reader to free the Duchess from the Duke's possessive 'My.' "
- Given the increasing gender frictions in Victorian England, the duke's objectification of the duchess becomes representative of such social inequalities in Browning's own historical moment.
- It is as if British patriarchy speaks: "I want to hold on to my world, my privilege."
- Quote 1825 treatise *Appeal of One Half the Human Race*.
- Quote *Woman and Her Master*, Sydney Owenson, Lady Morgan (1840).

Illustration 3

- By implicitly paralleling the young duchess and the wild horse in the two artworks, the poem also appears to critique a world in which men think of women as lower animals closer to nature, figures whose "wits" are not suited to the complex demands and discriminations of high culture and political life.

Interpretation 3

- In the duke's view, the duchess was too ignorant and "untamed" to understand proper decorum. She could not finally produce the proper level of aloofness and so needed to be "lessoned," or broken into service like the horse.
- An irony lies in the duke's myth of his own civility: he reveals himself as the uncivilized barbaric murderer, while his unlucky duchess practiced what seems like laudable courtesy.
- She does not appreciate or even comprehend, however, the duke's arbitrary codes of behavior based on class.
- She is an unqualified lover of natural phenomena such as "the dropping of the daylight in the West" (26) and "The bough of cherries" (27).
- She relishes simple amusements like "the white mule / She rode with round the terrace" (28–9); Browning, it would seem, seals the association between the duchess and simpler, lower animals with this image.
- Women, in the duke's paradigm—and in that of Victorian patriarchal culture—remain inherently of a lower realm, relegated to the domestic sphere or, worse, rendered part of a baser, more "natural" level.

- Quote Mary Wollstonecraft, *A Vindication of the Rights of Women* (1792) on education equality among the sexes.
- Research the misogynist assumption that women are somehow closer to nature.

Illustration 4

- The paired fresco and sculpture also expose the longstanding patriarchal belief that women need to be tamed, corralled, domesticated, kept. If not, they might disrupt the smooth operations of male culture—like wild horses running free.

Interpretation 4

- To the duke, the duchess transgresses the "appropriate" gender boundaries established by him and the aristocratic culture to which he belongs. She lacks proper reserve and tact and thus needs to be taught how to behave.
- The duke stresses what he feels are improper interactions with Friar Pandolf and even the "officious fool" who offers her a branch of cherry blossoms. Women, in other words, should be "lessoned" to behave in an appropriate manner.
- The artworks reinforce the notion of containment of wild, feminine energies. The duke has fixed her, contained her within the walls of his castle. She has literally become part of his extended domain, just as the Roman god contains and controls the sea-horse for his purposes.
- With the rise of feminist activism in Victorian England, many empowered British men felt as well the need to tame the reformist efforts, to quiet unruly women, to put them back in their proper, apolitical place.
- The artworks thus suggest how longstanding patriarchal privileges encouraged the damaging confinement and oppression of women in Victorian England.
- Introduce scholarship on the duke's ultimate inability to contain the duchess: "Male Authority and Female Subversion in 'My Last Duchess'" by Shifra Hochberg.

Illustration 5

- Finally, Browning's conversant artworks also suggest the patriarchy's right to preserve its position with force. Read against the violent subject matter of the sculpture, the fresco becomes a story of alleged transgression met with vicious punishment.

Interpretation 5

- In the duke's conception—as reflected by the subject matter of the sculpture—the duchess needed to be disciplined for not following the unspoken gender codes.
- Interestingly, the duke did not even attempt a less violent "educating" option. He moved directly from an awareness of perceived transgression to the ordering of

her murder, with no effort at a more amenable solution. (As he declares himself, any overt educational work on his part would have constituted "stooping.")

- Given the turbulent gender politics surrounding the poem's release, the duke's use of violence in the maintenance of his male privilege speaks directly to early Victorian-era clashes of the sexes, and the abusive treatment of women by domineering, unjust husbands.

- The poem remains rife with threats of punishment to those who—"if they durst"—cross the duke's self-established boundaries.

- The duke gives "commands," which, when read through the two mutually informing artworks, becomes synonymous with the violent enforcement of a male-centered status quo.

- Quote "S. E." (*Liverpool Mercury*) on wife pummeled with "the butt end of a [carriage] whip, till the great part of her body was beaten to a jelly."

- Quote Melissa Valiska Gregory on "a domestic problem of considerable importance to the Victorian period: the psychology of sexual violence."

- Locate more information on violence against women in early Victorian era.

Conclusion

- The poem's two artworks ultimately combine to offer a biting satire of men who believe that the only good woman is a civilized woman—one who understands and even intuits her subordinate place within the social hierarchy, and who thus willingly obeys the dictates of the male-centered culture to which she belongs.

- To the duke and the early Victorian-era patriarchal system that he represents, power over women must remain self-evident and natural.

- The very fact, however, that the duke only maintains his control in the imaginary world of art (the real duchess was uncontainable and, finally, had to be forcefully quelled; the horse is not yet broken) allows Browning to signal the changing landscape of gender politics in his mid-eighteenth-century British context.

Following the processes discussed in this section helps ensure that the actual paper—when you sit down to write it—will be the culmination of multiple, discrete, recognizable steps. These steps do not, however, demand rigid adherence. They are not systems, in other words, from which you should never deviate as an analyst. We respect that all writers possess their individual preferences with respect to process. We have simply suggested a set of options that have aided hundreds of students over the years. The full-sentence outline—one such organizing option—has many merits: it offers a clear view of what you intend to prove; it lets you see whether you have gathered enough evidence in each section of your study; and it helps you solidify your argumentation before you begin to craft your first draft. Such an orderly and intelligible outline (particularly at this late stage of the analysis) allows you to stay focused on your thesis and offer the proof necessary to persuade your audience.

18. Social class and "My Last Duchess"

Because this textbook has placed a high premium on the notion of multiplicity in meaning, we present for your consideration one more "big frame" and its relationship to the two artworks in "My Last Duchess." Just as we inflected the sign with issues of gender relative to Victorian England, so too can we situate the fresco and sculpture within the context of British class structures. Such a frame seems keenly relevant, too, given the duke's anxieties over status and rank. He obsessively protects his "nine-hundred-years-old name" and, thus, his claim to a privileged position atop an arbitrary and fiercely hierarchical system of social castes. The duke's problem with his last duchess, then, has as much to do with class proprieties as it does with notions of male superiority.

A class-based reading of the conversant artworks in Browning's poem also situates the text in its specific moment in the nineteenth century. Just as we did with our gender-focused example, we might begin this final framing option by tracing the contours of class history in England around the publication of Browning's poem. The fact that historians often refer to British history in the 1830s and 1840s as a "Time of Troubles"—with particular emphasis on class-centered clashes—seems especially meaningful to our purposes. With the Reform Bill of 1832, for example, came extended voting rights to men of the lower middle classes, as well as a redistricting of parliamentary representation. No longer could small townships and villages possess inordinately large representation in Parliament, simply because of outmoded traditions and nods to "the way things have always been." Thus, while the poem raises questions about the privileges accorded to social elites such as the duke, it also invites us to explore class struggles in England both before and during the early years of Queen Victoria's reign.

Many scholars, in fact, have studied the profound class-based transformations that transpired in England during the early nineteenth century. Anne Mellor notes in her landmark study *Romantic Irony*, for example, that "the rise of the middle classes during the seventeenth and eighteenth centuries challenged the traditional class system, as well as the prerogatives of the Crown."[40] She also calls attention to the ways in which events like peasant food riots and the beginnings of the Industrial Revolution "further attacked the rectitude of a class system."[41]

Similarly, Charles A. Endress declares in *History of Europe 1500–1848* that England had begun "a profound transformation into an urbanized industrial society" by the time Browning published his poem.[42] Ultimately, as Endress argues, the "emergence of an industrialized working class concentrated in the Midlands, an upper class of industrialists, and a middle class of managers [. . .] challenged the old landed and commercial interests for a proportional share of power."[43] "My Last Duchess," therefore, appeared during a time of profound social crisis in England, and the Brownings—both Robert and his wife—seem acutely aware of this fact.

During this period, for example, Elizabeth Barrett Browning wrote "The Cry of the Children," a 160-line poem condemning the "cruel nation" of England for its abuses of the underprivileged and innocent victims of an escalating industrial economy.[44] The children in Barrett's poem "die before [their] time" due to working in "the coal-dark underground" and in factories where "the iron wheels are droning" with a "cold metallic motion."[45] Consequently, we might suggest that both works of art in "My Last Duchess" depict innocents compelled to perform labors in the service of an established hierarchical structure—the one, a horse forcibly enlisted to pull the chariot of a mighty sea god; the other, a young duchess who loses her life after she fails to "work out" as an aristocratic spouse. Both artworks, in short, portray "laborers" forced to serve a powerful and uncompromising master. The sign alerts us, in short, to a godlike aristocrat in the process of domesticating the unruly energies of a reputedly lower order.

By situating the poem within the context of class struggles in the early 1800s, we might proceed to an overarching thesis such as the following:

> Through its references to two works of art that depict innocent beings overcome by powerful lords, Browning's poem subtly indicts unjust exercises of power by the rich; marshals public concern for the victims of wealth and privilege; and encourages reform of the reigning class structures in early Victorian England. The two mutually informing artworks, in other words, suggest how elites often use unwarranted privilege to wrestle down and tame unruly class energies. Together, the painting and sculpture subtly suggest the battles that raged along class lines during Browning's time.

As in our gender example above, we may note two key features of this thesis based on class divisions. First, the idea incorporates the historical "big frame" of social inequalities in Victorian England, bringing the poem's contemporary moment into relief. Second, it deploys an "in other words" follow-up that rearticulates the key assertion, which aids in reader understanding.

Our thesis suggests that the two artworks point to the abuse of social privilege and the problems of class stratification. That is, when interpreted as complementary to the sculpture of Neptune taming a horse, the fresco of the duchess becomes one of subjugation to the duke's aristocratic legacy. Just as the god forces the animal to do his bidding, so too does the duke force the lower-order duchess into his service, for he expects her to live up to his "nine-hundred-years-old name." From the duke's perspective, the duchess did not properly follow the mandates of class distinction. To the duchess—ignorant of the invisible and unspoken rules that govern the nobility and maintain class divisions—everyone and everything was equal: an innocuous comment by a painter, a beautiful sunset, a courteous if small gift from a laborer, a mule ride, and (much to his chagrin) even the duke's own respected name. The duchess—as portrayed by Browning—possessed no clear sense of class borders. She had not yet internalized the set of learned behaviors that help to maintain the distance between the elite class and all those who serve underneath them. What's more, as the duke argues, even if he *could* have explained to her how a noble woman should carry herself,

> and if she let
> Herself be lessoned so, nor plainly set
> Her wits to yours, forsooth, and made excuse,
> —E'en then would be some stooping, and I choose
> Never to stoop. (39–43)

Given our big frame involving class-consciousness, we can interpret this declaration by the duke to mean that the rules governing the behavior of the nobility must remain invisible. They must appear to everyone as natural and preordained. In Browning's presentation, the duke believes his power to be absolute in his domain, simply because that is the way of the world. Furthermore, he possesses the wealth to enforce that notion.

The irony, then, of situating these two artworks within the frame of social-class frictions also seems palpable. His young wife never learns the "correct" way of behaving in the duke's court. In Browning's portrayal, she is sadly too naïve, too ignorant of the proper codes assumed by her husband. Rather she is unconsciously egalitarian, someone who offers a gracious comment to anyone who shows her kindness, regardless of rank or occupation. Such behavior infuriates the duke, but there he faces a key dilemma. He cannot point out her alleged blunders (for that would make abundantly clear just how arbitrary and constructed the social system is), but he also desperately needs a duchess (any duchess, really) to continue his noble name. The duke's station, authority, and reputation remain contingent on a spouse. Without the last duchess—and the next and the next—he cannot maintain his status as an admired aristocrat. His title would lose all force.

Ingeniously, then, Browning makes clear that the duke's identity and "nine-hundred-years-old name" are much more fragile that we might at first surmise. They require an obedient "other"—a companion who will confirm his status and serve as a "sign" of his rightful place above the "officious fools," the friars, and the envoys who comprise the so-called lower orders. The problem with the last duchess resided in her treatment of everybody as "all one"—a nightmare dilemma for the duke. Consequently, he makes her disappear. Now, however, he needs a replacement—a new wife who will maintain proper appearances. Subtly, in this poetic "painting" of a Renaissance nobleman working anxiously to maintain his place at the top of culture, Browning exposes the precarious and unfixed nature of social power, particularly to a Victorian audience increasingly impatient with various class-based inequalities.

As the sculpture of Neptune's taming of the sea-horse illustrates, the duke remains haunted by his failure to control—through ideology, not force—his young former wife. The horse, remember, is not yet broken. By analogy, we see the duke's struggle and anxiety to maintain social class and to exert his will upon another. We also, however, come to understand the myth of such social hierarchies. Only in some imaginary realm of gods and fantastic beasts can the duke enjoy unquestioned power. He may have the means to order the death of his young wife (and almost anyone else who opposes him). But his place atop the social scale demands that he seek out another spouse to replace her. Put another way, through the two artworks, Browning's text reveals the illusion that class hierarchies are natural and inevitable ways of differentiating people.

As with our gender focus, we may now begin to marshal supporting evidence—our "illustrative" proofs—of a class-based interpretation related to the two artworks in the poem. Placed in the "big frame" of social hierarchy, the works of art appear to critique the following class-centered ideologies:

- the elite are naturally superior (social stratification is an unequivocal fact of human existence)
- those who serve underneath are objects, possessions of the elite class (and may be dealt with as the elites see fit)
- the elite may press into service the naturally inferior (the lower classes are more akin to animals, like those pulling Neptune's chariot)
- the elite are not obligated to explain their privilege (it is preordained)
- the elite possess, by tradition and even divine mandate, the right to use force in the maintenance of their privilege

With these illustrative proofs in hand, constructing a cogent analysis on the single-idea model becomes a matter of providing in-depth argumentation that explains the evidence and confirms the dominant thesis, just as we performed in the gender-framed analysis above.

19. Portrait of another adolescent

Alphonso II married Lucrezia di Cosimo de' Medici when she was 14. (She died just three years later.) Given the historical backdrop of Browning's text, we must regard the duke's "last duchess" as a very young wife indeed. In concluding this chapter, we turn to another poem that centers on an adolescent girl—this one the speaker of Rita Dove's "Adolescence-II." Dove's contemporary poem (the second of three works devoted to the transformative experiences of puberty) depicts a girl on the verge of womanhood, nervously awaiting her first menstrual bleeding. Each night, the poem's protagonist slips into the privacy of the bathroom to see if her period will finally arrive, and each night her imagination conjures up three bizarre visitors who seem to menace more than comfort her. The poem appeared in Rita Dove's first volume of poetry, *The Yellow House on the Corner*, published in 1980. Dove went on to win numerous awards for her writing, reaching the pinnacle of accomplishment by being named poet laureate of the United States in 1993. She served in the post until 1995. Here is the text:

Adolescence-II

Although it is night, I sit in the bathroom, waiting.
Sweat prickles behind my knees, the baby-breasts are alert.
Venetian blinds slice up the moon; the tiles quiver in pale strips.

Then they come, the three seal men with eyes as round
As dinner plates and eyelashes like sharpened tines.
They bring the scent of licorice. One sits in the washbowl,

One on the bathtub edge; one leans against the door.
"Can you feel it yet?" they whisper.
I don't know what to say, again. They chuckle,

Patting their sleek bodies with their hands.
"Well, maybe next time." And they rise,
Glittering like pools of ink under moonlight,

And vanish. I clutch at the ragged holes
They leave behind, here at the edge of darkness.
Night rests like a ball of fur on my tongue.[46]

In analyzing this poem for an English class, student Morgan Mileham considered the sign-selection options discussed in Chapter 2 and ultimately settled on a juxtapositional phenomenon in the text. Morgan noted the interesting tension between (a) the speaker's references to items from the safe, domestic sphere, and (b) her fantasy of the unfamiliar and otherworldly "seal men," who seem anything but soothing and homey. While Venetian blinds, dinner plates, forks, and licorice would all be familiar to a 12- or 13-year-old girl, the "sleek" seal men—inky, hybrid, and ephemeral—seem utterly alien, darkly unknown. Why, Morgan wondered, does the poem combine these contrastive images? What thematic concerns and underlying meanings stem from this unique juxtaposition? Morgan's paper assignment called for a single thesis, so she had a decision to make. She could try to create an umbrella thesis, or take a "big frame" approach. As you will see, she chose the umbrella (offering a final theory that unifies her five initial findings). On the other hand, student Eric Bickham—writing on the same text—selected a "big frame." Their essays appear below.

20. Student examples

An Evening Oddly Spent: Tensions between the Domestic and the Surreal in Rita Dove's "Adolescence-II"

Morgan Mileham

In her 1980 poem "Adolescence-II," Rita Dove repeatedly references the domestic sphere. She begins by situating her speaker in an everyday bathroom, and then presents images of "Venetian blinds," "tiles," "dinner plates," "tines," as well as a "washbowl," a "bathtub," and even "licorice" (3, 5, 6, 7). All of these articles hold strong ties to the domestic realm due to their associations with household locations such as the bathroom, kitchen, and dining room. In striking contrast, surreal, otherworldly images also emerge in the text. One example appears when the speaker details how the blinds "slice up the moon" and how the bathroom tiles "quiver in pale strips" (3). A more overt and telling instance occurs in the second stanza when Dove's speaker conjures "three seal men," later described as having "sleek bodies" that "glitter" (4, 10, 12). In the final stanza, more surreal images appear, including the "ragged holes" left behind by the vanished seal men and what appears to be a resting "ball of fur" on the narrator's tongue (13, 15).

Such a contrast of bizarre representations with common, household items creates a curious tension, especially in the context of a poem about an isolated adolescent girl fearfully awaiting her first menstruation during the night. In fact, the chilling details of her active and nearly nightmarish imaginings call attention to various fears associated with the physical change overcoming the speaker's body. Dove's poem, then, offers several ways of reading the young narrator's blending of the surreal and domestic: as reflective of the mystery surrounding menstruation for young girls; as creative compensation for her lack of knowledge about her impending period; as emblematic of the speaker's haunting solitude and isolation on the cusp of womanhood; as indicative of the complex transition from the "make believe" world of childhood to more mature spheres of consciousness; and—specifically in the conjuring of the "seal men"—as representative of her difficult entrance into the adult world of patriarchal authority. Most importantly, however, the poem's interplay between the domestic and the surreal, the ordinary and the fantastical, presents a young mind in active contest with the forces that render her ignorant. The struggle between the speaker and her anxious mixture of the domestic and the unreal becomes, in the final analysis, one of localized but significant resistance to the dominant myths of menstruation as a modern cultural taboo.

Perhaps most apparently, the tense interweaving of the domestic and the surreal displays the speaker's fears as a combination of the familiar and the unknown, underscoring how first menstruation often represents a mystery that stimulates wild speculation. Dove's adolescent initially fuses the everyday and the bizarre when she mentions that the "Venetian blinds slice up the moon" and that the "tiles quiver in pale strips" (3). Obviously, the blinds do not actually cut the moon, and the tiles do not legitimately quake. Nevertheless, the speaker's anxieties push reality so far out of focus that familiar bathroom blinds assume a strange, fractured quality, while the tiles seem weirdly to shiver and shake. The speaker also merges domestic items with the fabrications of her frightened mind when describing the three seal men as possessing "eyes as round / As dinner plates and eyelashes like sharpened tines" (4–5). Again, menstruation does not involve frightening figures with outlandish characteristics, yet this monumental change in any girl's life maintains its alien nature until the event finally transpires. In the meantime, as a way of making sense of the mystery, young girls like Dove's narrator conjure up grand explanations for what they cannot understand. Their explanations incorporate what they know (their home and its furnishings) and what they do not know (the change about to take place in their bodies).

Along similar lines, the poem's complex interaction between domestic and surreal imagery suggests that the speaker has not been properly prepared for this life-altering movement from girlhood to womanhood. That the speaker awaits her first period while sitting alone in the bathroom indicates that she possesses at least some knowledge about the coming event. She has clearly, however, taken her modicum of understanding to outrageous extremes. For Dove's young narrator, the anticipation of her first menstruation comes with manifestations of surreal, hybridized visitors—half seal, half men—who taunt and heckle her with the question, "'Can you feel it yet?'" (8). Underscoring the protagonist's ignorance about her situation, the poem indicates that she does not "know what to say, again" (9). At the same time, these mystifying figments of her imagination casually disperse themselves throughout the domestic setting of the bathroom. The speaker relates how "One sits in the washbowl, / One on the bathtub edge; one leans against the door" (6–7). Such outlandish beings do not belong anywhere near the everyday "washbowl" and "bathtub," but the young girl's lack of knowledge causes her imagination to run amok and craft these rather menacing creatures, which she inadvertently pairs with the domestic and associates with her coming period (6, 7). If the speaker were more informed about her first menstruation, the poem seems to suggest, then she might not have to endure repeated encounters with such freakish hecklers.

The poem's interesting linkage of the domestic and surreal additionally demonstrates how the speaker's apprehensions remain solitary and subjective, illuminating how Western culture frequently regards menstruation as a taboo and relegates it to a strictly private domain. Dove's protagonist emphasizes the privacy of her experience by positioning herself alone in the bathroom, presumably after everyone else in the house has retired to bed. Her experience then reveals itself as exceptionally subjective when the seal men arrive, for these odd forms exist only in the anxious mind of the speaker and nowhere else. Further, the intimate nature of the girl's fears becomes especially apparent when her senses betray her, offering even more instances of tension between the familiar and the strange. In the second stanza, for instance, the speaker claims that the seal men "bring the scent of licorice" (6). The mention of the candy's familiar scent orients itself within the domestic sphere and the world of childhood, even though the odor is attributed to the strange seal men. Dove therefore offers another sign of blurring subjective realities that mirror the confused and isolated narrator's mind.

In addition, the last line of the poem finds the speaker feeling as though "[n]ight rests like a ball of fur on [her] tongue" (15). Here, a common-enough substance found in households that include pets lends itself to the surrealism of the girl's experience by existing on her tongue, as if choking or silencing her. Because the speaker's senses of smell, touch, and taste all participate in her imaginative portrayal, she displays herself as fully engulfed in the privacy and subjectivity of the moment. Such an extreme immersion in the unreal suggests that Western culture has decreed menstruation to be a taboo; otherwise, Dove's speaker would not be so secluded, nor would she concoct the wild fantasies fed by her inability to discuss the inevitable physical transformation. Not a monumental secret or isolated phenomenon, the first period happens for every woman and only becomes daunting for adolescents when shrouded in mystery.

By merging the fantastical with the familiar, Dove's poem also signals the vast difference between the permitted fantasies of childhood and the real-world, adult responsibilities that await the protagonist. As a child, fantasies and daydreams practically characterize the everyday thought process, so much so that adults do not expect much more from children than imaginary playmates and invented games. The three seal men who come in the night to taunt Dove's protagonist bear similarities to childhood imaginings of the "bogey man" in the closet or the monster under the bed; even the "ragged holes / [the seal men] leave behind" hark back to traces of existence that children insist their monsters leave (13–14). A tension surfaces, however, when the speaker's current, childlike state seems threatened by the various domestic articles previously discussed: these confirm, in a sense, the roles that she will be expected to fill once she becomes a woman. According to traditional assumptions still present in 1980 and lingering to this day, women (particularly wives and mothers) belong in the domestic realm. Therefore, the gendered items in the poem— "dinner plates" and "tines," a "washbowl" and "bathtub"—act as reminders of the tasks of cooking and cleaning that will be expected of the adolescent speaker once she transitions into womanhood (5, 6, 7). With the arrival of her first period comes the loss of childhood fantasies, and the poem therefore captures a young girl's movement toward becoming a domesticated woman, one who concerns herself primarily with the household.

The relationship between the domestic and the surreal—with special emphasis on the arrival of the seal men—also represents a highly masculinized infringement upon a distinctively female experience. Such a gendered contest highlights how the transition out of girlhood marks a woman's initial exposure to patriarchy. As previously stated, Dove's adolescent sits in the bathroom, surrounded by female-oriented domestic items. Due to the fact that Dove portrays the girl as fearfully alone in the bathroom, the presence of others seems logically undesirable. The beings who finally arrive, however, are men said to have "eyelashes like sharpened tines" (dangerous and slightly phallic imagery), and one of the creatures "leans against the door," a stance that suggests a blockade to the speaker's possible escape (5, 7). As a result, the meaning of the surreal seal men's arrival shifts from mere imaginative conjuring to more of an invasion—a male interference in a strictly female experience. With her evolution into womanhood, Dove's poem troublingly suggests, the adolescent speaker enters the system of patriarchy, which may well expect her to conform and accept the roles devised for her.

"Adolescence-II" draws multiple connections between domestic representations and surreal imagery. The tension that emerges as these two semiotic
arenas interact throughout the poem calls attention to the mysterious nature
of first menstruation, and to the fears that often trouble adolescents on the
"edge" of adulthood (14). In addition, the imagistic overlap showcases the
problem inherent in American culture's treatment of menstruation as an
unspeakable topic: young girls imagine the worst and thus turn this natural,
life-altering experience into a surreal event and a difficult hurdle to overcome.
The poem's tension also demonstrates how a girl's first period represents a
time and space for introducing patriarchal standards regarding gender roles.
Ironically, then, the poem's curious inclusion of surreal imagery in the most
domestic of scenes and situations suggests just how "unnatural" and "foreign"
Western culture tends to deem menstruation. By interrogating the various
ways in which its young protagonist has been taught to repress her own bodily
experience, Dove's poem becomes one of reclamation. Ultimately, in other
words, "Adolescence-II" works to minimize the vexation, the anxiety, and
the frightful surrealism that often accompanies this natural transition into
womanhood. The poem seeks to wrestle with the various cultural practices
and tendencies that mystify and stigmatize menstruation, and that wrestling
match—between the young protagonist and her surreal imaginings—becomes
itself a sign of resistance against the multifaceted prejudice and marginaliza-
tion of the female body.

Beyond the Edge of Darkness: Imaginative Empowerment in Rita Dove's "Adolescence-II"

Eric Bickham

In earlier historical periods, menstruation signified an adolescent girl's
transition from childhood to womanhood. More modern attitudes, however,
have increasingly come to view menstruation as a crisis of hygiene, emphasizing personal cleanliness rather than a transformation into the adult sphere.
As Joan Jacobs Brumberg argues in "'Something Happens to Girls': Menarche
and the Emergence of the Modern American Hygienic Imperative," fewer adolescent girls in contemporary America learn about the passage into womanhood from their mothers or other women, and fewer receive information about
menstruation in a broader discussion of female sexuality. Moreover, male
child-health advocates and marketers of feminine products have supplanted
women and assumed central roles as educators, often regulating the maturation of adolescent girls in a scientific manner that focuses almost exclusively
on menstruation as a hygienic concern. Thus, Brumberg suggests, adolescent
girls learn about menstruation in a context that simplifies and stigmatizes the
complex meanings associated with their bodily changes (101, 103). Navigating
the expectations and the experiences of puberty—especially when American

culture often applies language such as "The Curse" and "Bloody Mary" to a benign, physiological function—seems increasingly difficult. The problem deepens, furthermore, when the facts of menstruation remain shrouded in secrecy, embarrassment, discretion, and fear.

Rita Dove's "Adolescence-II"—which appeared in her first poetry collection, *The Yellow House on the Corner* (1980)—captures several of the tensions associated with this modern cultural condition. The poem's young, female protagonist sits alone at night in the bathroom, awaiting her first period. She feels her body changing, for her "baby-breasts are alert" (2). Yet because many young women in her position do not learn to negotiate this life-changing experience under the tutelage of their mothers or other experienced women, the speaker must cope with this physical and psychological change in isolation "at the edge of darkness" (14). "Adolescence-II" thus serves as an exposé of the negative forces described by Brumberg. The poem suggests the secrecy and fear that have increasingly accompanied the onset of menstruation, with emphasis on night, obscurity, erasure, and solitude. Moreover, it points to the troubling presence of patriarchy during the passage from girl to woman, since the young speaker conjures "three seal men" (4) as menacing messengers from adulthood.

Although the poem deals with the bodily transformation about to unfold in its adolescent narrator, however, it tends more to stress her richly textured imagination. In other words, in portraying a key, physical passage out of adolescence, Dove underscores the creativity and psychological complexity of her speaker. Aside from the troubling "seal men" mentioned above—who possess "eyes as round / As dinner plates and eyelashes like sharpened tines" (4–5) and who "bring the scent of licorice" (6)—the narrator also imagines a strongly metaphorical world where "Venetian blinds slice up the moon" and "tiles quiver in pale strips" (3). In addition, the poem closes with the narrator "[clutching] at the ragged holes / [the seal men] leave behind" (13–14)—a complex blurring of absence and presence—before moving to the fantastical declaration that "Night rests like a ball of fur on [her] tongue" (15). Such an emphasis on imagination and highly detailed mental activity seems intriguing in a poem rooted in the body and its alteration. And yet, therein lies one of the crucial significances of the text. That Dove's speaker possesses such an active and potent imagination (in the face of ignorance and fear about her physiological changes) functions as a sign of hope and redemption. The poem, that is to say, presents an adolescent narrator whose powerful creative consciousness might help her to overcome stigmatizing dictates about menstruation. In the end, "Adolescence-II" portrays a woman-in-the-making whose unusually creative mind stands poised to challenge the societal forces that impinge upon her maturing female identity.

To illustrate how the creative imagination might finally help the protagonist confront the debilitating obscurity surrounding menstruation, Dove first endows her speaker with figurative language that emphasizes solitude and ignorance. From the start, the young narrator awaits the arrival of "it," a deliberately ambiguous pronoun. She remains alone in darkness, with only the faint illumination of moonlight cutting through the blinds. Dove conspicuously situates the poem at night, therefore, to reflect the prevailing ethos of secrecy and obscurity that surrounds female puberty. The speaker is in the dark, literally and figuratively, and ignorant of how to understand and manage her physical changes. This exacerbates her fears, the poem suggests, and adds to the overall distress that she experiences. Furthermore, the fact that the text closes with the simile of "Night [resting] like a ball of fur on [her] tongue" (15) suggests the difficulty of articulating the changes she faces: her mouth is clotted, and she seems gagged. In effect, the speaker knows that she dare not talk about "it," given the "menstrual taboo" that pervades American culture. She not only remains alone, then, but is also coerced into silence, as night stifles her speech and creates a heightened sense of isolation. The "edge of darkness" (14) consequently connotes more than a time of day. Rather, it calls attention to the speaker's ignorance concerning female maturation, while simultaneously signifying her internalization of negative attitudes regarding the experience of menarche. It is these forces—described by researchers such as Brumberg—that her creative mind will ultimately have to overcome.

Dove's portrayal of her speaker's intensely active—and even disorderly—imagination also presents the destabilizing sense of selfhood that often accompanies menstruation in the modern age. For the speaker, the dominant narrative that defines female adolescence remains egregiously insufficient, for it distorts and marginalizes pubescent girls' experiences, rendering them incoherent and disjunctive. Consequently, Dove imbues her speaker with highly metaphorical language as a way of voicing the nearly incomprehensible experience of "it," as well as to signal the protagonist's disjointed identity at a crucial moment in her life. The imagery of the poem seems jumpy, fragmentary, jagged—not unlike the speaker herself. What's more, the "ragged holes" (13) left by the freakish seal men become representative of the narrator's gap in fully understanding herself and the bodily transformations coming over her. Her identity seems brimming with fissures, and she appears to lack self-possession. The paucity of knowledge regarding menstruation engenders cognitive dissonance and causes her to refigure her world and populate it with semicoherent images. The nearly cartoonish descriptions of the seal men—"with eyes as round / As dinner plates and eyelashes like sharpened tines" (4–5), plus the fact that they "bring the scent of licorice" (6)—all illustrate how the speaker's mind remains bewildered. That the Venetian blinds "slice up the moon" and the tiles "quiver" (3) additionally suggest the instability of the narrator's experience. The strange images that the speaker conjures, in other words, illustrate an active but confused imagination as it wildly attempts to make sense of the conversion about to take place.

At the same time, Dove's focus on her narrator's lively imagination may also underscore how the young girl has already internalized the misogynist notion of a menstrual taboo. What she conjures seems akin to an interrogation, one in which she stands already guilty. The specifics of the closed room, particularly the blinds that "slice" (3) the scant moonlight, lend a sinister and even threatening air to the scene. In that foreboding space, Dove's speaker summons her own interrogators, who ask if she can "feel it yet" and even "chuckle" when she cannot answer in the affirmative (8–9). Through the speaker's imaginative "mock trial"—complete with heckling judge and jury—the poem indicates what lies ahead for the speaker as she enters womanhood. Adults will monitor and scrutinize her every move, especially the most intimate ones.

Given that the speaker's vivid imagination projects internalized feelings of guilt supports what many sociologists have observed in young women's attitudes toward menses. In "The Personal and Interpersonal Significance of Menarche," for example, Elissa Koff, Jill Reirdan, and Stacy Jacobson demonstrate how the American narratives of secrecy, discretion, and embarrassment surrounding menses have potently affected pubescent girls' understandings of their bodies and their burgeoning sexuality:

> Menarche [for contemporary American girls] is an intensely experienced, highly significant and potentially traumatic event. The girls [interviewed for the study] portrayed menarche as a primarily negative event [. . .] and expressed grave concerns about altered relations with family and peers, self-consciousness and embarrassment, intense apprehensions they would be discovered and feelings of shame. (156-7)

Read in this light, the three seal men reflect the speaker's fear of being stigmatized and relegated to the category of the irreparably dirty, after "it" comes. Furthermore, the speaker's imagination places one of the patronizing seal men "in the washbowl" (6), while another assumes a position "on the bathtub edge" (7). By pairing two of the three seal men with objects utilized for cleansing, Dove's speaker confirms the centrality of hygienic concerns in the minds of adolescent girls with respect to this important transitional moment. The young speaker's metaphorical constructions, in other words, serve to confirm the extent to which she has already internalized dominant and debilitating narratives about menstruation.

The protagonist's imaginative fantasies, her wild metaphor-making, and her exaggeratedly active mind signal another problematic condition of female puberty: the struggle of individual mental freedom in the context of larger patriarchal forces. Through the narrator's active imagination, the poem places special emphasis on the power of male-centered ideology and gender politics to organize identity, define emotional life, and dictate movement. The mobility of the young speaker's imagination—with its emphasis on "slicing" and "quivering" (3) and with the sleek seal men who "chuckle" (9) and "glitter" (12)—stands in sharp contrast to her own lack of agency. She merely "[sits] in the bathroom, waiting" (1). By contrast, the seal men exude confidence in her space, and possess knowledge of her bodily experience, a fact that gives them authority within her world. That she imagines one "[leaning] against the door" (7), for example, suggests how thoroughly patriarchal culture suppresses her mobility. These nightmarish and hybrid animal-men effectively control her experience, as they define what "it" is and will be for the young female speaker. Without them, she remains "at the edge of darkness" (14) and thus wholly dependent on their authority. Fittingly, she can only "clutch at the ragged holes / They leave behind" (14–15)—an imaginative illustration of how this young girl has learned to filter specifically female experience through a patriarchal lens. Her fertile mind, it would appear, serves ironically to seal her within a dominant, male-centered ideology that relegates female maturation to isolation and mortification. In this way, Dove produces a vision of a youth struggling to comprehend a natural and biological phenomenon that, due to prevailing patriarchal views about female experience, evokes feelings of shame, disgust, and fright.

Finally, however, Dove's focus on her narrator's wild imagination may also suggest redemption, a way for women to reclaim and refigure narratives of menstruation. True, the speaker's imaginings remain anxious and destabilizing, so much so that her surroundings "quiver" (3), while absences like "ragged holes" (13) accrue a potent presence. Her imagination, however, also hints at how she might overcome the cultural problem of misogyny in relation to menstruation. Modern American culture—with its prevailing myths surrounding female biology and sexuality—still seems reluctant to engage in open discussions about inevitable, natural, and developmental progressions inherent in women. Thus, adolescent females experience the onset of puberty in a manner decreasingly shaped by loving, supportive female family and friends. Dove's decision to invoke "seal men" rather than "seal women," seems fitting, then, as a representation of the extent to which male-dominant culture controls the narrator's experience.

Still, even the seal men cannot weaken her imaginative powers—which prove strong enough to render dynamic the concrete world around her. The "quivering" tiles, for example, might also suggest how radically transformative her imagination remains. The ominous hybrid nature of the seal mean, too, may point as well to the generative powers of her mind, able to transcend strict categories of existence. Finally, the fact that the young narrator imagines "clutching" at "holes" serves as proof of her mind's capability to redefine the either-or polarity of presence and absence. The saving grace of the poem, it would seem, lies in its insistence on imaginative hybridity and elasticity, and its rigorous treatment of "the edge" of these life-altering experiences.

In "Siting the Poet: Rita Dove's Refiguring of Traditions," Susan R. Van Dyne posits that Dove's poems often serve as a "refiguring of tradition" (68). With "Adolescence-II," the poet refashions traditional constructions of adolescent speech through metaphors that dramatize and even threaten female empowerment. The "edge of darkness" in the poem comes to signify a space of self-construction, where the speaker imaginatively creates an identity that conforms to representations of female adolescence. Unfortunately for many prepubescent girls growing up in contemporary America, the discourse surrounding menstruation has not significantly altered. Dove's focus on her narrator's anxious summoning of strange figures encapsulates the secrecy, embarrassment, and fear that accompany the young girl's biological change. Even as it confirms her absorption of debilitating narratives regarding menarche, however, the young narrator's fertile imagination also offers some degree of hope, a sense that the power of her mind might yet claim ownership of the experience and the future. And though the narrator cannot define the "it" about to occur, the poem nonetheless stages her consistent grappling with the event. She cannot yet articulate her feelings about the mysterious event, but she remains in control of the poem's language and imagery, and therefore fills the silence in which many girls find themselves at the "edge" of their passage into womanhood.

Works Cited

Brumberg, Joan J. " 'Something Happens to Girls': Menarche and the Emergence of the Modern American Hygienic Imperative." *Journal of the History of Sexuality*. 4.1 (1993): 99–127.

Dove, Rita. "Adolescence-II." 1980. *The Yellow House on the Corner*. 2nd ed. Pittsburgh: Carnegie-Mellon UP, 1989.

Koff, Elissa, Jill Rierdan, and Stacy Jacobson. "The Personal and Interpersonal Significance of Menarche." *Journal of the American Academy of Child Psychiatry*. 20.6 (1981): 148–58.

Van Dyne, Susan R. "Siting the Poet: Rita Dove's Refiguring of Traditions." *Women Poets of the Americas: Toward a Pan-American Gathering*. Ed. Jaqueline Vaught Brogan and Cordelia Chavez Candelaria. Indiana: U of Notre Dame P, 1999. 68–87.

6

Analytical Exercises

As we have suggested throughout this textbook, university-level analytical writing requires students to push past the obvious, to craft the kinds of statements that educated readers—those with formal training in semiotic analysis—might make about specific cultural or literary phenomena. This work takes time and effort, energy and discipline, but the rewards can often prove profound. In the 1983 film *Educating Rita* (which dramatizes these very rewards), literature professor Dr. Frank Bryant, played by Michael Caine, tells his new student that she needs to "discipline" her mind. A suffering alcoholic, a poet who has abandoned his craft, a self-described "appalling" teacher, and a bungler of romantic relationships, Frank seems like the last person to offer advice about discipline.[1] Yet Rita, a 26-year-old hairstylist determined to earn a degree, takes his words seriously and not only becomes a savvy interpreter of both literature and the world around her, but also helps Frank climb out of his personal and professional mire.

Though Rita's early essays turn out to be, in her own phrasing, "crap," she persists. By the end of the film, she has learned to read closely, study diligently, and think independently (hardly easy tasks, especially since her educational aspirations cause strife at home). Ultimately, Rita writes papers insightful enough to impress her professor, her peers, and most importantly, herself. Julie Walters, the British actress who played Rita and earned a Golden Globe Award for her performance, once noted that "Self-worth is everything. Without it, life is a misery."[2] As *Educating Rita* suggests, self-worth often arises from learning to read and write with critical awareness and flair.

In this sixth and final chapter, we introduce ten analytical approaches designed to stimulate thought, build confidence, and promote academic self-worth. All of the exercises have been devised and written by semioticians teaching at a range of universities, in a host of educational contexts. Some of the calisthenics explore cultural signs, others delve into literary texts, and all strive to help you expand your interpretive options and deepen your arguments about meaning. By testing out the approaches that follow, and applying the methods laid out in Chapters 1 through 5, you will no doubt make strides as a writer and thinker, and find yourself increasingly able (as the title of our book suggests) to analyze anything.

1. Analyzing spectacle

Gwen Davidson, MA, MLS

In his 1985 novel *White Noise*, Don DeLillo takes several playful potshots at the semiotic analysis of popular culture. Consider this quote from one of DeLillo's most memorable characters, Murray Jay Siskind, a cultural semiotician teaching at a small US college: "I understand the music, I understand the movies, I even see how comic books can tell us things. But there are full professors in this place who read nothing but cereal boxes."[3] Despite this casual satire on scholars who abandon so-called high-culture texts (such as literary novels or philosophical treatises), Murray plays a center role in DeLillo's keen-eyed examination of the power of signs—all kinds of signs—in the shaping of human cultures and personal identities. In an early passage, for example, Murray takes the protagonist Jack Gladney on a drive to "the most photographed barn in America"—a send-up of the ubiquitous roadside attraction. Jack "counts five signs" advertising the barn before they actually reach the site, and he is generally impressed with the swarms of tourists on the viewing platform. The hype about the barn—the signage, the spectacle of it all—even seems to overshadow the barn itself, which, in DeLillo's coverage, is completely ignored. Murray, in fact, declares as much to Jack: "Once you've seen the signs about the barn, it becomes impossible to see the barn."[4]

This kind of hype and spectacle—where the signs *about* the barn subsume the *actual* barn—were especially interesting to French cultural theorist Jean Baudrillard in the latter part of the twentieth century. For Baudrillard, simulations—through media such as television and film, or even in theme parks like Disneyland—possess the power to eclipse the original reality. Disneyland's "Main Street," for example, may resemble a typical thoroughfare in any American town with its shop fronts and sidewalks, fire hydrants and flower gardens. Disney's version, however, is hyperrealized, *more real*—as Baudrillard might say—*than real*.[5] Most American Main Streets, for example, do not include life-sized topiary animals, quaint "choo-choo" trains, or uniformed candy makers eager to please every desire for sweets. Disneyland's simulation of Main Street, then, is also a distortion, one that can finally achieve a life of its own, detached from its ties to any actual place. Just like Murray's barn, that quaint "Main Street" exists only in the imagination, in the spectacular simulations that we observe.

Spectacles, however, need not be large-scale theme parks. Consider, for example, how marketers sell tickets to sporting competitions, live concerts, and theater productions. What about the "one-time only" signs pointing you toward some "Close-Out Sale" or "Savings Extravaganza"? Spectacles, in other words, exist in packaging, in the signs that condition us to see things as *worth seeing*. Becoming sensitive to the ways in which culture creates these spectacles, and the uses to which they are put, will help you to see with Murray-like analytical vision.

Exercise: Locate a sign that appears to have reached "spectacular" status. Note the surrounding signs that point you toward the spectacle and that begin to condition your responses to its presence. Then, à la Murray, "speculate about the spectacle." In other words, offer plausible insights that address how the spectacle may shape the desires and outlooks of viewers; how it helps to define its community or culture at large; how it functions, perhaps, to override or dissuade critical analysis; and so on.

2. Analyzing ads

Rod McRae, MA

I possess a power that is out of the ordinary. And like all powers that go beyond those of the everyday, it is both a blessing and a curse. My power is that I am no longer beguiled by advertising—by that, I mean any ad in any medium. While this may not sound like anything extraordinary, experts have concluded that each of us is exposed to thousands of ads every day, explicit or otherwise. My power enables me to see advertising for what it truly is: a carefully constructed fiction that reflects a clear agenda. As I said, this situation is both good and bad. I automatically snoop out the motivation for the message. I cannot simply watch a commercial: the apparent "entertainment value" no longer disguises the context and content of the ad. Yet I did not acquire my power through some radical science experiment gone awry. Mine came simply from overexposure.

This extended contact came from copywriting for a major American-owned radio company in New Zealand. Working with sometimes erratic personalities, I wrote dozens of ads each week for several types of stations in many different markets across the country. This combination meant that I had to frame each message to suit the presumed demographics of the target listeners. Before each script, I had to consider the context and the content, the client's goal and the target audience, not to mention every element of the ad itself: jingle with a voice-over or a cast of characters, the voice of the client or that of a disc jockey, background music, speed of the dialogue, voice effects, sound effects, soft sell, hard sell, and so on. Basically, I always asked myself: who's doing the talking, how, and about what?

Finding just the right words and ideas to fit within 15, 30, or 60 seconds sounds tough, but I found it exciting. These tiny acts of persuasion demanded attention to language, marketing, and motivational psychology. My job, however, was not to be a linguistic artist but a careful coaxer, talking the listeners into parting with their money. And even if I thought that the ad might fail in the marketplace, I still ensured that what hit the air was the embodiment of the client's desire for increased awareness (and usually sales). When I handed the script to the production team, I expected that they would also be as attentive to the final stages of production. The finished product required approval from not just the salesperson but also the client—both of whom can be rather fickle at the best of times. If either one disapproved, I started over. Many people, in other words, had to come together to work on the ad before any listeners ever heard it.

Luckily, my unusual power is not difficult to develop. The same methods that I used for creating a radio ad, for instance, also apply to scrutinizing a full-page ad in a major magazine. Looking at the elements of the content, you can move to the context. Then the task of analysis becomes a matter of asking why the ad features that person or those people, how the lighting changes what you see, what objects are noticeable and notable in their presence or even in their absence. You can also ask what the ad reveals about the magazine's presumed readership or the motivations behind the message.

Consider a current trend in television advertising: a good many ads—selling everything from fast cars to fast food—seem intent on ridiculing the male figure. Up until the last generation, the father was viewed as the center of familial authority, but modern advertisers appear willing to undermine that once-esteemed position. Dad, for example, has filthy hands and sees his teenage daughter's short shorts hanging on the line. He smiles as he wipes his hands with the shorts, hoping they'll end up in the trash, but the clever mom reaches for a bottle of detergent; then the daughter emerges from the bedroom, all thighs and smiles, much to her father's confusion and dismay. The advertising company that created this ad carefully selected each part—from the actor playing the father to the style of his daughter's shorts. In looking at this trend as a whole, we can ask ourselves a few questions: in what ways does the characterization of the patriarchal figure display or distort cultural expectations, and to what ends? How does this type of advertising reveal the irony of America's current view of family power structures? What insecurities does the advertisement hope to exploit, and why?

Exercise: To start developing the special power described above, choose an ad from a major magazine—preferably one whose content lies outside your own interests. Once you have located an ad, focus on one particular facet of the composition: choice of main character, setting, even typographical indicators such as font and text color. Then offer speculations as to why the advertisers may have chosen that specific element. Be sure to read beyond the content to the context below.

3. Analyzing metaphor

Adrian Matejka, MFA

Before I became a creative writer, I wanted to be an emcee. My best friend and I spent the hours between basketball practice and dinner in his living room, working a Casio keyboard and writing rhymes over programmed handclaps and beats. A velvet painting of a half-dressed woman with a black panther hung on the wall above a plush purple couch. The beats we made in that living room were basic, and our verses were equally mundane, yet the acts of creating and communicating thrilled us.

Even though I gave up rhyming after ninth grade, I never lost my affection for hip-hop. I love beats that clatter like street noise and samples that retrieve snippets from the past and turn music into a conversation about history. More than anything, I love the innovative ways in which hip-hop communicates: invented words, slant rhymes, playful innuendoes, all fused in a mixture that reaches listeners from countless walks of life, in communities and countries across the globe.

That particular type of hip-hop mishmash—that energized collage or pastiche—relies a great deal on metaphor. Sure, good emcees use metaphor to express ideas in ways that their audiences can understand, but their metaphors also help us recognize new possibilities embedded in language. Take, for example, British-American rap artist MF DOOM's "Kon Karne" and the savvy with which the song compares sampling to stealing a car. Both jacking and sampling, according to DOOM, require "straight pliers" and "vise grips," which turns music-making into a kind of deviant vandalism.[6] Conversely, stealing—whether cars or samples—becomes a creative activity, a clever way to "acquire nice whips," as the wheels of both the turntables and cars spin.

DOOM's lyrics use the same metaphorical strategies that traditional literary writers deploy, only with a bit more swagger. Suddenly, stealing a car assumes the power and prestige of an art form (like sampling), while sampling appears illicit and dangerous (like stealing). At the same time, the metaphor signals respect. Thieves only swipe cars that carry status and value, and by comparison, sampling becomes a sincere form of tribute. While the metaphor serves to familiarize listeners with an act that is most likely unfamiliar (stealing cars), it also redefines and reinterprets another act that remains poorly understood (mixing on turntables). In the end, the hip-hop metaphor reassigns meaning to both practices, creating a common space, a middle ground between the extremes of stealing cars and pilfering samples.

In fact, cultural theorist Homi Bhabha suggests that entire cultures and communities may participate in hybrid forms of creativity—"mishmashes" and mixtures that challenge strict binaries and simple categories. Hybrid cultures—much like hip-hop itself—often lead to startlingly new understandings and identities, even though they often emerge from strife and difficulty. The key, in Bhabha's mind, is dialogue between parties: the colonized and the colonizers, but also—more generally—those assumed to be in power and those who feel disenfranchised. Each side must listen to the other, and hip-hop's inventive forms of metaphor beguile us into hearing more and more attentively. Such metaphors help us, in short, to "hybridize" our ears and minds.[7]

Exercise: Take a hip-hop song, and focus on one particular metaphor. As always in sign selection, generate multiple possibilities before deciding on one. Then, discuss the ways in which the metaphor or simile ("this is that" or "this is *like* that") redefines the objects under inspection. What is the effect of that redefinition, particularly to the music's target audience? Who does the song—by way of the chosen metaphor—appeal to, and why? What cultural work does this specific figure of speech accomplish? As a follow-up exercise, try to locate a particularly interesting metaphor in, say, a country, metal, or pop song. How might the different genre of music affect the metaphorical constructions in the lyrics?

4. Analyzing gender

Bonnie Adams, MA

In a 2006 episode of NBC's *The Office*, an employee brings her baby to work, beaming proudly as she cuddles the infant, who is bundled snugly in a puffy pink jacket. The mother's smile quickly turns to a scowl, however, when a fellow employee approaches the baby and exclaims, "Oh, she's absolutely adorable!" The woman snaps, "*He*," while her embarrassed coworker can only stammer weakly, "Oh—sorry. He's—he's dressed all in pink."[8]

The humor in this awkward encounter stems from the mother's deeply offended reaction to what the audience would recognize as an understandable assumption, one that viewers themselves probably shared upon seeing the baby clad in pink. After all, everyone knows that mothers dress boys in blue and girls in pink; to do otherwise is abnormal, right? Or is it? In reality, no biological imperative or natural law underlies these color-coded associations. Rather, culture has conditioned us to recognize blue as a sign of masculinity and pink as a marker of femininity—and this is only the beginning.

Consider the toys we tend to give children: sports gear, Matchbox cars, and sometimes plastic guns for boys; baby dolls, dress-up clothes, and "play" kitchen equipment for girls. Notice the ways in which these toys establish— and perpetuate—gender-related stereotypes. Our culture encourages men to be competitive (hence the sports-themed toys) and authoritative (fake guns tend to be accompanied by an emphatic "Stick 'em up!"), while women are expected to be nurturing (those baby dolls and Easy Bake ovens offer good practice) and refined (what is more beautiful and sophisticated than a tiara?).

When we analyze gender, though, we have to be careful not to confuse it with sex. A person's sex is a biological fact, whereas his or her gender is considered by cultural theorists to be a social role—a performance of certain behaviors that a given society considers "masculine" or "feminine." To change one's sex requires surgical procedures and hormonal regimens that alter the physical body. But shifting or "bending" gender comes much more easily: one need only adopt a set of behaviors culturally associated with a particular gender.

For a pop-culture example, consider Arnold Schwarzenegger in *Kindergarten Cop* (1990), a film that features the recognized tough guy transformed into a nurturing, feminized character. Or what about films such as *Lara Croft: Tomb Raider* (2001), in which the hyperfeminized Angelina Jolie straps on a holster and plays the steely eyed, authoritative archeologist (a role typically associated with men)? For an extreme example of cinematic gender slippage, think of the Wayans brothers' release *White Chicks* (2004), where two black male detectives go undercover as spoiled white heiresses. While these cases focus on professional actors in big-budget films, when it comes to gender, theorists suggest that we are all actors in our everyday lives. We *act* according to the gender *scripts* established by our culture. Gender is theatrical, in other words: we can "put on" or "play" different gender roles at will, because these are not fixed categories of natural reality. Rather, they are social constructions recognizable via a multitude of signs and perpetuated through invisible ideologies.

The examples above all reveal a liberating (and often comical) flexibility inscribed in gender roles. Yet gender bending—when played out in the real world rather than on the silver screen—can sometimes produce troubling consequences. Gender-coded signs are so deeply ingrained in our cultural consciousness that when an individual chooses to step outside of the accepted gender signifiers, the result is oftentimes social alienation. Consider your reaction if one of your fellow male students showed up to class wearing makeup and high heels. Or what if a female friend shaved her head and adopted the profile of what gender theorist Judith Halberstam refers to as a "tough street butch"—a woman who performs a hypermasculine identity?[9] Would you accept these acts as personal choices and not give them a second thought? Maybe, but you might also do a double take and perhaps even distance yourself. Thus, culture not only conditions us to *read* the signs of gender (makeup and high heels as feminine; cropped hair and beefy biceps as masculine) but also to *perform* our gender, or run the risk of being ostracized.

Exercise: Gender scripts and assumptions permeate the worlds of marketing and advertising. For this exercise, pick a specific gender-coded product within one of the three following categories: Beauty and Hygiene (deodorants, soaps, shampoos, etc.); Food and Drink (breakfast cereals, snacks, energy drinks, alcoholic beverages, etc.); and Clothing and Accessories (sweaters and slacks, shoes and sneakers, backpacks and purses, etc.). Visit the official website of your chosen product and identify five invisible gender assumptions embedded within the site. Then ask yourself: Does the web space simply reinforce standard views about gender, or does it strive in any way to redefine—or "bend"—established ideologies?

5. Analyzing slang

Peter F. Murphy, Ph.D.

As a boy growing up in northern New York State in the 1960s, I was exposed to an array of offensive slang terms, most of them still spoken today. The list includes *slut, piece of ass, wimp, faggot*, and dozens more. In many ways, this type of slang dictated my behaviors and policed my options as a young male. Its underlying messages pronounced men's power over women as well as over other men. Such slang also made it difficult to imagine alternative ways of acting in the world. And while it is possible to change the way we talk about women and men—and to create new visions of gender and gender-based behaviors—such change is not easy.

In my book *Studs, Tools, and the Family Jewels: Metaphors Men Live By*, I analyze a host of slang terms in an attempt to understand how the discourse of male bonding shapes the choices that young men make.[10] I began the project by remembering slang phrases from my youth and jotting them down in a journal. Once I had a sizable list, I looked up each of the terms in various slang dictionaries as a way to learn about their multifaceted uses. I also traced their histories using the *Oxford English Dictionary* (*OED*), which gives a broader perspective on the evolution of English words. When were the terms first used? What did they mean initially? How have their definitions shifted over time? All of this knowledge is available for you to investigate.

I consider myself a feminist, and one important dimension of feminist cultural analysis suggests that "the personal is political." So while researching and writing the book, I also jotted down notes from my immediate experience of having voiced a given phrase myself or having heard someone else use it. Recording my personal usage was central to the project. I took notes alongside each term in my journal, trying to recall not only when and how I had used it or heard it used, but also how I felt when it was uttered. One main idea behind my theoretical writing is the assumption that if we understand the sources of slang terms, their histories, and the complexity of their meanings, then we can begin to comprehend our deeper and more ideologically based motivations for adopting them. Within this broad critical context, we can begin to recreate the language with which we discuss gender, and expand our identities as men and women. If, as I believe, masculinity and femininity are largely social constructions, then we can affect their meanings and bring about positive change. How we talk about ourselves as men and women, in other words, can alter the way we live as men and women.

Exercise: Compile a list of gender-based slang derived from your personal experience. After you have collected several terms, choose one and look up its history in slang dictionaries, the *OED*, and other texts and websites devoted to word origins. Take notes on first usage, initial meanings, and changes in definition over time. Then use your research to help you theorize why the term continues to be deployed. What power does the term appear to offer the user, or what anxieties might it help the user address? For example, a young man might claim that he "bagged" his date the night before. What does such a phrasing imply? That women are game or prey that need to be hunted down? That he is an adept (and hence successfully masculine) predator? That his date is a trophy, and that he deserves the accolades of his male friends? That sex becomes a confrontation with a clear-cut winner and loser? You get the idea.

6. Analyzing tomorrow

Angela Insenga, Ph.D.

In his book *Keywords: A Vocabulary of Culture and Society*, theorist Raymond Williams encourages thinkers to begin by closely analyzing what they believe they already know.[11] And what could be more familiar to us than the world of school—bound to it, as we are, for the better part of our early lives? With Williams's idea of close scrutiny in mind, consider M. T. Anderson's presentation of school in his sci-fi young-adult novel *Feed*:

> Now that School™ is run by the corporations, it's pretty brag, because it teaches us how the world can be used, like mainly how to use our feeds. Also, it's good because that way we know that the big corps are made up of real human beings, and not just jerks out for money, because taking care of children they care about America's future. It's an investment in tomorrow. When no one was going to pay for the public schools anymore and they were all like filled with guns and drugs and English teachers who were really pimps and stuff, some of the really big congloms got together and gave all this money and bought the schools so that all of them could have computers and pizza for lunch and stuff, which they gave for free, and now we do stuff in classes about how to work technology and how to find bargains and what's the best way to get a job and how to decorate our bedroom.[12]

Here, Anderson rereads the sign of school by placing it in a vastly different historical context—a future where knowledge and learning have strangely metamorphosed. "School™" is now a proper noun, a brand, taken over and trademarked by large corporations for which higher learning equals teaching children how to be consumers who can spot bargains and redecorate rooms. In this world, schoolchildren no longer memorize facts and figures or learn to read and write, and no one thinks critically because the "feed"—a kind of internal internet implanted at birth—makes decisions for them. As a result of these observations, we could argue that Anderson's rereading of school critiques our present world's educational system by including some familiar aspects of it but also adding information that is slightly skewed. The result is a future where we recognize some of the attributes normally assigned to school but are uneasy about others.

Exercise: Building on Anderson's playful yet disturbing take on school as a cultural institution, identify another institution with which you are familiar. It could be retail sales, law enforcement, organized sports, transportation, recycling programs, and so on. Then, imagine what these institutions might look like in the future. Perhaps, for instance, we will not use cash or even credit cards to make retail purchases, but will instead simply allow a retinal scanning machine to verify our identity. Next, analyze that vision of the future in terms of what it might suggest about our present concerns. We could argue, for example, that a version of the future in which no money ever changes hands, and our physical bodies do the work of credit cards, allows us to critique our culture's relentless move toward ease of consumption, frictionless purchasing. Buying something these days is already much less cumbersome than even 50 years ago, but what happens when we take that desire for convenience to an absurd level?

7. Analyzing consumption

Debra Ann MacComb, Ph.D.

Early in Edith Wharton's 1913 novel *The Custom of the Country*, the *nouveau riche* heroine Undine Spragg frets about which stationery to use in responding to a dinner invitation from one of New York's social elite: "She had read in the 'Boudoir Chat' of one of the Sunday papers that the smartest women were using the new pigeon-blood notepaper with white ink [. . .]. It was a disappointment, therefore, to find that Mrs. Fairford wrote on the old fashioned white sheet, without even a monogram."[13] For a moment, Undine's pen "wavered." What if white paper were really "newer" and "more stylish?"[14] Caught between contending authorities concerning a sign of social consecration, Undine elects to model her response on the latest evidence and takes out a "plain sheet" of paper on which to formulate her reply.

Undine's quandary over what seems a supremely unimportant matter is nevertheless a familiar one: how do our things or our avocations speak for us? What do possessions—from shoes to cars to notepaper—signal about an individual's cultural identity, values, and status? In his sociological survey *The Theory of the Leisure Class* (1899), Thorstein Veblen coined the term "conspicuous consumption" to explain consumer habits as submerged rituals proclaiming social power. In barbaric cultures, argues Veblen, trophies of war or the successful raid on a neighboring tribe provided tangible proof of superior prowess, but such actions in the modern world would be unacceptable means of demonstrating one's preeminence. According to Veblen, although the barbaric impulse remains, it has been sublimated into economic rather than overtly aggressive expression; wealth makes it possible to purchase signs of power—those goods that exceed the "subsistence minimum"—and display them "as evidence of the prepotence of the possessor of these goods over other individuals in the community."[15] If you have ever chuckled at the bumper sticker proclaiming, "He who dies with the most toys wins," you are well on your way to understanding Veblen's concept of "conspicuous consumption."

In the modern competition for status, however, the sheer *quantity* of possessions as a mark of social distinction gives way to idioms of *quality* as signs of enhanced power: workmanship, rarity, and newness mark "successes scored in the game of ownership,"[16] because consumption of such goods bespeaks the possessor's superior discrimination—hence Undine's concern that she employ the latest fashion in note paper as a sign of her social worthiness. We all "know" that handmade is better than machine made, that diamonds trump cubic zirconias, and that *new* ____ (fill in any product, from shampoo to lawn mowers) surpasses last year's formula or model, yet few of us ever question the truth of this conventional wisdom.

Veblen goes one step further in theorizing the ultimate sign of "pecuniary prowess" afforded by conspicuous consumption, asserting that "waste"—the "expenditure of superfluities"—confers the greatest social distinction.[17] Rather than the fixed possession of a few luxury items, the continuous renewal and disposal of goods confers the greatest status. Simon Patten, a contemporary of Veblen's and professor at the University of Pennsylvania's Wharton School of Economics, asserts the patently Veblenesque argument that "the standard of life is determined, not so much by what a man has to enjoy, as by the rapidity with which he tires of the pleasure. To have a high standard means to enjoy a pleasure intensely and tire of it quickly."[18] Do ideas such as these begin to explain our cultural fascination with the lifestyles of the rich and famous? the desire for always newer—and hence better—*things*?

Undine Spragg, aspirant to the ranks of New York's social elite, ultimately consumes her way to the top, disciplining her "floating desires" so that she is always poised to have "the best" on the market.[19] Each time she believes herself in possession of the "real thing," however, her confidence is "spoiled by a peep through another door" that reveals "something still better beyond [. . .] more luxurious, more exciting, more worthy of her."[20] Haunted by the thought "that there were other things she might want if she knew about them," Undine cease-lessly renegotiates her self—an identity predicated on a succession of ephemeral possessions.[21]

Exercise: Look over your personal possessions, and identify ten that you feel are absolutely necessary to your life. Then make a list of ten other items without which you *could* live, but that you chose to purchase based less on need and more on desire. From those, choose one item that seems the most "conspicuous," carries the most explicit status, and calls attention to itself and you. Now analyze in detail what that particular item signifies beyond its functionality. What does it say not just about itself as a product, but about you as its owner? The "posh" name-brand purse, the "cool" piece of electronic gear, the "stunning" pair of high heels, tickets to the "right" concert: what signals do they send and why? Be sure that the item is meant not just to be "used" but also to be "seen."

8. Analyzing beauty

Margaret Mitchell, Ph.D.

Everyone knows that we live in a beauty-obsessed culture. But what does it mean to say so, and why do we assume that this is a dangerous state of affairs? How do we define beauty? Is it an essential quality that happens to exist in certain people, things, or ideas, or is it—as we like to say—in the eye of the beholder? What leads us to identify something—or someone—as beautiful, and what kind of power does the thing in question derive from this designation?

What seems destructive about our current cultural fixation with physical beauty is our assumption that it is a fixed standard, something that might just be within our grasp if we can only acquire the right clothes, the right hair, the perfect skin; starve or sculpt our imperfect bodies into submission; erase signs of age, of sun, of difference. This is an expensive proposition, of course, and the fact that a multibillion-dollar industry exists to satisfy (and fuel) these desires suggests that someone stands to benefit considerably from this state of perpetually anxious imperfection.

But glancing through the art of the past few centuries reveals that our understanding of beauty is far from static. Peter Paul Rubens's voluptuous models would be packed off to the gym in no time if they lived in our midst, while the towering, angular runway models of today might have seemed downright freakish in other eras. A look at fashion magazines from the past few decades reveals shifts nearly as dramatic. If beauty is not an essential quality but a fluid concept, if aesthetic values are historically and culturally specific and constantly changing, then how are we to understand beauty—what it is, what it means, what it does?

Philosophers have considered these questions for thousands of years, and have offered countless ways of understanding beauty, both as an abstract quality and as a fundamental element of human experience. They have debated its relationship to virtue, to goodness, to perception and desire. Writers, too, have explored these questions, complicating the issue further by seeking to express an essentially visual quality through language alone. Moreover, by spinning beauty into narrative, writers assign beauty to particular characters, or to places or objects of significance, thereby aligning it with certain moral qualities, values, plot trajectories. Beauty is always an elusive idea. It demands particularly careful interpretation, however, when represented in literary texts, entangled in already ambiguous layers of meaning and signification.

When it is deployed in narrative, beauty tends to have consequences: it elicits reactions, demands responses, sets events in motion. Contemporary scholar Elaine Scarry provides one way of thinking about this. In *On Beauty and Being Just*, Scarry proposes that beauty "incites deliberation," that "[s]omething beautiful fills the mind yet invites the search for something beyond itself, something larger or something of the same scale with which it needs to be brought into relation."[22] Hers is an idealistic conception of beauty; Scarry insists that the human response to beauty is not the desire to possess, to consume, or even to destroy, as some have posited; nor is it a neutral or passive reaction, such as pure, self-contained pleasure. Scarry conceives of the perception of beauty as a *relationship* between the perceiver and the possessor of beauty—and, specifically, as a "starting point for education."[23]

Consider Mr. Darcy in Jane Austen's 1813 novel *Pride and Prejudice*. Upon first sight, the aloof and supercilious Mr. Darcy scorns Elizabeth Bennet as merely "tolerable," and declines to ask her to dance.[24] The next time he finds himself in her company, he is surprised by his new reaction:

> No sooner had he made it clear to himself and his friends that she had hardly a good feature in her face, than he began to find it was rendered uncommonly intelligent by the beautiful expression of her dark eyes [. . .]. Though he had detected

with a critical eye more than one failure of perfect symmetry in her form, he was forced to acknowledge her figure to be light and pleasing [. . .]."[25]

The immediate result of Mr. Darcy's reluctant reassessment is that "he began to wish to know more of her."[26]

Although Mr. Darcy's sudden interest in Elizabeth Bennet is, on one level, simply a necessary stepping stone in this elaborate but not unpredictable courtship plot, and while Elizabeth's good looks certainly do not set her apart from the general run of novel heroines in the nineteenth century, Austen's depiction of Elizabeth's beauty and Darcy's response to it is freighted with subtler meanings, too. To "know" Elizabeth is to overcome his aristocratic distaste for her "vulgar" family, to reassess his lifelong assumptions about the importance of birth and breeding, to learn to find virtue, kindness, and other admirable qualities in a social realm where it would not have occurred to him to look.

The novel makes Mr. Darcy's response to Elizabeth's dark eyes a "starting point for education" in the broadest sense—in Mr. Darcy's case, ultimately bringing about a radical alteration of his worldview. Here, as in other literary texts, beauty has a crucial narrative function that also offers a productive starting point for analysis.

Exercise: Choose a literary or cultural text in which the representation of beauty features prominently. Examine closely the language used to convey beauty, and consider what values, ideals, or judgments are associated with it. How might beauty be said to incite "the search for something beyond itself," or to act as a "starting point for education"? Or does it resist this framework, and if so, how and why? What kind of ideological work do you think the representation of beauty performs in the text? What cultural assumptions does it challenge or reinforce?

9. Analyzing captivity

Rebecca Harrison, Ph.D.

Mary Rowlandson's 1682 captivity narrative—a cornerstone in colonial studies and the first American best seller—documents the trials and survival of an affluent woman taken as a prisoner by the Narragansett Indians, after witnessing the devastation of her community during King Philip's War. While this text was clearly used to justify colonial expansion and violence against native populations, it simultaneously documents—through Rowlandson's contact with and adjustment to the Narragansett—the sometimes liberating potential of being removed from one's home culture. This story, like many female captivity narratives, reveals a woman capable of breaking the boundaries of "civilized" culture while captive. She finds strength, agency, and, at times, freedoms not assigned to her in her own community; she discovers the monetary value of her labor; and she is mournful upon her return to white, Christian culture. Consequently, her captive body in this text subtly subverts her home culture while attempting to stand as a model of Puritan womanhood. Various signs in her text—such as Rowlandson's stealing of food literally from the mouth of a starving, captive English child—invite us to question such binary categories as "civilized" and "savage," "superior" and "inferior," and "free" and "captured."

Rowlandson's narrative represents only the beginning of a long line of texts by women participating in the discourse of captivity—a cultural mythology that allows women to address their place in and against social confinement. Kate Chopin's 1899 novella *The Awakening*, for instance, documents a married (and socially and spiritually captive) woman named Edna Pontellier, who interacts with Creoles during a summer vacation. Edna's newly found consciousness and sense of liberty leads her on a quest for autonomy in a world where such a state is all but impossible for a woman. In the face, however, of the unrelenting captivity of marriage and "true womanhood"—as defined by the strict Southern culture to which she originally belongs—Edna ultimately resists what she terms "soul's slavery" by drowning herself in the sea.[27]

Not surprisingly, signs of female captivity continue well into the twentieth century. Jane Campion's 1992 film *The Piano*, for example, centers on Ada McGrath, a nineteenth-century single mother married off by her father to a man whom she has never met. Thrust upon the foreign coast of New Zealand as Alisdair Stewart's bride, Ada comes into contact with the native Maori and George Baines, a white settler living among them. Baines manipulates Ada at first via the possession of her beloved piano, but she eventually discovers her own passion and needs through him. Baines's character crosses cultures, resists patriarchal systems, and recognizes Ada's authentic voice—her piano playing.

Ada's husband attempts to force her into accepting the role of his wife, and she consents, but only after sending a parting note to Baines, which Stewart intercepts. As a violent reminder of her status as his property, to do with as he will, Stewart severs one of Ada's fingers (and thus her musical "voice") to reestablish his claim on her body. Alisdair does give Ada to Baines—much like a piece of property—but she resists her continued social imprisonment by attempting to drown herself, along with her piano, in the sea. Unlike Chopin's Edna, though, Ada does not die. In the silent depths of the ocean, she chooses to save herself and define her own path in life, even if that means social ostracism. Baines restores her artistic voice by fashioning her a metal fingertip, and Ada embraces her revised identity as a woman of difference. "I'm quite the town freak," she remarks, "which satisfies."[28]

Exercise: As the above texts demonstrate, the experience of captivity makes the captive (and the reader) question the very nature of who is free, to what end, and under what circumstances. For this exercise, select a text featuring a female protagonist "caught in" or "captured by" a foreign culture—even if that "culture" is the family of her fiancé or members of a different class. Contemplate how the work represents, repeats, challenges, or transforms the signs of captivity and liberation. To what ends? What meanings arise through your chosen text's semiotic relationship to the genre of captivity narratives?

10. Analyzing disability

Susannah Mintz, Ph.D.

The Clint Eastwood film *Million Dollar Baby* created a firestorm of debate when it appeared in 2004. Described by critic Roger Ebert as a "masterpiece," the movie nearly swept the Oscars that year, earning four awards, including Best Picture and Best Director. But its controversial ending did not please all viewers, and so offers us a compelling example of how the meanings of textual signs can shift depending on perspective.

Million Dollar Baby follows Maggie (Hilary Swank) from her poor beginnings in the Ozarks to stardom as a boxer under the guidance of trainer Frankie (Eastwood). In the final segment, Maggie's neck is broken during a title match, and she ends the film a quadriplegic, one leg amputated because of bedsores. In a scene clearly intended to be heart-wrenching, Maggie tells Frankie, "I can't be like this . . . Don't let 'em keep taking it away from me. Don't let me lie here till I can't hear those people chanting no more."[29] At Maggie's own request, and against his initial religious misgivings, Frankie administers a fatal injection of adrenaline, and Maggie dies.

Film critics praised the movie's cinematic technique, and sports fans appreciated its dramatic momentum. But other groups had vastly different reactions. Some Christian viewers worried about the endorsement of euthanasia, which Eastwood's own character acknowledges as a sin. Conservative commentators cited euthanasia as evidence of a liberal political agenda. Some feminist viewers celebrated Maggie's success in a male-dominated arena; others decried the implication that when women tread on men's terrain, the consequences may be lethal. Class-conscious watchers denounced the portrayal of Maggie's opportunistic family as a caricature of "white trash" stereotypes. And finally, members of the disability community lambasted *Million Dollar Baby* for its assertion that life with disabilities is not worth living. Eastwood, many protested, had missed an opportunity: rather than capitalizing on his prominence as a filmmaker to suggest a range of possibilities for Maggie's life after spinal cord injury, he had instead perpetuated the worst of American attitudes toward impairment and pain.

What these various reactions show is that the signs of the body become meaningful within the powerful narratives of ideology and discourse. Maggie's physicality is hypervisible, but how we respond to the movie's treatment of her bodily markers, even how we *name* those markers (is she working class or "hillbilly"? injured or damaged? a boxer or a "girl"?), depends in part on the stories we have internalized about which attributes legitimize us as people. From a disability-studies perspective, this means that we might pay particular attention to the arc of the movie's plot, because it exaggerates a symbolic dichotomy between Maggie's pre- and post-fight sense of who she is. Going into that final bout, Maggie is at the top of her game, her picture "in magazines," her fans shouting her name. But afterward, though she is very much alive, she imagines herself disappearing, vital parts of herself—her able body; her boxing name—"taken" from her. Once a fighter, she equates paralysis with passivity and is terrified by seeming helpless or weak. In her own words, she "can't be like this," as if her condition were worse than death.

Viewed through the lens of disability theory, the "script" of *Million Dollar Baby* is not just a screenplay; it is also a manifestation of certain prevalent assumptions about embodiment. Though few of us will achieve the status of elite athleticism, we are nonetheless urged by numerous forces—advertising and healthcare, for instance—to discipline our bodies: to diet, exercise, beautify, and heal ourselves in an attempt to achieve accepted norms, and to experience anything from the common cold to sensory impairment or immobility as a deviation from who we "really" are or ought to be. Such efforts to tame the body are connected to what is known as the "medical model" of disability, the belief that disabilities are individual problems requiring physical rehabilitation or medical cure. When the problem cannot be "fixed"—like Maggie's paralysis or blindness or cerebral palsy—a typical social response is pity or even fear. This is because disability, in its many forms, reminds us that no matter how hard we work to maintain control over our physical selves, bodies are inherently vulnerable and unpredictable.

Some viewers of *Million Dollar Baby* suggested alternate endings. For example, what if Frankie had refused Maggie's request and encouraged her to go to school? Maggie simply cannot imagine pursuing her life as a person with severe impairments, but we might argue that this is not because disability is *obviously* catastrophic; rather it is because Maggie has no good examples of what living well with disability might be like. Had Maggie, now a wheelchair user, been transported from Los Angeles to Berkeley, California—the birthplace of the Independent Living movement—she would have found herself in an environment that facilitates rather than obstructs her mobility: every curb has wheelchair cuts, the classrooms of the University of California are easily accessible, and there is an elaborate network of social-service resources. In such an environment, Maggie is neither radically "other" nor particularly disabled, since Berkeley is open (literally and figuratively) to a wide range of bodily types.

What this scenario demonstrates is that disability may be *contextual*—a function of widespread attitudes and infrastructure—more than individual or even medical. Scholars call this the "social model" of disability, and it shifts our attention away from the habit of stigmatizing impairment as a sign of insufficiency or failure and onto the social codes that frame bodies in certain ways.

Exercise: As some scholars say, disability is everywhere: in literature, film and TV, classrooms, neighborhoods, families. Choose and analyze a text for how disability has been presented. Can you discern bias against bodily difference? Could you offer alternative ways of understanding or reacting to disability in this instance? You might also focus on some element of your typical surroundings (your home, your campus) that reveals the way physical space is constructed according to the dictates of "ableism."

11. Student example

Disrupting Narratives of Impairment: Disability in Flannery O'Connor's "Good Country People"

Erica Lynn Rohlfs

At the age of 25, Flannery O'Connor was diagnosed with lupus, the incurable disease that caused her father's death at age 40. By 1955—the year "Good Country People" was published and just five years after her diagnosis—she needed the assistance of crutches, and in 1964, lupus took her life. While many scholars focus on O'Connor's Catholic responses to living in the Protestant South, perhaps equally significant are her literary confrontations with disability, which often remain overlooked. Such a situation seems unfortunate, given that O'Connor offers a unique understanding of the role that disabled characters play in literature. As Sharon L. Snyder writes, O'Connor is "an author who wrote eloquently out of her experience of lupus" (179). This essay explores how O'Connor challenges metaphors of the "freakish" and "grotesque," and how "Good Country People," moves beyond conventional and religious treatments of disability. By affording Joy-Hulga, the story's disabled protagonist, the opportunity to reimagine her extraordinary body, O'Connor creates a disruptive narrative that exposes how culture responds to physical impairment.

"Good Country People" structures itself around Joy-Hulga's missing leg and engages the cultural responses to such an impairment. In this bizarre tale, Manley Pointer—a conman posing as a simple and decent Bible salesman—seduces the crippled Joy-Hulga and steals her wooden leg. Given that bodily deformity is often linked to moral depravity in literature, many critics equate Joy-Hulga's missing limb with a lack of spiritual wholeness. In this approach, "Good Country People" serves as a faith-based caution against idolizing the earthly rather than the divine. These readers understand the juxtaposition of Joy-Hulga's stated atheism with her external deformity as a way of connecting her physical "grotesqueness" to her allegedly "deviant" soul. According to Kathleen Feeley, for example, Manley's theft of the wooden leg "readies [Joy-Hulga] for grace" (24). In other words, the conman's "streak of diabolism" rids Joy-Hulga of the false idol that she has created out of her prosthesis.

In *Mystery and Manners*, O'Connor herself appears to perpetuate this theological reading of the amputee hero who is violently reawakened to grace. "Early in the story," O'Connor writes, "we're presented with the fact that [Joy-Hulga] is spiritually as well as physically crippled. She believes in nothing but her own belief in nothing, and we perceive that there is a wooden part of her soul that corresponds to her wooden leg" (99). Through this rather ubiquitous reading, the disabled body becomes a metaphor that accounts for the presence of evil and the ultimate triumph of salvation. From such a conventionally religious perspective, then, O'Connor's protagonist must engage with a nefarious person in order to attain grace. The story, in fact, suggests that there may be a brutal side to grace—an almost sadistic facet that causes the protagonist to embrace God's glory.

To reach grace, it would seem, the protagonist must assume an extraordinary form not found in the so-called normal world. As in the case of Joy-Hulga, the disabled body becomes a metaphor necessary to reveal the character's religious identity (Grimshaw 8). In fact, Feeley describes O'Connor's texts as "full of freaks" (ix) and asserts that the characters inhabiting her fiction often "have a physical deformity which is symbolic of a spiritual one" (22–3). Moreover, O'Connor affirms that "the freak" in her fiction may serve as a "figure for our essential displacement" (*Mystery* 44). She continues by suggesting that "to be able to recognize a freak, you have to have some conception of the whole man, and in the South the general conception of man is still, in the main, theological" (45). Thus, while her statement appears to sustain the theological discourse that reproduces "disability as religious metaphor," it also suggests that her grotesque characters "lean away from typical social patterns, toward mystery and the unexpected" (40).

Moving beyond the religiously coded metaphor of impairment, however, allows the disabled character and the audience an opportunity to experience disability more directly. Such metaphors (like the theologically based trope in "Good Country People") often problematically turn language away from the disabled person's experience and foreclose further debate. In his essay "Narrative Prosthesis," David T. Mitchell notes that "dependency of literary narratives on disability" establishes the "notion that all narratives operate out of a desire to compensate for a limitation or to reign in excessiveness" (20). Mitchell also argues that stories depend on "bodily deviance" or disability to serve as a "metaphoric signifier of social and individual collapse" (16), and that the "pervasive nature of disabled images [. . .] catches unaware even the most knowledgeable scholars" (18).

Furthermore, he declares that the trite use of disability as a metaphor for deviance expunges the disabled body's experience in "terms of its own significance" (25). The adoption of disability as a metaphor for what O'Connor describes as Joy-Hulga's "maimed soul" (*Habit* 171) exemplifies Mitchell's argument. The metaphor, in other words, causes the disabled person to be defined by her limitations, establishes an automatic devaluation of Joy-Hulga's body, and reproduces an age-old misrepresentation of the impaired individual as a freakish deviant. Moreover, the standard interpretation of good and evil in "Good County People" creates problematic symbolic imagery within disability studies. If, for example, the Christian metaphor seems to explain Joy-Hulga's impairment, then its elimination allows for a recasting of the story as a disability narrative. The extraordinary body, in other words, may be considered on its own terms.

Disrupting the "normal" (because conventionally religious) approaches to Joy-Hulga's missing leg also offers a chance to experience disability through the authorship of a disabled writer. Through multiple narratives within "Good

Country People," O'Connor exposes the social construction and reproduction of the embodied identities of so-called normals and their reactions to the disruptive "freak." Certainly, the text contains many scenes where abled and disabled characters interact. When Manley himself appears at Mrs. Hopewell's doorstep in a contorted shape, for example, the narrator reflects that his black suitcase "weighted him down so heavily on one side that he had to brace himself against the door facing" (277). Furthermore, Manley divulges to Mrs. Hopewell that he may not live long due to a heart problem. Mrs. Hopewell becomes sentimental as soon as he reveals his illness, and inwardly exclaims, "He and Joy had the same condition!" In effect, she creates an immediate bond between the two based on impairment. Suddenly, Manley and Joy-Hulga are assumed to share something outside the "normal." In addition, although Manley appeals to Joy-Hulga's intellect, he reinforces a more deeply encoded assumption by asking, "don't you think some people was meant to meet on account of what all they got in common and all?"—thus playing on the notion of some natural bond between two disabled people.

Joy-Hulga, for her part, imagines that she will seduce Manley the next day, since, according to her, "true genius can get an idea across even to an inferior mind." She even envisions herself "tak[ing] all his shame away and turn[ing] it into something useful" (284). Yet, Manley instigates the seduction, not Joy-Hulga: "he put his hand on her back again and drew her against him without a word and kissed her heavily" (285). Manley's startling action creates Joy-Hulga's first break from the common stereotype of the asexual cripple, a prejudice that dismisses the disabled person's ability to give and receive sexual pleasure. Indeed, Joy-Hulga herself internalizes this asexual view and reads intimate contact as a "matter of the mind's control" (286). Nevertheless, Manley pulls the disabled figure out of the asexual and into the sexual realm. Ultimately, she cannot ignore her instinctual bodily desires.

Both her education and her wooden leg initially allow Joy-Hulga to disregard her disabled body. Once Manley removes the leg, however, the narrator remarks that "this boy, with an instinct that came from beyond wisdom, had touched the truth about her [. . .]. It was like losing her own life and finding it again, miraculously, in his" (289). Manley apparently sees beyond the able-bodied world, and—while expressing an extraordinary interest in her wooden leg—does not possess the typical culturally conditioned response to Joy-Hulga's body. He seems not to support, for example, the social inscription of her freakish body as evil, and the relative ease that he displays regarding her disability compels Joy-Hulga to surrender to him. Once Manley steals her prosthesis, however, Joy-Hulga is left alone in the barn with her one-legged body. Manley, an outside force that ruptures normalcy, brings disability to the fore and provokes a radical recognition of impairment. The disruptive narrative of Manley's ruse, in other words, forces Joy-Hulga to reenter the "normal" sphere without her prosthesis, signaling a new relationship to her environment and, in fact, a new identity.

Manley's actions force Joy-Hulga to understand that her "normal" body only has one leg—that her disability, in other words, is normal, and that all humans are enabled differently. Hence, Joy-Hulga's experience is not about overcoming a disability, or what Thomas Couser calls a "rhetoric of triumph" (111). Rather, it is more about accepting her particular impairment. In short, Joy-Hulga is forced to reimagine her disabled body. Through Manley's radical theft, Joy-Hulga becomes reembodied. Although his response to disability is extraordinary, Manley's action presumably shakes Joy-Hulga, her family, and O'Connor's audience out of the customary complacencies that surround bodily impairment.

Interestingly, "Good Country People" offers two contrastive approaches to disability: one rooted in direct bodily contact, the other characterized by indirect and at times condescending speech. Manley might question Joy-Hulga's physical ability to climb the barn ladder, and he might gaze at her "as if the fantastic animal at the zoo had put its paw through the bars" (286). His direct engagement with her disability, however, differentiates him from the conventional and evasive attitudes and language of Mrs. Hopewell and Mrs. Freeman. Even though Manley's actions appear despicable, they provide for Joy-Hulga's reengagement with her distinct physical form. Thus, while Manley steals Joy-Hulga's wooden leg and spotlights her extraordinary body, Mrs. Hopewell and Mrs. Freeman reveal how culture often speaks about disability, encoding it as aberrant or casting it into mystery. At one point, for example, Mrs. Freeman engages in a discussion with Mrs. Hopewell regarding diversity, one which clearly condescends to Joy-Hulga:

> "Everybody is different," Mrs. Hopewell said.
> "Yes, most people is," Mrs. Freeman said.
> "It takes all kinds to make the world."
> "I always said it did myself."
> [Joy-Hulga] was used to this kind of dialogue for breakfast and more of it for dinner; sometimes they had it for supper too. (273)

In this instance, the dialogue between the two women is not only alienating to Joy-Hulga but also demonstrates their everyday, insincere responses to her disability. The narrator's words clearly suggest that Joy-Hulga receives daily doses of condescension from them, but the conversation also reveals the way in which "able" people use language to conceal their anxieties about impairment. The masking of fear, then, establishes Mrs. Hopewell and Mrs. Freeman as figures of repression within the disability narrative.

Not only do these two female characters demean Joy-Hulga's unusual physicality, they also critique her personal choices. To Mrs. Hopewell and Mrs. Freeman, in other words, Joy-Hulga's freakishness extends far beyond her body. Her doctorate in Philosophy, her atheism, and perhaps especially her name open the protagonist to their conventional doubts and ridicule. Such attitudes come into view, for instance, when "without warning one day, [Mrs. Freeman] began calling her Hulga" (274), disrespecting her by lopping off the "Joy" in her hyphenated name. The act causes Joy-Hulga to "scowl and redden" because she "consider[s] the name her personal affair." Meanwhile, Mrs. Hopewell—Joy-Hulga's mother—ignores her daughter's decision to keep private the story of her dismemberment, and proceeds to offer "the details of the hunting accident, how the leg had been literally blasted off, how she had never lost consciousness" (275). Mrs. Freeman and Mrs. Hopewell, then, appear trapped inside a language system that constructs disability as freakish and wrong, and both fail to acknowledge Joy-Hulga's perspective.

In her landmark 1997 study *Extraordinary Bodies*, Rosemarie Garland-Thomson examines Western literature's portrayal of the physically disabled. Her book seeks to "defamiliarize these identity categories ["able-bodiedness" and "disability"] by disclosing how the 'physically disabled' are produced by way of legal, medical, political, cultural, and literary narratives that comprise an exclusionary discourse" (6). For Garland-Thomson, the concepts of the "normal" and "abnormal" body in literature create a problematic situation in which "one is beautiful or perfect [and] one is grotesque or ugly" (8). Furthermore, she argues that "the physically disabled body becomes a repository for social anxieties about such troubling concerns as vulnerability, control, and identity" (6). Joy-Hulga's reembodiment in the barn affords her an opportunity to establish her own disability narrative. The extent to which she and others can reimagine her impairment, however, will obviously be threatened by the "exclusionary discourses" described by Garland-Thomson. Yet, readers of "Good Country People" are clearly challenged to rethink their own relationships to figures like O'Connor's protagonist. They are also challenged to re-read—with new interpretive lenses—literary works by disabled authors such as Flannery O'Connor.

Works Cited

Couser, G. Thomas. "Signifying Bodies: Life Writing and Disability Studies." *Disability Studies: Enabling the Humanities*. Ed. Sharon L. Snyder, Brenda Jo Brueggemann, and Rosemarie Garland-Thomson. New York: MLA, 2002. 109–17.

Feeley, Kathleen. *Flannery O'Connor: Voice of the Peacock*. New York: Fordham UP, 1982.

Garland-Thomson, Rosemarie. *Extraordinary Bodies: Figuring Physical Disability in American Culture and Literature*. New York: Columbia UP, 1997.

Grimshaw, James A. *The Flannery O'Connor Companion*. Westport, CT: Greenwood, 1981.

Mitchell, David T. "Narrative Prosthesis and the Materiality of Metaphor." *Disability Studies: Enabling the Humanities*. Ed. Sharon L. Snyder, Brenda Jo Brueggemann, and Rosemarie Garland-Thomson. New York: MLA, 2002. 15–30.

O'Connor, Flannery. *The Complete Stories*. New York: Farrar, Straus and Giroux, 1971.

—. *The Habit of Being*. Ed. Sally Fitzgerald. New York: Farrar, Straus and Giroux, 1979.

—. *Mystery and Manners*. Ed. Sally and Robert Fitzgerald. New York: Farrar, Straus and Giroux, 1969.

Snyder, Sharon L. "Infinities of Forms: Disability Figures in Artistic Traditions." *Disability Studies: Enabling the Humanities*. Ed. Sharon L. Snyder, Brenda Jo Brueggemann, and Rosemarie Garland-Thomson. New York: MLA, 2002. 173–96.

Notes

Chapter 1

1. Benjamin Franklin. Qtd. in *The Home Book of American Quotations*. Ed. Bruce Bohle. New York: Random House, 1967. 220.
2. Benjamin Franklin. *The Autobiography of Benjamin Franklin*. Ed. Louis P. Masur. 2nd ed. Boston: Bedford/St. Martin's, 2003. 38.
3. Ibid. 39.
4. Lorraine Hansberry. *A Raisin in the Sun*. New York: Vintage, 1959. 4.
5. Ibid. 81.
6. Ibid. 80.
7. Ibid.
8. Ibid. 81.
9. Ibid. 38.
10. Ibid.
11. Socrates. Qtd. in "The Apology of Socrates." *The Last Days of Socrates*. Plato. Trans. Hugh Tredennick. New York: Penguin, 1969. 50.
12. John Keats. "Letter to George and Tom Keats, 21 Dec. 1817." *Selected Letters of John Keats: Based on the Texts of Hyder Edward Rollins*. Ed. Grant F. Scott. Cambridge, MA: Harvard UP, 2005. 60.

Chapter 2

1. Ibid.
2. Robert Frost. "The Road Not Taken." *The Poetry of Robert Frost*. Ed. Edward Connery Lathem. New York: Henry Holt and Company, 1969. 105.
3. Ralph Waldo Emerson. "Self-Reliance." *Emerson: Essays and Lectures*. New York: Library of America, 1983. 261.
4. Ibid. 265.
5. Robert Frost. "Letter to Louis Untermeyer, 9 Sep. 1915." *The Letters of Robert Frost to Louis Untermeyer*. New York: Holt, Rinehart and Winston, 1963. 14.

6. Frank Lentricchia. *Modernist Quartet*. Cambridge: Cambridge UP, 1994. 72.

7. Stephen Graham Jones. "Discovering America." *Bleed into Me*. Lincoln, NE: U of Nebraska P, 2005. 139–42.

8. William Wordsworth. "Lines Composed a Few Miles Above Tintern Abbey, On Revisiting the Banks of the Wye During a Tour, July 13, 1798." 103–7.

9. F. Scott Fitzgerald. *The Great Gatsby*. New York: Scribner, 1925. 88.

10. Ibid. 92.

11. Ibid. 91.

12. Ibid. 29.

13. Ibid. 49.

14. Ibid. 6.

15. Ibid. 72.

16. Mary Shelley. *Frankenstein*. Ed. Johanna M. Smith. 2nd ed. New York: Bedford/St. Martin's, 2000. 60.

17. Ibid. 61.

18. William Blake. *Selected Poetry and Prose of Blake*. Ed. Northrope Frye. New York: Random House, 1953. 132.

Chapter 3

1. Francis Bacon. "Of Discourse." *Francis Bacon: The Major Works*. Ed. Brian Vickers. Oxford, UK: Oxford UP, 2008. 406.

2. Albert Einstein. Interview with William Miller. *LIFE Magazine*. May 2, 1955.

3. Stephanie Rosenbloom. "Good Girls Go Bad, for a Day." *New York Times*. Oct. 19, 2006.

4. Marc Lacey. "A Revolutionary Icon, and Now, a Bikini." *New York Times*. Oct. 9, 2007.

5. Penelope Green. "What's in a Chair?" *New York Times*. Mar. 6, 2008.

6. Fitzgerald, *The Great Gatsby*, 28.

7. James Holt McGavran. *European Romantic Review* 11.1 (2000): 46–67.

Chapter 4

1. Herman Melville. "Letter to Evert A. Duyckinck, 3 Mar. 1849." *The Letters of Herman Melville*. Ed. Merrell R. Davis and William H. Gilman. New Haven: Yale UP, 1965. 79.

2. Ibid.

3. Ralph Waldo Emerson. *A Year with Emerson*. Ed. Richard L. Grossman. New York: David R. Godine, 2005. 19.

4. Ibid.

5. Ben Hogan with Herbert Warren Wind. *Ben Hogan's Five Lessons: The Modern Fundamentals of Golf*. 1957. New York: New York Times Special Services, 1985.

6. Linus Pauling. Qtd. in *Dictionary of Quotations in Communications*. Ed. Linda K. Fuller and Lilless M. Shilling. Santa Barbara: Greenwood, 1997. 112.

7. Mihaly Csikszentmihalyi. *Creativity: Flow and the Psychology of Discovery and Invention*. New York: Harper Perennial, 1996. 113.

8. Gary Gildner. *Blue Like the Heavens: New & Selected Poems*. Pittsburgh: U of Pittsburgh P. 3.

9. Emily Dickinson. *The Complete Poems of Emily Dickinson*. Ed. Thomas H. Johnson. Boston: Little, Brown and Co., 1960. 350.

10. Emily Dickinson. "Letter to Abiah Root, 31 Jan. 1846." *The Letters of Emily Dickinson*. Vol. 1. Ed. Thomas Johnson. Cambridge: Belknap UP, 1965. 27.

11. Emily Dickinson. "Letter to Helen Hunt Jackson, Mar. 1885." *The Letters of Emily Dickinson*. Vol. 3. 866.

12. Craig Raine. "A Martian Sends a Postcard Home." *Collected Poems 1978–1999*. London: Picador, 2000. 95.

13. Ibid.

14. Ibid.

15. Shelley, *Frankenstein*, 57.

16. Ibid. 58.

17. Ibid. 60–1.

18. Ibid. 93.

19. Ibid. 40.

20. Ibid. 87.

21. Ibid.

22. Ibid.

23. Ibid. 57.

24. Ibid. 93.

25. Ibid. 177.

26. Ibid. 60–1.

27. William Godwin. *Enquiry Concerning Political Justice*. New York: Penguin, 1985. 184.

28. Mary Wollstonecraft. *A Vindication of the Rights of Women*. London: Walter Scott, 1891. 203–4.

29. Naomi Tadmor. *Family and Friends in Eighteenth-Century England: Household, Kinship, and Patronage*. Cambridge: Cambridge UP, 2001. 34.

30. Ibid.

31. Charles Dickens. *Oliver Twist*. London: Macmillan, 1962. 4.

32. See Judith Herman. *Trauma and Recovery*. New York: Basic Books, 1997.

33. Shelley, *Frankenstein*, 184.

34. Anne Mellor. *Mary Shelley: Her Life, Her Fiction, Her Monsters*. New York: Methuen, 1988. 1.

Chapter 5

1. Henry David Thoreau. *Walden: A Fully Annotated Edition*. Ed. Jeffrey S. Cramer. New Haven: Yale UP, 2004. 317.

2. Ibid. 36.

3. "Emily in Wonderland." *The Gilmore Girls*. Dir. Amy Sherman-Palladino. Perf. Lauren Graham and Alexis Bledel. WB Television Network, 2007. DVD.

4. 50 Cent. "In Da Club." *Get Rich or Die Tryin'*. Aftermath, 2003. Music video. Dr. Phillip Atwell. www.youtube.com. July 20, 2011.

5. Cornel West. "On Black Sexuality." *The Cornel West Reader*. New York: Basic *Civitas* Books, 1999. 514–20. 514.

6. Ibid. 514.

7. Robert Browning. *The Poetry of Robert Browning*. Ed. Jacob Korg. Indianapolis: Bobbs-Merrill, 1971. 58–9.

8. William Shakespeare. *Romeo and Juliet*. *The Riverside Shakespeare*. Boston: Houghton Mifflin, 1974. V.iii.92–6.

9. Kenneth Maclean. "Wild Man and Savage Believer: Caliban in Shakespeare and Browning." *Victorian Poetry* 25.1 (1987): 1.

10. Laurence Lerner. "Browning's Painters." *The Yearbook of English Studies* 36.2 (2006): 96–108. 99.

11. Robert Browning. Qtd. in "A Conversation with Browning." William Lyon Phelps. *ELH* 11.2 (1944): 154–60. 155.

12. Robert Browning. "Letter to W. G. Kingsland, Nov. 27, 1868." *Letters of Robert Browning*. Ed. Thurman L. Hood. New Haven: Yale UP, 1933. 128–9.

13. Louis S. Friedland. "Ferrara and *My Last Duchess*." *Studies in Philology* 33 (1936): 656–84. 656.

14. Ibid. 681–2.

15. Ibid. 677.

16. Ibid. 678.

17. "The Browning-Howard Connection." *The Wilson Quarterly* 23.1 (1999): 108–14. 108–9.

18. George Gordon Byron. *Lord Byron: Selected Letters and Journals*. Ed. Leslie. A. Marchand. Cambridge, MA: Belknap UP, 1984. 213.

19. British Women's History Timeline. www.historyofwomen.org/feministcuttings.html

20. Lady Morgan. *Woman and Her Master*. London: Henry Colburn, 1840. 11.

21. Elizabeth Barrett Browning. Qtd. in "The Least 'Angelical' Poem in the Language": Political Economy, Gender, and the Heritage of *Aurora Leigh*. Lana L. Dalley. *Victorian Poetry* 44.4 (2006): 525–42. 526.

22. Ashby Bland Crowder. "Browning and Women." *Studies in Browning and His Circle* 14 (1986): 91–134. 107.

23. Ibid. 114.

24. Ibid. 121.

25. Ibid. 125.

26. Ibid. 124.

27. Ibid. 134.

28. Ibid. 132.

29. Judith Weissman. "Women without Meaning: Browning's Feminism." *The Midwest Quarterly* 23.2 (1982): 200–14. 201.

30. Ibid. 202.

31. Ibid. 205.

32. Ibid. 203.

33. Shifra Hochberg. "Male Authority and Female Subversion in 'My Last Duchess.'" *Lit: Literature Interpretation Theory* 3.1 (1991): 77–84. 84.

34. Ibid. 82.

35. Ulrich Knoepflmacher. "Projection and the Female Other: Romanticism, Browning, and the Victorian Dramatic Monologue." *Victorian Poetry* 22.2 (1984): 139–59. 155.

36. Ibid. 155.

37. Melissa Valiska Gregory. "Robert Browning and the Lure of the Violent Lyric Voice: Domestic Violence and the Dramatic Monologue." *Victorian Poetry* 38.4 (2000): 491–510. 491.

38. Ibid. 492.

39. Ibid. 494.

40. Anne Mellor. *Romantic Irony.* Cambridge, MA: Harvard UP, 1980. 3.

41. Ibid. 3.

42. Charles A. Endress. *History of Europe 1500–1848.* New York: Barnes & Noble Books, 1975. 275.

43. Ibid.

44. Elizabeth Barrett Browning. "The Cry of the Children." *The Complete Poetical Works of Mrs. Browning.* Boston: Houghton Mifflin, 1900. 158.

45. Ibid. 157.

46. Rita Dove. "Adolescence II." 1980. *The Yellow House on the Corner.* 2nd ed. Pittsburgh: Carnegie-Mellon UP, 1989.

Chapter 6

1. *Educating Rita.* Dir. Lewis Gilbert. Perf. Julie Waters, Michael Caine, and Maureen Lipman. Acorn Pictures, 1983. DVD.

2. Julie Walters. Internet Movie Database. https://www.imdb.com/name/nm0910278/

3. Don DeLillo. *White Noise.* New York: Penguin, 1985. 10.

4. Ibid. 12.

5. See Jean Baudrillard. *Simulacra and Simulation.* Trans. Sheila Faria Glaser. Ann Arbor, MI: U of Michigan P, 1995.

6. MF DOOM. "Kon Karne." *MM. Food?* Rhymesayers, 2007.

7. See Homi Bhabha. *The Location of Culture.* New York: Routledge, 1994.

8. "The Convict." *The Office.* Dir. Jeffrey Blitz. Perf. Steve Carrell and John Krasinski. NBC Universal, 2007. DVD.

9. Judith Halberstam. *Female Masculinity.* Durham, NC: Duke UP, 1998. 196.

10. See Peter F. Murphy. *Studs, Tools, and the Family Jewels: Metaphors Men Live By.* Madison: U of Wisconsin P, 2001.

11. See Raymond Williams. *Keywords: A Vocabulary of Culture and Society.* Oxford, UK: Oxford UP, 1976.

12. M. T. Anderson. *Feed*. Cambridge, MA: Candlewick, 2004. 109–10.

13. Edith Wharton. *The Custom of the Country*. 1913. New York: Charles Scribner's Sons, 1941. 18

14. Ibid. 19.

15. Thorstein Veblen. *The Theory of the Leisure Class*. 1899. New York: Dover Publications, 1994. 18.

16. Ibid.

17. Ibid. 60.

18. Simon N. Patten. *The Consumption of Wealth*. Philadelphia: U of Pennsylvania, 1901. 51.

19. Wharton, *The Custom of the Country*, 48.

20. Ibid. 54.

21. Ibid. 59.

22. Elaine Scarry. *On Beauty and Being Just*. Princeton, NJ: Princeton UP, 2001. 29.

23. Ibid.

24. Jane Austen. *Pride and Prejudice*. 1813. Oxford, UK: Oxford World's Classics, 1991. 9.

25. Ibid. 19.

26. Ibid.

27. Kate Chopin. *The Awakening*. 1899. Ed. Nancy Walker. New York: Bedford/St. Martin's, 2000. 138.

28. *The Piano*. Dir. Jane Campion. Perf. Holly Hunter, Harvey Keitel, and Sam Neill. Miramax, 1992. DVD.

29. *Million Dollar Baby*. Dir. Clint Eastwood. Perf. Clint Eastwood, Hilary Swank, and Morgan Freeman. Warner Brothers, 2004. DVD.

Index